STATE GOVERNMENT

STATE GOVERNMENT

CQ's GUIDE TO CURRENT ISSUES AND ACTIVITIES
1990-91

edited by Thad L. Beyle

The University of North Carolina
at Chapel Hill

Congressional Quarterly
1414 22nd Street N.W.
Washington, D.C. 20037

Congressional Quarterly

Congressional Quarterly, an editorial research service and publishing company, serves clients in the fields of news, education, business, and government. It combines Congressional Quarterly's specific coverage of Congress, government, and politics with the more general subject range of an affiliated service, Editorial Research Reports.

Congressional Quarterly publishes the *Congressional Quarterly Weekly Report* and a variety of books, including college political science textbooks under the CQ Press imprint and public affairs paperbacks on developing issues and events. CQ also publishes information directories and reference books on the federal government, national elections, and politics, including the *Guide to the Presidency,* the *Guide to Congress,* the *Guide to the U.S. Supreme Court,* the *Guide to U.S. Elections, Politics in America,* and *Congress A to Z: CQ's Ready Reference Encyclopedia.* The *CQ Almanac,* a compendium of legislation for one session of Congress, is published each year. *Congress and the Nation,* a record of government for a presidential term, is published every four years.

CQ publishes *The Congressional Monitor,* a daily report on current and future activities of congressional committees, and several newsletters including *Congressional Insight,* a weekly analysis of congressional action, and *Campaign Practices Reports,* a semimonthly update on campaign laws.

An electronic online information system, Washington Alert, provides immediate access to CQ's databases of legislative action, votes, schedules, profiles, and analyses.

The Library of Congress cataloged the first edition of this title as follows:

Beyle, Thad L., 1934-
    State government.

    Bibliography: p.
    Includes index.
        1. State governments—Addresses, essays, lectures. I. Congressional Quarterly, inc. II. Title.

JK2408.B49   1985   320.973   85-9657
583   1990

ISBN 0-87187-550-0
ISSN 0888-8590

Contents

V. STATE LEGISLATURES

VI. GOVERNORS AND THE EXECUTIVE BRANCH

VII. STATE BUREAUCRACIES AND ADMINISTRATION

VIII. STATE COURTS

IX. STATE ISSUES

Boxes, Tables, and Figures

BOXES

TABLES

FIGURES

Foreword

As the fiscal crisis deepens and the budget knives sharpen in Washington, the states are faced with greater financial and programmatic challenges than ever before—and more than ever before, they are on their own. The years of the Bush presidency almost certainly will bring little fiscal relief and more transferred costs to the states, continuing and perhaps accelerating the trend of the last dozen years. The Reagan era in particular ushered in a massive shift in the balance of federalism. Enormous responsibilities—and the accompanying burden—were transferred from the nation's capital to the state capitals, and the change was dramatic.

While Washington drastically cut back many of its basic social programs, struggled with massive deficits, and seemed almost incapable of putting its governmental house in order, the states considerably expanded their activities, operating with balanced budgets in most cases and taking the necessary steps, however painful—such as raising taxes—to meet their obligations. The energy, enthusiasm, and willingness to experiment observed today at the state level is reminiscent of earlier, happier eras in the national government's existence; the contrast between past and present is stark.

Thad Beyle, one of the country's foremost scholars of state government, has been skillfully charting the trends that are reshaping state government and politics in this series for Congressional Quarterly. The carefully selected articles in this latest compendium recount the results of the 1989 elections for state offices and look forward to the 1990 contests. Updates on current governors, legislatures, bureaucracies, and state courts are included, as are discussions of some overriding issues on the states' agendas, from abortion and the environment to education and AIDS.

In an age when the federal government is retrenching, both the national government and the localities are looking to the states as never before for leadership. State governments are facing unprecedented challenges, and we need to be more attentive than ever to their agendas. This informative volume, the sixth in the series, helps us to keep up with the states—the new cutting edge of the federal system.

Larry J. Sabato
Charlottesville, Virginia

Preface

State governments are no longer sleepy backwater operations located in far-off capitals where few people know or care what they are doing. They are big-time organizations on a par with many "Fortune 500" companies. Comparing the states and their 1987 general revenues with the nation's largest businesses based on their 1987 sales finds 17 states in the top 50 of these largest organizations.[1] In fact, 28 states have revenues equal to or greater than the top 100 companies in the "Fortune 500" listing.

The "Reagan revolution" contributed to the states' increased visibility and influence. State governments were asked to shoulder more of the domestic policy burden as the federal government coped with the national debt and defense. The states' response to the fiscal challenges of the 1980s became an issue of national as well as local importance. And this heightened role is projected to continue into the 1990s as we see state after state grappling with budgetary problems often caused by having to pick up some of the fiscal slack created by a federal government "preoccupied by the problems of subtraction"[2] and cutting back its support of domestic programs.

Richard Nathan of Princeton University and Martha Derthick of the University of Virginia recently reviewed what they now see happening in the states: "State governments are on a roll ... they are reforming education and health systems, trying to convert welfare to workfare and building new roads and bridges and other public works." They found that most elected state officials loved this new activism, often seeing governors and legislatures competing "with one another to do more, do it better, and do it faster." Even state attorneys general were coming alive "with populist flair" as they were "fighting mergers that the [U.S.] Justice Department finds acceptable" and "challenging allegedly deceptive advertising by fast-food chains and commercial airlines." Nathan and Derthick argued that one of the most important legacies of the Reagan years would be "this increased activism in state governments" as responsibilities have gravitated from both the national and local levels to the states.[3]

The 1990-91 edition of *State Government: CQ's Guide to Current Issues and Activities* includes recent articles from state journals and other publications by those in state government and public interest organizations attempting to define and analyze state issues and agendas.

Short background essays introduce the articles and highlight developments in the states.

The organization of this book parallels that of state government texts. First is politics: the most recent election results, and the roles of direct democracy, political parties, and the media. Next are the institutions: legislatures, governors, bureaucracies, and state courts. Finally are some of the issues of primary concern to the states today: abortion, AIDS, education, hazardous waste, and foreign investment in the states. A reference guide for further study also is included.

There are many to thank for their assistance in developing this book. Among them are David R. Tarr, the director of the Book Department at Congressional Quarterly, for his support, and Larry Sabato at the University of Virginia for his recommendations and kind words in the Foreword. This edition reflects the hard work of CQ editors Nancy Kervin and Ann O'Malley. To them, and to the managing editor of the Book Department, Nancy Lammers, I offer my appreciation.

This is our sixth compilation of the *Guide,* and there is much we have yet to learn. Any errors you find are mine. I hope you will send your comments and suggestions so we might be able to improve the 1991-92 edition.

Thad L. Beyle
Chapel Hill, North Carolina

Notes

1. California ($55.9 billion) fell between fourth place IBM ($59.7 billion) and fifth place General Electric ($49.4 billion); New York ($44.6 billion) was between sixth place Mobil Oil ($48.2 billion) and seventh place Chrysler ($35.5 billion); Texas ($19.6 billion) fell between thirteenth place Shell Oil ($21.1 billion) and fourteenth place Occidental Petroleum ($19.4 billion); Pennsylvania ($18.9 billion) was between fifteenth place Procter & Gamble ($19.3 billion) and sixteenth place United Tech ($18.1 billion); Michigan ($17.5 billion) and Illinois ($17.3 billion) fell between seventeenth place Atlantic Richfield ($17.6 billion) and the three companies tied for eighteenth place at $17.0 billion—Eastman Kodak, Boeing, and RJR Nabisco; Ohio followed these corporations and tied twenty-first place Dow Chemical at $16.7 billion; New Jersey ($15.9 billion) fell between twenty-second place Xerox ($16.4 billion) and twenty-third place USX ($15.8 billion); Florida ($14.4 billion) and Massachusetts ($13.2 billion) were between twenty-fifth place McDonnell Douglas ($15.1 billion) and twenty-sixth place Pepsico ($13.0 billion); North Carolina (slightly under $9.8 billion) fell between fortieth place ALCOA ($9.8 billion) and forty-first place General Dynamics ($9.6 billion); Virginia and Wisconsin ($9.2 billion) were between forty-fourth place ConAgra ($9.5 billion) and forty-fifth place Johnson & Johnson ($9.0 billion); Minnesota and Washington ($8.8 billion) and Georgia at a little under $8.6 billion were between two corporations tied for forty-seventh place—Anheuser-Busch and Unoco ($8.9 billion) and Sun ($8.6 billion), with Maryland ($8.4 billion) following Sun, ahead of forty-ninth place Coca-Cola ($8.3 billion) on the *Fortune* "100" listing. From "The 'Fortune' 100," *USA Today*, April 5, 1989, 4B; also refer to *State Policy Data Book '89* (Alexandria, Va.: State Policy Research, 1989), Table C-10.

2. Carl E. Van Horn, ed. *The State of the States* (Washington, D.C.: CQ Press, 1989), ix.

3. "Federalism," *State Policy Reports* 5:24 (December 31, 1987): 23.

I. THE 1989-90 ELECTIONS

State officials continue to debate the timing of U.S. elections. Some argue that national, state, and local elections should be held at different times to keep separate the issues, candidates, and political concerns of each level. Following this argument, national elections for president, vice president, U.S. senators, and U.S. representatives would be held in even years, as they are now; exactly which year would depend on the length of the term—that is, representatives every two years, presidents every four years, and senators every six years. State-level elections for governor and other executive officials, state legislators, and state constitutional amendments and referendums would be held in "off-years" (nonpresidential election years) or possibly in odd-numbered years. And local elections would be at another time, preferably not in conjunction with either state or national elections.

Others advocate holding all elections at the same time to maximize voter interest and turnout and, not inconsequentially, to increase the importance of the political party as the main determinant of voters' decisions from the top of the ballot to the bottom. But there is not a single Republican party or a single Democratic party to influence voters' choices. At least fifty different Republican and Democratic state parties reflect the unique political culture, heritage, and positions of the fifty states. Add to that the increasing number of independents and other voters who split their tickets, and it is clear that this political party rationale for simultaneous elections will not hold up in the practical world of politics.

Neither side of the timing argument has predominated. During the 1988 presidential election year, forty-four states elected their legislatures, but only twelve elected their governors. Of these twelve states, New Hampshire, Rhode Island, and Vermont elected their

governors to two-year terms, which means that their gubernatorial elections alternate between presidential and nonpresidential election years. In 1986, Arkansas switched its gubernatorial elections to the even, nonpresidential years and granted the governor a four- rather than two-year term. Indeed, most states hold their gubernatorial elections in even, nonpresidential years, as in 1990, when thirty-six governors will be elected, along with forty-four state legislatures; or in odd years, as in 1989, when New Jersey and Virginia held their state elections, and in 1991, when Kentucky, Louisiana, and Mississippi will be holding theirs.

A major reason why some states have shifted their elections to nonpresidential years is because the personalities, issues, and concerns evident in presidential elections often spill over into state-level contests. While presidential elections are stirring events that bring the excitement of politics to the American populace and lead to higher turnout among voters, some state officials fear that the "coattail effect" of the national elections will change the results of their elections and, most important, obscure the state issues that voters should consider on election day.

In 1988, there was an interesting political change as twenty states moved to hold their presidential primary elections on the same date—on the March 8 "Super Tuesday." The twelve states holding state elections in 1988 still ran their primaries and caucuses at the normal time in their political calendars, and thereby kept their national and state political processes separate. It is too soon to determine the effects of this shift on state politics, but one fact is clear: there was an additional primary election in these states. This addition strained fragile political resources, resulting in a diminished pool of those who would work in political campaigns, those who would provide contributions to political campaigns, and, unfortunately, those who would vote in a state primary. Over the next few years, watch the state legislatures in these states to see if they make some changes in these primary processes; some already have.

State Campaigns: 1986-89

During the 1986-89 electoral period, there was an uncertainness about our political system. President Ronald Reagan, having been reelected for his second term in 1984, was a political "lame duck": a powerful national politician with no further chances to demonstrate this power at the ballot box. His administration was being shaken by allegations of scandal, and the beginnings of the Iran-contra affair raised questions about his leadership. In response, politicians at all levels of government, especially Republicans, began to put some political distance between themselves and the president. Local and state issues began to dominate the contests for these offices. To date, the 1988 election of Republican George Bush as president, and the Bush administration, have not seemed to have an impact on elections at lower levels of government.

In 1986, of the thirty-six states holding gubernatorial elections, twenty-one new governors were selected, with fifteen of the eighteen incumbent governors winning reelection. The campaigns were often dominated by economic and local- or state-based issues. Despite the fact that Democrats won nineteen of the races and Republicans seventeen, there was growth in Republican gubernatorial strength from sixteen seats to twenty-four seats.

This increase was somewhat balanced by the wins of Democrats in state legislative races, who claimed nearly 180 new legislative seats across the country and gained control of two more state legislatures, raising their total to twenty-eight. This configuration of party wins

and losses resulted in split political leadership in twenty-nine states, where the governor belonged to one party and one or both houses of the legislature were controlled by the opposing party.

However, in this same election year, thirty-four U.S. Senate contests led to some dramatic Democratic wins that changed the partisan makeup of the U.S. Senate to 55-45 Democratic, from 53-47 Republican. Interestingly, many of these Senate campaigns were fought over local or statewide issues such as the plight of the farm economy in the Midwest, which reversed the 1984 trend whereby local issues too often were swamped by the national campaign. These campaigns often became very negative and nasty through media advertising as candidates attempted to smear the reputations of their opponents.

The 1986 general elections provide an excellent profile of the American voter and the trend toward split-ticket voting at the state level. With thirty-six governorships and thirty-four Senate seats up for election, twenty-five of these states had contests for both seats. According to an ABC News election day exit poll, 24 percent of those who voted Democratic for governor voted Republican in the Senate race, and 23 percent of those who voted Republican for governor voted Democratic in the Senate race.[1]

Some of the results in particular states demonstrate how wide an impact split-ticket voting can have on specific elections. Eleven of these twenty-five states elected a governor from one party and a U.S. senator from the other. For example, in New York, Democratic gubernatorial candidate Mario M. Cuomo won with 65 percent of the vote while Republican senatorial candidate Alfonse M. D'Amato won with 57 percent of the vote—a vote swing of twenty-two points! Likewise, in Illinois, Republican gubernatorial candidate James R. Thompson won with 57 percent of the vote while Democratic senatorial candidate Alan J. Dixon won with 65 percent of the vote. In both of these cases, all the winning candidates were incumbents. Vote swings in Oregon and South Carolina totaled sixteen points each, in California thirteen points, and in five other states vote swings totaled more than four points.[2] Clearly, party-line voting was not the overriding rule guiding the voters in the 1986 statewide elections.

The three states that held elections in 1987 are traditionally one-party Democratic states: Kentucky, Louisiana, and Mississippi. Democrats again won the major gubernatorial races and continued their control over the state legislatures. Each gubernatorial race was unique. The most lopsided victory was in Kentucky where new Democratic governor Wallace G. Wilkinson, a self-made millionaire businessman with a lack of political experience, conducted the most expensive gubernatorial campaign in the state's history, stressing his "new ideas" approach to governing and winning 65 percent of the vote.[3]

Louisiana's new Democratic governor, Buddy Roemer, a U.S. representative from the Shreveport area, promised a "revolution" in state government, and barely defeated incumbent governor Edwin Edwards (33 percent to 28 percent) in that state's unique open first primary. For Edwards, a controversial and tainted political figure, this loss was the handwriting on the wall. He declined to challenge Roemer to a runoff. This seemed to end Edwards's "Louisiana Hayride" style of governing under the Cajun-French slogan *Laissez les bons temps rouler* (Let the good times roll), but there are rumors he may attempt a comeback in 1991.[4]

In Mississippi, the rise of Republican party strength was apparent as Democratic state auditor Ray Mabus received only 53 percent of the vote in defeating a moderate Republican challenger. The state has not had a Republican governor since the Reconstruction era and times are clearly changing in Ole Miss. Mabus's narrow victory also reflected a reaction against his "high-profile efforts to promote efficiency and honesty in government [which] ruffled some feathers in the courthouse cliques."[5]

The impact of women on the ballot at the highest levels continued to increase in 1986 as Republican Kay A. Orr of Nebraska won that state's governorship and Democrat Madeleine M. Kunin of Vermont was reelected to her second term. Women also won forty-two other statewide elected offices, including twelve secretaries of state, ten treasurers, six lieutenant governors, and six state auditors.[6] These women can attribute their success to better fund raising, aid from other office holders who are women, more active financial support and counseling from female corporate executives, and more active support for top female candidates from men.[7]

To some observers, this set of victories by women represents the third wave of recruitment of women into state politics. The first wave, up to the early 1970s, consisted of women winning as widows, wives, or daughters of established male politicians. The second wave through the 1970s consisted of women active in civic affairs shifting their volunteer work and contacts into political affairs. The third wave now evident is of women who have moved up the political ladder by defeating other candidates while keeping their eyes on a higher political goal such as the governorship, much as men have. In other words, the third wave consists of upwardly mobile politicians who happen to be women.[8]

In 1988, when elections in the states coincided with a presidential election, there were legislative elections in most states but only twelve gubernatorial contests. The main message of the 1988 results in the states is stability.

For example, an all-time low of 16 percent of elected state legislators are "new," while the rest are incumbents who were re-elected. This low turnover suggests our state legislatures are starting to resemble the U.S. Congress, with its 8 to 15 percent turnover rate of recent decades.[9] In gubernatorial races, eight incumbents were able to retain their seats and only one incumbent, Arch Moore of West Virginia, was defeated in his attempt to stay in office. Only four new governors were elected: in Indiana, Montana, New Hampshire, and West Virginia. Presidential politics seemed to help the GOP, as seven of the twelve winners were Republican (58 percent) compared to zero in 1987 and seventeen of thirty-six in 1986 (47 percent).

As in 1986, there were three states in which split-ticket voting was evident as voters elected a governor and a U.S. senator of opposite parties. Voters in Vermont returned Democratic incumbent Madeleine M. Kunin to office with 56 percent of the vote and elevated Republican representative James M. Jeffords to the U.S. Senate with 69 percent of the vote—a twenty-five point swing. In Indiana, Democratic secretary of state Evan Bayh was elected governor with 53 percent of the vote while Republican Richard G. Lugar was returned to the U.S. Senate with 68 percent of the vote—a swing of twenty-one points. In Washington state, Democratic incumbent governor Booth Gardner won with 63 percent of the vote while former Republican U.S. senator Slade Gorton claimed victory for a return to the Senate with a close 51 percent of the vote—a swing of fourteen points. In 1989, there were two states in which gubernatorial elections took place: New Jersey and Virginia. Voters in Virginia also were electing their legislators and New Jersey voters were electing members to their lower house, the General Assembly. The Democrats were victorious in both states: in the gubernatorial races, James

J. Florio (N.J.) and L. Douglas Wilder (Va.) were elected, and in the legislative races, Democrats retained their hold over the Virginia legislature and recaptured the lower house in New Jersey.

But the focus in the 1989 elections was on abortion. In July 1989, midway through these campaigns, the U.S. Supreme Court announced a major decision on abortion.[10] In effect, the Court began the process of reversing the standard set in an earlier decision, *Roe v. Wade* (1973), which had provided women the right under the U.S. Constitution to choose an abortion within a certain time period.[11] This earlier decision also had the effect of giving governors and "state legislators the opportunity not to choose sides in a wrenching political debate."[12]

The impact of the decision was almost immediate as candidates for office in the states were asked their positions on the issue: were they prolife or prochoice? The governor of Florida even called a special fall session of his legislature to tighten up that state's abortion laws. The legislators met, but decided not to act on the issue, much to the governor's embarrassment.

The abortion issue hurt the Republican candidates for governor in both New Jersey and Virginia since they held prolife views, in contrast to the more prochoice views of the Democratic candidates. But as the Republicans began to feel the heat of the rapidly growing ranks of the prochoice activists—even from within their own party—and as they saw the numbers in their polls rising against them, they waffled on the issue, moving away from their previous prolife stand. That strategy seemed to hurt them even more.

Virginia's gubernatorial race was significant for more than how abortion affected that state's politics. The Commonwealth's voters had the opportunity to elect the nation's first elected black governor, Lt. Governor L. Douglas Wilder (D). Wilder worked his way up through Virginia politics, winning a state senate seat in 1969, then lieutenant governorship in 1985.

There are two stunning messages from these elections: blacks can seek and win major offices as politicians instead of as civil rights warriors; and abortion is a major issue that can help or hurt candidates depending on their views and how they handle the abortion question on the campaign trail.

The Issues

As evidenced by the 1989 New Jersey and Virginia gubernatorial races, abortion has become the political issue of the next decade. Until 1989, issues in state campaigns varied considerably, not only from state to state but also among offices being contested. For example, campaigns for state legislative seats tended to focus on the individual candidate as he or she sought to achieve name recognition among the voters. Some candidates shied away from taking a position on specific issues, preferring instead to endorse economic development, reduction of crime, better education, and other broad issues. Others used specific issues such as antiabortion, tax repeal, or growth limits to achieve the name recognition they needed to win. On the whole, however, candidates preferred to take a position on broad issues rather than commit themselves to a specific issue that could alienate potential supporters. As *State Policy Reports* has pointed out,

> Campaigns rarely reveal candidate positions on the difficult questions of state policy. The easy question is whether candidates are for lower state and local taxes, better educational quality, higher teacher pay, and protecting the environment while stimulating economic growth. The candidates generally share these objectives. The hard question is what to do when these objectives collide as they often do.[13]

As a result, the average voter has a hard time discerning where the candidates stand on specific issues, and attempts to survey state legislative candidates on specific issues usually are not successful. One public interest organization in North Carolina does provide voters with information on how incumbents are rated by their peers, lobbyists, and the media covering the legislature in addition to information on the legislation they sponsored and their votes on key bills. However, no information of this kind can be provided on nonincumbent legislative candidates.[14]

But the days of noncontroversial state campaigns appear to be over with the emergence of the abortion issue in state politics. The abortion issue has become the driving force behind many state political campaigns, and prolife and prochoice advocates are "educating" the voters about candidates, depending on which side of the abortion argument the candidates stand. How candidates stand on this single issue rapidly is becoming the litmus test on which way the electorate will vote— just as politicians had feared.

The first article in this section is by Beth Donovan of Congressional Quarterly who reviews the thirty-six gubernatorial campaigns of 1990. Rhodes Cook and Bob Benenson of Congressional Quarterly examine the results of the New Jersey and Virginia elections. These late 1980s elections, and those to be held in 1990, are important in that they will put into office those responsible for redrawing congressional and state legislative district boundaries after the 1990 Census.

Notes

1. Survey by ABC News, November 4, 1986, reported in *Public Opinion* 9:4 (January-February 1987): 34.
2. Adapted from Walter Dean Burnham, "Elections Dash GOP Dream of Realignment," *Wall Street Journal*, November 26, 1986, as cited in note 1.

3. Caroline Ashley, "History Is on the Side of the Democrats . . . in Kentucky's and Mississippi's Elections," *Congressional Quarterly Weekly Report,* October 31, 1987, 2689.

4. Bob Benenson, "The Edwards 'Hayride' Ends; Rep. Roemer to Be Governor," *Congressional Quarterly Weekly Report,* October 31, 1987, 2687.

5. Ashley, "History Is on the Side of the Democrats," 2688-2689, and "The Elections of 1987," *State Policy Reports* 5:21 (November 16, 1987): 26.

6. "1987 Statewide Elected Women—44," *Women in State Government Newsletter,* December 1986, 4.

7. Meg Armstrong, "WSEG Campaign News," *Women in State Government Newsletter,* May 1986, 4.

8. Comments of Celinda Lake, Candidate Services Director of the Women's Campaign Fund, at a National Conference of State Legislatures seminar as reported by David Broder, "Hard-earned Credentials Give Female Candidates an Edge," [Raleigh] *News and Observer,* September 15, 1986, 13A.

9. Karl T. Kurtz, "No Change—For a Change," *State Legislatures* 15:1 (January 1989): 29.

10. *Webster v. Reproductive Health Services* (1989).

11. *Roe v. Wade* (1973).

12. Wendy Kaminer, "From *Roe* to *Webster*: Court Hands Abortion to States," *State Government News* 32:11 (November 1989), 12. (This article has been reprinted in this volume on pp. 209-212.)

13. *State Policy Reports* 2:20 (October 31, 1984): 11.

14. North Carolina Center for Public Policy Research, *Article II: A Guide to the N.C. Legislature,* (Raleigh, N.C.), published biennially.

'90 Gubernatorial Contests Give Key Clues to Future

by Beth Donovan

The 1990 round of gubernatorial elections are the most important in recent memory, with 36 seats at stake and national political forces playing an unusual and pivotal role.

These governorships are all coming up for grabs in a year when there is no presidential contest to define the national mood, and in a year when states stand on the brink of a redistricting process that could reshape the face of Congress and the state legislatures.

A number of next year's gubernatorial contests will feature battles over one of the most contentious issues in modern-day America—abortion policy. In addition, crafty strategists for both national parties will be seeking an upper hand in drawing congressional district lines by electing more governors, who are "gatekeepers" of the redistricting process in nearly every state.

New Lines, New Forces

The states electing governors in 1990 account for nearly 80 percent of all U.S. House seats. Governors will be chosen in all five Sun Belt states that are expected to gain House seats after the 1990 census—Arizona, California, Florida, Georgia and Texas. Also electing governors are the five Frost Belt megastates that are likely to lose two or more

House seats—Illinois, Michigan, New York, Ohio and Pennsylvania.

Republicans currently hold the governor's office in all three states slated to gain three or more seats—California, Florida and Texas—while Democrats now control three of the four states likely to be big losers in reapportionment—Michigan, Ohio and Pennsylvania.

Governors typically hold veto power over the new congressional maps that will be drawn by the state legislatures. Thus, a governor can be either insurance against a partisan gerrymander or the seal of approval for it. As a result, the national parties will get intensely involved in numerous campaigns. "Redistricting is the guiding force next year," says Michele Davis, executive director of the Republican Governors Association.

The U.S. Supreme Court's July [1989] ruling in *Webster v. Reproductive Health Services*, which gives states more power to regulate abortion, is drawing new political forces into the arena of gubernatorial elections. In recent years, governors' contests have come

---

Beth Donovan is a staff writer for the *Congressional Quarterly Weekly Report*. This article appeared September 23, 1989, 2486-2489.

Legislative and Gubernatorial Control, 1990

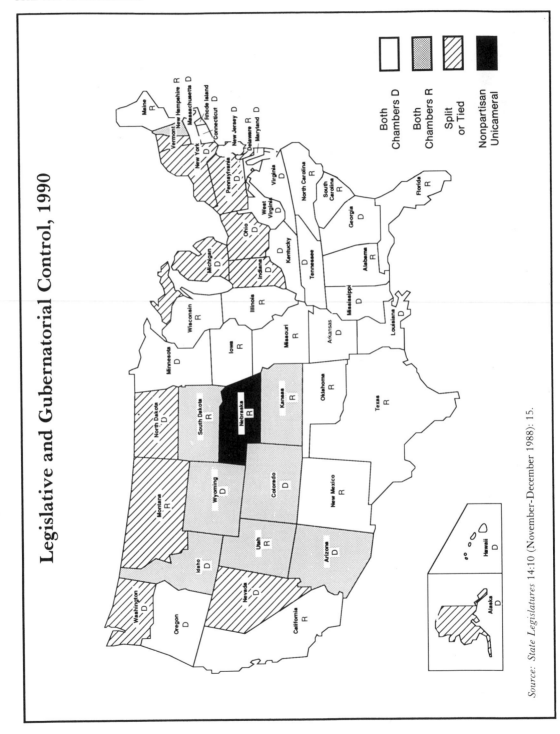

Source: *State Legislatures* 14:10 (November–December 1988): 15.

to turn primarily on nuts-and-bolts issues of state management, not on matters of fierce philosophical debate. So it is not surprising that in their 1990 campaigns, many chief executives and challengers are struggling to come to grips with the highly sensitive issue of abortion.

Higher Ambitions

Whatever the governors' elections may mean for the shape of House districts in the 1990s, they are likely to have an immediate impact on the makeup of the next Congress.

That is because one senator and eight House members are already laying the groundwork for gubernatorial campaigns. Several other members are weighing their options.

While it is fairly common for governors to try for the Senate, the uncommon power of California's governorship has tempted GOP Sen. Pete Wilson to move in the opposite direction—from Washington to Sacramento. Wilson, who was re-elected to a new six-year Senate term last year, would have the power to appoint his Senate successor if he wins the governorship. He also would have an important voice in shaping the congressional districts of California's huge House delegation, which may grow to 51 members after the next census.

The last time a senator left midterm to become governor was in 1938, when Democratic Sen. Arthur Harry Moore won the New Jersey governorship just two years after coming to the Senate.

From the House, Democrats Bill Nelson of Florida, Ronnie G. Flippo of Alabama [and Bruce A. Morrison of Connecticut] have already begun their 1990 gubernatorial bids, while Democrats ... Wes Watkins of Oklahoma and Bill Richardson of New Mexico are considering statewide campaigns.

The gubernatorial aspirations of GOP Reps. Tommy F. Robinson of Arkansas and John G. Rowland of Connecticut are the subject of intense speculation in their states. [Although] Republican Rep. Mike DeWine of Ohio ... formed an exploratory gubernatorial committee, [he decided to run for lieutenant governor].

Two House members [faced] off in one of the gubernatorial elections that [was] held [in 1989]: Democratic Rep. James J. Florio [beat] GOP Rep. Jim Courter in New Jersey. The other 1989 contest [was] in Virginia, where Democratic Lt. Gov. L. Douglas Wilder [defeated] Republican J. Marshall Coleman.

Holding Steady

Though the stakes of next year's gubernatorial elections are high, neither party at this point is predicting dramatic change in the overall partisan breakdown of the nation's 50 governorships. Democrats now hold 28 of the 50, and they are defending the majority of the seats at stake in 1990—20 to 16.

The best-case scenario for the GOP, according to Davis, is a net gain of two seats for the GOP. Chuck Dolan, executive director of the Democratic Governors' Association, paints a similar picture for his party.

These predictions are essentially borne out in Congressional Quarterly's [1989] state-by-state election analysis. From this early vantage point, not a single governor's office seems highly vulnerable to partisan turnover in 1990, though in numerous states the party currently in power begins as just a slight favorite.

Other contests could be more competitive by [the fall of 1990]. But absent a significant downturn in the national economic forecast, it appears likely that to succeed, challengers will need incumbents to stumble badly.

Open seats traditionally present the best opportunity for partisan change, but 1990 offers fewer open seats than in the past. In 1986, when most of the governors up [for re-

Table 1 Gubernatorial Elections: 1977-1989

| | | Democratic winner | | Number of incumbent governors | | | | | | | | | Where lost | |
| | | | | Eligible to run | | Did run | | Won | | Lost | | | | Primary | General election |
Year	Races	#	%	#	%	#	%	#	%	#	%			#	#
1977	2	1	50	1	50	1	100	1	100	—	—			—	—
1978	36	21	58	29	81	22	76	16	73	6	27			1[a]	5[b]
1979	3	2	67	0	0	—	—	—	—	—	—			—	—
1980	13	6	46	12	92	12	100	7	58	5	42			2[c]	3[d]
1981	2	1	50	0	0	—	—	—	—	—	—			—	—
1982	36	27	75	33	92	25	76	19	76	6	24			1[e]	5[f]
1983	3	3	100	0	0	—	—	—	—	—	—			—	—
1984	13	5	38	9	69	6	67	4	67	2	33			—	2[g]
1985	2	1	50	1	50	1	100	1	100	—	—			—	—
1986	36	19	53	24	67	18	75	15	83	3	18			1[h]	2[i]
1987	3	3	100	2	67	1	50	0	0	1	100			1[j]	—
1988	12	5	42	9	75	9	100	8	89	1	11			—	1[k]
1989	2	2	100	0	0	—	—	—	—	—	—			—	—
TOTALS	163	96	59	120	74	95	79	71	75	24	26			6 (25%)	18 (75%)

[a] Michael S. Dukakis, D-Mass.
[b] Robert F. Bennett, R-Kan; Rudolph G. Perpich, D-Minn.; Meldrim Thompson, R-N.H.; Robert Straub, D-Ore.; M. J. Schreiber, D-Wis.
[c] Thomas L. Judge, D-Mont.; Dixy Lee Ray, D-Wash.
[d] Bill Clinton, D-Ark.; Joseph P. Teasdale, D-Mo., Arthur A. Link, D-N.D.
[e] Edward J. King, D-Mass.
[f] Frank D. White, R-Ark.; Charles Thone, R-Neb.; Robert F. List, R-Nev.; Hugh J. Gallen, D-N.H; William P. Clements, Jr., R-Texas
[g] Allen I. Olson, R-N.D.; John D. Spellman, R-Wash.
[h] Bill Sheffield, D-Alaska
[i] Mark White, D-Texas; Anthony S. Earl, D-Wis.
[j] Edwin Edwards, D-La.
[k] Arch A. Moore, R-W.Va.

election in 1990] were elected, 12 incumbents had served the maximum number of terms permitted by state law. In 1990, just three incumbents are ineligible to seek re-election—Georgia Democrat Joe Frank Harris, New Mexico Republican Garrey Carruthers and Ohio Democrat Richard F. Celeste.

The Georgia race tantalizes national Republicans. Four of the five states that border Georgia have GOP governors, and state Democrats seem headed for a divisive primary. Conversely, in New Mexico, the Democrats have lured at least one high-profile competitor into the race, while the GOP field is still vague.

In Ohio, Democrats may actually fare better without Celeste; his administration has been battered by allegations of corruption in his second term. But the GOP campaign task will be tougher because the object of voter ire is not on the ballot.

The situation is similar in most of the six states where the incumbent is voluntarily retiring. Massachusetts Democrat Michael S. Dukakis and Illinois Republican James R. Thompson plummeted in popularity after calling for tax increases this year. Neither is seeking re-election, but their parties still start with better than even-money chances to hold power in 1990.

The stagnant oil economy has undermined three governors—Alaska Democrat Steve Cowper, Oklahoma Republican Henry Bellmon and Texas Republican William P. Clements Jr. All are stepping down. But in the contests to replace them, neither party has a pronounced advantage.

Californian Republicans were very worried when George Deukmejian announced his retirement. Though his popularity had slipped, he looked like the GOP's strongest contender in this critical state. But when the popular Wilson stepped into the race, Republican prospects improved greatly.

Standing Pat

In the electorate, the mood for change does not seem very strong, a reflection of the general sense of national economic well-being. In hard times, state chief executives are the first to bear the brunt of voter unrest. But when the economy is sound and jobs are available—as is the case in most parts of the country—governors are the first to reap the benefit.

The political landscape today looks very different from 1986. That year, the industrial Midwest was just emerging from the 1982 recession and the farm crisis and oil slump were big news. For those and other reasons, it was not a good year for the party in power: Fourteen governorships changed partisan hands, and the GOP scored a net gain of eight seats.

Since then, much has changed. The farm and industrial states have made steady progress, and in most cases the state budgets are flush. Nebraska's Republican Gov. Kay A. Orr finds herself under fire not for any weakness in the state economy, but rather for her tardiness in returning the budget surplus to taxpayers. Republican incumbents in Iowa and Wisconsin are well-positioned for re-election, as are their Democratic counterparts in Pennsylvania and Michigan.

In the Sun Belt, which continues to prosper, the GOP hopes to build on its successes in 1986, when it seized seven governorships from Democratic control and lost only one GOP-held seat. In addition to Georgia, a top GOP target is Arkansas, where Democratic Gov. Bill Clinton is now in his ninth year in office. Clinton may be weakened by a primary challenge, but the GOP has two well-financed party switchers—including Rep. Robinson—who are waging even more cutting campaigns.

Democrats have a chance to retake the

Abortion Issue . . .

When the Supreme Court [in 1989] handed down its decision in the *Webster v. Reproductive Health Services* case, it handed the nation's governors power that few of them wanted. Most of them won office on the strength of their managerial skill and personal image, not because of their strong ideological passions. Some had never even taken a public stand on abortion.

But *Webster*—which gives states latitude in setting abortion policy—has made abortion a hot topic in many 1990 gubernatorial contests. Despite the national Democratic Party's firm support for abortion rights and the national Republican Party's outright opposition to the procedure, candidates and voters in both parties seem more conflicted about the issue than this rigid party alignment suggests.

Some Democratic politicians, such as New York Gov. Mario M. Cuomo, deal with these tensions by supporting abortion rights while stating their personal opposition. Others support certain restrictions on access to the procedure.

In the 1989 gubernatorial contests, New Jersey Democratic nominee Rep. James J. Florio and his counterpart in Virginia, Lt. Gov. L. Douglas Wilder, . . . both suggested they would not reject legislation requiring parental notification for minors seeking abortions. The GOP nominees in those states—New Jersey Rep. Jim Courter and former Virginia Attorney General J. Marshall Coleman— . . . suggested that despite their opposition to abortion, they would not seek to change state laws permitting it. . . .

In Florida . . . the reaction was swift and largely negative when, following the *Webster* ruling, GOP Gov. Bob Martinez called for a special legislative session to test the limits of allowable abortion restrictions. As the October session approache[d], Martinez . . . softened his stand, but his influence . . . [was found to be lacking when the Legislature declined to consider] bills to ban abortion in public hospitals, require fetal viability tests after the 20th week of pregnancy and impose tougher regulations on clinics that perform abortions.

Unlike Martinez, Illinois Attorney General Neil Hartigan, the . . . Democratic nominee for governor in 1990, did not volunteer for a front-line position in the abortion battle. But the issue came his way, when the U.S. Supreme Court accepted a case involving an Illinois law requiring clinics to meet standards similar to hospitals'. . . . Hartigan, like his chief GOP opponent

---

GOP's Sun Belt jewel, Florida. While the state GOP there has made great strides since 1986 (the U.S. House delegation is now majority Republican), Republican Gov. Bob Martinez has been plagued by problems of his own making. Early in his first term, he flip-flopped on taxes, and in recent months his call for a special legislative session to restrict access to abortion has disquieted even many in his own party. Democratic Rep. Nelson is his

party's front-runner.

In New England, economic growth has slowed enough to squeeze state budgets, but not enough to make unemployment a serious problem. Like his neighbor in Massachusetts, Connecticut Democrat William A. O'Neill raised taxes to the great detriment of his own popularity. Unlike Dukakis, O'Neill is saying he will seek another term.

For GOP Gov. Edward D. DiPrete of

... a Quandary

for governor, supports a woman's right to choose abortion. But the Democrat defends Illinois law, saying it will not close clinics, but simply make abortions safer. . . . [The law, which was opposed by abortion-rights groups as medically unnecessary, was to be defended by Hartigan's office, but the case was settled out of court two weeks before it was to be argued. The resolution was negotiated by Hartigan.]

In other Midwestern industrial states where white, ethnic voters are pivotal to Democratic success, anti-abortion candidates have long been welcomed at the party table. All of the top Democratic contenders in Ohio oppose abortion, and Pennsylvania Gov. Robert P. Casey is a leading anti-abortion Democrat. [Since] the Pennsylvania Legislature [passed] sweeping new abortion restrictions [in October 1989], this is a priority race for abortion-rights activists. A number of Republicans hope to exploit this potential problem for the Democrats by embracing a candidate who supports abortion rights.

[The legislative-gubernatorial drama in Idaho caught everyone's attention when that state passed anti-abortion legislation drafted specifically to test the earlier Supreme Court abortion decision, *Roe v. Wade* (1973). Democratic Gov. Cecil D. Andrus, a long-time pro-life supporter, finally decided to veto the bill as being too restrictive. He faces a re-election fight in 1990.]

In much of the rest of the country, however, abortion-rights activists are making their presence felt in Democratic politics, much as anti-abortion activists have been a force in the GOP throughout the 1980s. In Massachusetts, Boston Mayor Raymond L. Flynn has stayed out of the Democratic gubernatorial fray in part because his opposition to abortion is untenable to primary voters. In Kansas and Iowa, Democratic opponents of abortion are facing stern primary opposition.

In the post-*Webster* era, however, both sides in the abortion dispute may have trouble extracting absolute commitments of support. In past gubernatorial contests, most candidates have succeeded by emphasizing their political pragmatism over their philosophical purity. It is not at all clear that the abortion issue will alter this fundamental electoral fact.

Source: "Abortion Issue a Quandary," *Congressional Quarterly Weekly Report,* September 23, 1989, 2488. Updated by editor.

Rhode Island, ethical questions raised in the 1988 campaign continue to be his biggest obstacle to re-election.

Incumbent Advantages

For most incumbents, the strength of the national economy plus the perquisites of office provide plenty of political insulation. In addition to the publicity and fund-raising machines most officeholders enjoy, governors usually have patronage powers and control of their state party.

These resources—along with some artful personal campaigning—may enable a few governors to buck their states' partisan tradition. Guy Hunt in 1986 became the first Republican since Reconstruction to win Alabama's top office, but he is personally popular, and the Democrats are heading toward a bitter primary. In predominantly Republican Arizona,

Democratic Gov. Rose Mofford is the clear favorite to win her first full term. She was elevated to the governor's office in April 1988, after Republican Evan Mecham was impeached and removed from office by the Legislature.

In Idaho, another Republican-heavy state, an expanding economy is putting Democrat Cecil D. Andrus well on his way to a fourth (non-consecutive) term. Three other governors are favored to win third consecutive four-year terms, something voters are often reluctant to award—Iowa Republican Terry E. Branstad, Michigan Democrat James J.

Blanchard and New York Democrat Mario M. Cuomo.

In Minnesota, Democratic Gov. Rudy Perpich is contemplating a third consecutive term, but a feud within his own party has weakened his position. His salvation may be the disarray in the GOP.

Nevada Gov. Bob Miller will be seeking his first full term [in the fall of 1990]. He was promoted from lieutenant governor after his predecessor, Democrat Richard H. Bryan, was elected to the Senate in 1988. But if the GOP fails to recruit a candidate with statewide experience, Miller will be hard to unseat.

Wilder Win Marks Differences of Old Dominion and New

by Rhodes Cook

In his razor-thin victory in the Virginia gubernatorial race Nov. 7, [1989,] L. Douglas Wilder essentially won the "New Virginia" but lost the old.

He carried the fast-growing suburbs and cities of Northern Virginia and the Tidewater, where newcomers tend to outnumber natives in many jurisdictions. But Wilder, the state's lieutenant governor, lost the heart of the "Old Dominion," the more rooted Virginia of small towns and Confederate monuments.

As the votes were counted on election night, Wilder, who becomes the nation's first elected black governor, rolled up a lead of nearly 100,000 votes in Northern Virginia and the Tidewater, then saw it whittled away to virtually nothing in the rest of the state.

In complete but unofficial returns from The Associated Press, Wilder had 896,283 votes (50.15 percent) to 890,750 votes (49.85 percent) for former Republican state Attorney General J. Marshall Coleman—a slim lead of 5,533 votes. A recount is likely, but the result is expected to hold up. Still, the numbers meant that Wilder's historic election was achieved with neither the breadth nor emphasis that most polls and commentators had predicted.

Race and 'Old Virginia'

Wilder showed more statewide reach in his 1985 victory for lieutenant governor. Then, he carried not only the Washington, D.C., suburbs of Northern Virginia and Tidewater population centers such as Norfolk, Portsmouth, Hampton and Newport News, but also much of the Shenandoah Valley, the mountainous western panhandle and the conservative Southside.

But that was a low-budget, less closely watched race, featuring Wilder crisscrossing the state by car. And in winning the largely ceremonial lieutenant governor's office with 52 percent of the vote, it's likely that Wilder drew some coattail pull from the victorious Democratic gubernatorial candidate, Gerald L. Baliles, who won with more than 55 percent.

With Virginia's one-term-and-out law forcing Baliles to the sidelines, Wilder was at the top of the ticket this year, and the racial aspect of the vote was unmistakable.

During the campaign, the race issue

Rhodes Cook is a staff writer for the *Congressional Quarterly Weekly Report.* This article appeared November 11, 1989, 3101-3102.

17

probably benefited Wilder. The historic nature of his candidacy helped him draw contributions from across the country and press coverage from around the world. Exasperated, Coleman complained in a news conference that news reporting of Wilder's campaign was too favorable, making Coleman the victim of a "double standard."

But on Election Day, the racial issue probably cost Wilder more votes than it won him. If anything, the results seemed to show that pre-election opinion polls measuring the support for black candidates running against whites can be extremely unreliable.

To Wilder's advantage, Virginia does not have a history of racially polarized voting. The state's black population of nearly 20 percent is a significant voting bloc, but not large enough to be particularly threatening to the white majority. Wilder won roughly 40 percent of the white vote to go along with an estimated 95 percent of the black vote.

Still, Wilder ran well behind his two white Democratic ticket mates. Falls Church Volvo dealer Donald S. Beyer Jr. was an upset winner in the lieutenant governor's race with 54 percent of the vote. State Attorney General Mary Sue Terry was easily re-elected with 63 percent.

Election-eve surveys and Election Day exit polls had forecast a comfortable Wilder victory—about 5 to 10 percentage points—but the actual vote was a virtual dead heat. Analysts speculated that a number of white Virginia voters told pollsters they intended to vote for Wilder and then didn't.

In a news conference the day after the election, Wilder discounted race as being a major factor in the unexpectedly close outcome. Several pre-election polls had shown a large undecided vote, and Wilder was the target of a barrage of negative attacks from Coleman throughout the final weeks of the campaign that could have sent late-deciding

voters scurrying to Coleman.

But those who saw race as a crippling factor for Wilder pointed to a comparison of his vote with Beyer's. Both Democrats emphasized a pro-choice stance on abortion; both were well financed. The major difference between the two was that Wilder is black and Beyer is white.

Wilder's vote tally was close to Beyer's in the strongholds of the New Dominion. Both swept vote-rich Northern Virginia with roughly 60 percent of the vote, and both carried the populous Tidewater with roughly 55 percent.

But in "Old Virginia," ticket-splitting was more evident, and Beyer clearly ran better.

Beyer won southwest Virginia with 54 percent; Wilder drew 47 percent. Beyer won metropolitan Richmond, which is dominated by the conservative suburbs of Chesterfield and Henrico counties, with 52 percent; Wilder lost it with 47 percent.

Beyer won the Southside with 51 percent; Wilder took 46 percent there.

And while both Democrats lost the historic base of the Virginia GOP, the Shenandoah Valley, Beyer ran 4 percentage points better there than Wilder.

Coal and Abortion

If there was a major disappointment for Wilder, though, it was probably his loss in southwest Virginia. And the vote there was probably due as much to pocketbook issues as to race. While there are relatively few votes in this rural region compared to the suburbs, the coal fields along the West Virginia border have provided Democrats a strong base in recent gubernatorial elections.

But this year, the miners have been on strike and openly hostile to the Baliles administration for deploying state troops to enforce Virginia's right-to-work law.

The United Mine Workers (UMW) endorsed Wilder, but the political mood was so volatile in the coalfields that a local UMW official ran as a write-in candidate for the state Legislature against a veteran Democratic incumbent and won easily. The legislator's son, a judge, had imposed more than $30 million in fines against the union for illegal strike activities.

Democratic statewide candidates normally count on carrying southwest Virginia. That Wilder apparently won without it is a tribute to his strength in Northern Virginia and the Tidewater. Wilder tapped the large pool of black votes in the Tidewater, which is roughly one-third black, and apparently made points in congested Northern Virginia by attacking Coleman as a pawn of real-estate developers; developers reportedly contributed at least $3 million to Coleman's campaign.

In both places, abortion emerged as a winning issue for Wilder. While Coleman tried to downplay his anti-abortion stance, Wilder skillfully featured his abortion-rights position within the framework of Virginia's historic concern for individual rights. The issue not only helped Wilder win the votes of economically conservative, socially liberal suburban voters, but also enabled him to control debate in the final weeks of the campaign.

While Coleman struggled to portray Wilder as a closet liberal, who was weak on crime and personally untrustworthy, Wilder maintained the veneer of a genteel moderate, who was basically pro-abortion rights, pro-death penalty and pro-right-to-work. And Wilder was quick to respond to attacks by Coleman with attacks of his own.

The negative tone of the campaign drew brickbats from editorial writers around the state, but did not drive down the turnout. The number of votes cast was actually up nearly 450,000 from the 1985 gubernatorial election. And the turnout of 1.79 million easily eclipsed

Finally, Florio Is Governor

In a remarkable turnabout of partisan voting patterns, Democratic Rep. James J. Florio scored a crushing victory over GOP Rep. Jim Courter in New Jersey's Nov. 7 [, 1989,] gubernatorial contest.

Florio's 61 percent tally against Courter came just four years after Republican Thomas H. Kean won a second term as governor with a state-record 70 percent of the vote. Kean's coattails in 1985 helped the GOP sweep to a state Assembly majority....

... [T]he issue that turned the election definitively in Florio's favor was abortion. Outspoken in his support of letting a woman choose abortion, Florio had strong backing from abortion-rights activists enraged by the Supreme Court's July 1989 ruling in *Webster v. Reproductive Health Services*.

Courter, who had voted consistently in opposition to abortion in the House, wavered on the issue.... With state polls showing widespread opposition to restrictive laws on abortion, Courter stated that abortion was not a priority issue for him—infuriating anti-abortion activists. Later, he said he opposed abortion, but would not seek to overturn state provisions permitting the procedure.

Attacks by Florio on Courter's inconsistency continued when Courter stumbled over the "gay rights" issue. In August, Courter implied the state should discourage employment of homosexuals in jobs where they would work with children. When accused of favoring discrimination, Courter said he was not proposing job-limiting laws. At one point, the candidate bolted from a news conference where the question was pressed.

Source: Bob Benenson, "Finally, Florio Is Governor; Democrats Take Assembly," *Congressional Quarterly Weekly Report,* November 11, 1989, 3103-3104.

the previous record for a Virginia governor's race of 1.42 million, set in 1981 when Democrat Charles S. Robb rebuffed Coleman's first bid for the governorship.

History Hat Trick

. . . For the 58-year-old Wilder, election as governor would mark the third history-making event of his career. In 1969, he was the first black elected to the Virginia Senate since Reconstruction. His election as lieutenant governor four years ago made him the first black since Reconstruction to capture a major statewide office in the South. Now, he becomes the first black in the nation to be elected governor. (He is not the first black governor, though. That honor goes to Pinckney B. S. Pinchback, who served as acting governor of Louisiana for slightly more than a month during the Christmas holiday season of 1872.)

Wilder's victory also completes the Democrats' third straight sweep of state elective offices this decade. No Republican has won a state office since the late John Dalton was elected governor and Coleman attorney general in 1977.

Republicans did gain four seats in the lower house of the Virginia Legislature, but Democrats maintain hefty majorities in both chambers. Wilder's victory assures the Democrats control of all the political power points in the upcoming redistricting process.

II. POLITICS:
DIRECT DEMOCRACY

Colorado Citizens Rewrite Legislative Rules

Voters in some states do more than choose candidates for state offices; they also vote directly on particular issues. Rather than have their elected representatives make the policy decisions, the voters themselves decide. This is called *direct democracy*. The concept of direct democracy has had a long history in the Midwest and West and at the local level in New England communities, where citizens and leaders often assemble in town meetings to determine the town budget as well as other policy issues.

There are three specific vehicles for citizens to use in states with direct democracy: *initiative, referendum,* and *recall.* In seventeen states, citizens may change the state constitution by initiating constitutional amendments to be voted on in a statewide referendum. In twenty-one states, an initiative provision allows proposed laws to be placed on a state ballot by citizen petition; the proposal is then enacted or rejected by a statewide vote. Thirty-seven states have a referendum provision in their constitutions that refers acts passed by the state legislature to the voters for their concurrence before they become law. Most amendments to state constitutions are referred to the voters for approval. In fifteen states, a recall provision allows voters to remove a state elected official from office through a recall election.[1]

The provisions for the initiative vary among the states, the most important difference being the role of the legislature. In fourteen states the initiative process is direct: no legislative action is required to place the proposal on the ballot once the requisite number of signatures on the petition is secured. In 1988, South Dakota voters ratified an amendment to their state constitution removing the legislature as part of the initiative process. In four other states the process is more indirect: the petition with the necessary signatures is submitted to the legislature, which then can (1) enact the proposal directly without a vote of the electorate, (2) alter the proposal before placing it on the ballot, or (3) place it on the ballot as submitted. Three states provide for both types of initiative—direct and indirect. Another important difference is the number of signatures required on the petition for an initiative to be considered.[2]

Like the initiative, provisions for a referendum on state legislation vary from state to state. In nineteen states, a referendum is required on certain types of bills, usually those related to state debt authorization (bond issues). In twenty-four states, a citizen petition can place an issue on the ballot for a vote by the electorate to approve or disapprove. In practice, this usually proves to be an attempt to reject an act already passed by the legislature, although many states restrict the type of legislation that can fall under this provision. Finally, fourteen states allow their legislatures to voluntarily submit laws to the voters for their concurrence or rejection.[3]

Provisions for the recall of all elected officials are included in only fifteen state constitutions. Eight states have provisions allowing the removal of all officials, six exclude judicial officials, and Montana includes all public officials, elected or appointed. Considerably more signatures are required for a recall to be placed on the ballot than for an initiative or a referendum.[4] The success of recent recall efforts indicates that this vehicle for direct democracy can be more than the "loaded shotgun behind the door" to keep elected officials on their toes. In 1983, two Michigan legislators were recalled after voting for a tax increase during the state's severe recession, and in 1977, a Wisconsin judge was recalled for his insensitive remarks during a rape trial.

The importance of the voters' right to recall an elected official was recently demonstrated in Arizona. The words and actions of Governor Evan Mecham, elected in 1986, angered many Arizonans sufficiently so that a recall petition was circulated to remove him from office. Their drive was successful and was part of the series of events that led to Mecham's removal from office in April 1988, after having served only seventeen months in office. Mecham had won a three-candidate race by gaining only 40 percent of the general election vote. This situation led to voter approval of a 1988 constitutional amendment calling for a runoff election should no candidate receive a majority vote in the general election—that is, no more plurality vote governors. However, the 1988 Arizona legislature failed to adopt the so-called "Dracula clause" in that state's constitution that would have barred Mecham, as an impeached official, from ever seeking or holding office again. As a result, Mecham is seeking the governorship again in 1990.

Immediate Effects

The effects of direct democracy can be far reaching, affecting not only the state that has the initiative, referendum, or recall provision, but also other states and the broader political milieu in which state government operates.

When California voters adopted Proposition 13 in 1978, they sent a message to elected officials across the country. This successful initiative put the brakes on state and local governments in California by restricting their ability to fund governmental programs and services. Property taxes were reduced to 1 percent of property value rate (a 57 percent cut in property tax revenues); future assessments were limited to an annual rise of only 2 percent; and a two-thirds vote of the state legislature was required for the enactment of any new state taxes.

The voters' message to state and local governments was clear: We have had enough! We want less government, fewer programs, and greatly reduced taxes. You have become our problem because of the tax burden we must shoulder. We have asked you to do something about this; nothing has been done, so we are restricting the amount of money you can raise through taxes and placing this restriction in the constitution where you will not be able to tamper with it. This message—from what had been considered the most progressive electorate and state government among the fifty—prompted a widespread reevaluation of the goals of state and local governments. To what extent should elected officials expect the taxpayers to pay to achieve these goals?

There were other signals besides Proposition 13 for decision makers to consider. Opinion polls at the beginning of the 1980s reported that more than 70 percent of the public felt that income taxes were "too high"; only 45 percent felt this way in 1962. Those who felt that "the government wastes taxpayers' money" rose from 45 percent in 1956 to 80 percent in 1980,[5] and dropped to only 76 percent in 1986.[6] In some states, elected officials heeded their electorates' call to reduce taxes; in others, tax increases for governmental services and programs were postponed. Although Proposition 13 did not spark a nationwide tax revolt, it set the possibility of such an occurrence high enough on state policy agendas to get the attention of politically concerned policy makers.

State elected officials might be wary of a "ripple-effect" of the successful recall effort conducted against Arizona Governor Mecham. Will voters in those fourteen other states with a recall provision in their constitutions take a more critical view of their elected officials and be willing to recall them from office for cause? Will there be efforts in the other thirty-five states to add recall provisions to their constitutions? Politically, this would be difficult as most states require the legislature to place constitutional amendments on the ballot, and legislators may be unwilling to provide voters with an additional means of removing them from office. There are sixteen states, however, in which an amendment to the constitution can be brought before the voters by the initiative, so that the legislatures in those states could be circumvented politically. Nine of these states do not have a recall provision.[7]

Pragmatic Decisions

Initiatives are now being placed on state ballots and voted on at the highest rate since World War II. In 1986, there were 226 referenda on the November ballots in forty-three states, and in 1988 there were 230 on the ballots in forty-one states. The initiative and referenda processes are not only becoming more prevalent in the states but more complex and expensive as well. One estimate of the cost of fighting for and against the twenty-nine referenda on the 1988 general election ballot in California was $100 million, or $4 per capita![8] Initiative and referenda politics are becoming big business.

In a study of 199 initiatives acted on between 1977 and 1984, *Initiative News Report* found that the vehicle was being used by interests at both ends of the ideological spectrum. Seventy-nine initiatives were backed by those on the liberal side of the political spectrum, seventy-four by those on the conservative side, and forty-six were not classifiable in ideological terms (usually because the initiatives concerned narrow, business-related issues). The approval rates for both the liberal and the conservative initiatives were about the same, 44 percent and 45 percent, respectively. Two-thirds of the initiatives between 1980 and 1984 qualified for the ballot through volunteer efforts alone; the others used "paid petition circulators" in addition to volunteers. The

importance of using only volunteer or grass-roots support was clear: 51 percent of these initiatives passed.[9]

The referenda considered in 1988 indicate just how varied these questions can be across the states. Lotteries were approved in four states (Idaho, Indiana, Kentucky, Minnesota), English was adopted as the official state language in three states (Arizona, Colorado, Florida), taxpayer-funded abortions were banned in two states (Arkansas, Michigan), and tax revolt initiatives failed in three states (Colorado, South Dakota, Utah). Maine voters made their state constitution gender neutral, Arizonans voted to remove a constitutional requirement that constitutional officers be male, while Oregonians revoked their governor's executive order protecting state employees from sexual discrimination.[10]

Several state electorates took aim at their state legislatures. Voters adopted referenda shortening legislative sessions in Colorado and Missouri while Montana voters refused to let the legislature meet annually—all actions directed at maintaining part-time citizen legislatures. Colorado voters approved the GAVEL (Give A Vote to Every Legislator) initiative that directs how bills are processed by committees and reduces the power of committee chairs.[11] And voters in Arizona and Massachusetts voted down legislative pay raises.[12]

In 1989 there were at least twenty-one referenda votes conducted in six states; eleven passed and ten failed. West Virginia's governor lost in his attempt to change the political topography of that state when the voters soundly rejected his proposals to eliminate the statewide elective offices of secretary of state, state treasurer, and agricultural commissioner, as well as eliminate the state board of education and state superintendent of education as constitutional offices, all in favor of more gubernatorial appointments.[13] Voters in West

Virginia also rejected the governor's proposal to give more autonomy to local units of government.[14]

The legislature fared poorly in Texas when the voters rejected proposals to give legislators a raise in salary and expense allowances. Maine voters turned aside an attempt to limit the spending in gubernatorial campaigns.[15]

Bond issues were approved in Maine (juvenile corrections), in Rhode Island (environment and mental health), in Texas (water, corrections, and mental health), in Utah (planning for hosting the Winter Olympics), but one failed in Maine (adult corrections). Two proposed options for a sales tax increase were defeated in Michigan, and the governor of Washington was unable to convince voters in his state to support a major tax increase for education. Rights of crime victims were the subject of two successful referenda in Texas and Washington state.[16]

In this section, Amy Young of Common Cause discusses how the nature of initiative campaigns has become much like other political campaigns. Bob Benenson of Congressional Quarterly demonstrates how difficult it is to get control of how money is spent in political campaigns, even through referenda. An article from *State Policy Reports* looks at the grand initiative and referenda state of California and the impact of its tax and spending limits. Finally, in *State Legislatures,* journalist Fred Brown investigates how the Colorado GAVEL

constitutional amendment played out in the state's legislature.

Notes

1. *The Book of the States, 1988-89* (Lexington, Ky.: The Council of State Governments, 1988), 17, 217-220.
2. Ibid., 217.
3. Ibid., 218-219.
4. Ibid., 220.
5. Susan Hansen, "Extraction: The Politics of State Taxation" in *Politics in the American States: A Comparative Analysis,* 4th ed., ed. Virginia Gray, Herbert Jacob, and Kenneth N. Vines (Boston: Little, Brown, 1983), 441-442.
6. Survey by the *New York Times,* December 14-18, 1985, reported in *Public Opinion* 9:6 (March-April 1987): 27.
7. *The Book of the States, 1988-89,* 17, 220.
8. "The Long Ballot in California," *State Policy Reports* 6:15 (August 1988): 27-28.
9. Reported in "Liberals, Conservatives Share Initiative Success," *Public Administration Times* 8:4 (February 15, 1985): 1, 12.
10. Elaine S. Knapp, "Voters Like Lotteries, Reject Tax Cuts," *State Government News* 31:12 (December 1988): 26.
11. Sandra Singer, "Voters Dabble with Legislative Details," *State Legislatures* 15:1 (January 1989): 30.
12. Knapp, 27.
13. "West Virginia Setbacks," *State Policy Reports* 7:18 (September 1989): 23-24.
14. Ibid., 23.
15. "Election USA: 1989," *USA Today,* November 9, 1989, 6A-7A.
16. Ibid.

The Changing Nature of Initiative Campaigns

by Amy E. Young

Statewide initiatives—which enable citizens and others to take their legislative agendas directly to the voters—have grown from a Progressive-era reform into an increasingly controversial political tool.

Generally the initiative process involves obtaining a prescribed number of petition signatures to get an issue on the ballot, followed by a public awareness campaign to inspire support. Not every state has an initiative process, but during the 1987-88 election cycle, 67 initiatives appeared on ballots in 23 states, the largest number in more than 50 years.

With this flood of popular lawmaking has come a rise in spending, which critics say has gotten out of control and is undermining the grassroots nature of the initiative process. The Supreme Court ruled in 1978 that spending limits on initiative campaigns are unconstitutional.

In California alone initiative spending exceeded $129 million in 1988. Roughly $100 million went toward a bitter battle over insurance reform, the subject of five different ballot measures. Critics charge that the complex issues surrounding insurance reform do not lend themselves to simplified ballot proposals, and furthermore that misleading slogans and claims by some of the initiatives' sponsors caused confusion among voters. While ultimately a pro-consumer measure passed, its sponsors had scrambled to raise more than $3 million for their campaign.

Despite these problems, defenders of the process believe that the initiative plays an important role in enabling citizens to have their say. Dave Schmidt, executive director of the Initiative Resource Center, a nonprofit group, maintains that "not only is the initiative process still practical; it is the strongest way for public interest groups to have an impact on the legislature."

In California, for example, the insurance reform campaign was inspired in part by the legislature's failure to respond to consumer frustration with high insurance rates. Similarly, [Common Cause of California] mounted a campaign to enact campaign finance reform because the legislature refused to act on the issue.

An initiative campaign makes sense, points out Scott Trotter, executive director of

Amy E. Young is an editorial assistant for *Common Cause Magazine*. This article is reprinted from *Common Cause Magazine* 15:4 (July/August 1989): 43. © 1989 by *Common Cause Magazine,* Washington, D.C.

[Common Cause of Arkansas] "when a good citizens' proposal becomes mired in the legislative process or when you see that the legislature is stymied."

Last year Arkansas enacted two important reforms in the process. Monthly financial disclosure statements are now required, revealing the names of and amounts given by financial backers of an initiative, and the secretary of state's office will review initiative proposals for constitutionality and possible conflict with existing laws.

Financial disclosure statements can help citizens identify an initiative's supporters in campaigns involving groups with misleading names. For example, a group opposing a proposed container-deposit ballot measure in Montana last year dubbed itself Montanans for Voluntary Recycling. [Common Cause of Montana] invoked that state's "truth in PAC-labeling" law and forced the group to change its name to the Committee Against Forced Deposit—Montana Grocers, Bottlers and Recyclers.

Truth in labeling, however, didn't end confusion stemming from ads sponsored by the anti-bottle-bill coalition. A last-minute, expensive advertising blitz by the beverage industry was a major factor in the measure's 79 to 21 percent defeat, says [Common Cause of Montana] Executive Director C. B. Pearson. "From an exit poll at the November election we know that 24.3 percent of the voters heard only negative advertising," he says. "The beverage industry was really bad about [running] misleading advertising [that claimed] only con-

venience stores would be able to take the containers . . . and bars would *have* to recycle. It was simply not true."

"When people see the ad, they need to know who's paying for it to evaluate the truth of the ad," comments the Initiative Center's Schmidt, author of *Citizen Lawmakers: The Ballot Initiative Revolution*.

With limited knowledge of an issue, the general public can be easily swayed by 30-second TV ads that focus on only some emotionally charged point, reform advocates say. Because of this trend, [Common Cause of West Virginia] is opposed to bringing the initiative process to the state. "The system would oversimplify issues, provide inappropriate choices based on a lack of information and subject people to undue pressure tactics by special interest groups," says Bob Hall, executive director of [Common Cause of West Virginia]. "The opportunity in this process is for the abuse of the democratic process."

Other [Common Cause] state organizations favor adoption of the initiative process. Last year the [Common Cause] National Governing Board approved a request by [Common Cause of Pennsylvania] to work for an initiative process in that state. But Barry Kaufman, the state organization's executive director, doesn't believe proposed legislation can be created overnight. Explaining the need to take into account other state statutes and their strengths and weaknesses, he predicts a several-year process, adding, "We want to ensure that appropriate safeguards are incorporated into the recommendation."

Changing Money's Role
Is No Easy Task

by Bob Benenson

Given their lack of progress in legislative elections since the last redistricting, California Republicans appear to have only a long-shot chance of gaining control of the Legislature before the 1990s redistricting. But a change in the state campaign-finance law, forced by the passage of Propositions 73 and 68 on the June 1988 ballot, has introduced at least an element of unpredictability to the 1990 election cycle.

The ballot initiatives were ostensibly aimed at limiting skyrocketing legislative campaign expenditures, which far exceed those in any other state. In the enormous state Senate districts (there are 40, fewer than the state's 45 U.S. House seats), the winning candidates spent an average of $277,000 in 1988, according to the California Fair Political Practices Commission. State House elections were not cheap either, with the winners spending an average of $190,000.

The new law created by the initiatives limits individual, corporate and political action committee (PAC) contributions to legislative candidates. But in terms of political effect, the initiatives' biggest impact will be to eliminate the campaign committees controlled by the leaders of the Democratic and Republican caucuses in the Legislature.

During the 1980s, the Democrats' persis-tent majorities have let them build their legislative "leadership funds" into mighty fund-raising machines. During the 1987-88 campaign cycle, Assembly Speaker Willie L. Brown Jr. spent $2.74 million, very little of which he used in his own routine re-election campaign; most went to other Democratic Assembly candidates. Senate President Pro Tem David Roberti, who also had a routine win, collected and spent $1.2 million. But Brown and Roberti will no longer be able to exercise such financial clout, because of an initiative provision that bars cash transfers between legislators' campaign treasuries, including the leadership funds.

Though the ballot propositions had the support of many "good government" organizations, some Democrats believe these groups were co-opted by Republicans, whose purpose was to limit the influence of the Democratic legislative leaders. "The real goal, . . . to limit the ability to funnel money from one candidate to another within the caucuses, is an attack on the Democratic majority," said Democratic U.S. Rep. Vic Fazio.

Bob Benenson is a staff writer for the *Congressional Quarterly Weekly Report*. This article appeared November 4, 1989, 2987.

However, California's new laws have their share of loopholes that will allow the Legislature's top dogs to stay involved. For example, there is apparently nothing in the law to prevent Brown and other Democratic (or Republican) legislative leaders from appearing at fund-raisers for individual candidates. Nor are they barred from giving guidance to PACs and other major contributors. These in turn may form "independent expenditure committees" that can spend whatever they want in behalf of targeted candidates, as long as their efforts are not coordinated with the candidates' campaigns.

Campaign-finance experts predict that such independent committees will proliferate before the 1990 campaign, just as occurred after Arizona passed a similar law. "Money is an inevitable element in politics," said Fazio. "Push it down here, it comes up there. The drafters [of the 1988 propositions] may not have solved all the problems."

Arizona: The Consequence of Reform. Proponents of restraining campaign spending in Arizona scored what they claimed was a big victory in November 1986 with the passage of their ballot initiative, Proposition 200. But it quickly became obvious in the 1988 state elections—the first after the law passed— that the flow of campaign money could find a way around reformers' obstacles.

Under the measure, an individual contributor can give only $200 to a legislative candidate and is limited to $2,000 in contributions to all candidates in a campaign year. PACs also are limited to $200 per candidate, except for so-called "super PACs" (those that raise at least $10 apiece from 5,000 people), which can give up to $1,000. Candidates can receive no more than $5,000 from all PACs.

This venture in campaign-spending reform has had unintended consequences. Barred from their traditional method of giving, the interest groups that had regularly been among the biggest campaign donors redirected their money into independent expenditure committees, which are not limited under the law. As in California, these committees can spend as much as they want in behalf of individual candidates, as long as they do not coordinate with the candidates' campaigns.

While there have been independent committees in U.S. politics for some time, their prominence in Arizona increased dramatically after Proposition 200 passed. "They expanded to fill a huge void caused by the restrictive campaign law," said Rick DeGraw, a Phoenix political and marketing consultant who helped organize independent committees in 1988 for Democratic-oriented interests. More than a dozen such committees were active in the 1988 campaigns, including business groups with Republican leanings and labor unions and professional organizations favorable to Democrats.

The committees stirred considerable controversy. Candidates portrayed negatively in independent campaigns cried foul, and editorialists joined the chorus. As a result, several candidates supported by independent campaigns were forced to disavow activities or rhetoric over which they had no control. "The candidate supposedly being helped is terrified of that committee screwing up," said Democratic state Rep. Peter Goudinoff.

But DeGraw rejects the view that such campaigns are too negative or unnecessarily provocative. He said a typical mailing addressing a Republican incumbent's legislative agenda can be seen as "either an attack piece or a comparison of record." He also said fellow Democrats who decry the independent committees are overlooking their results. "1988 was the first time the Democratic Party utilized independent campaign committees in any forceful way" in legislative campaigns, he said. "They won four new seats."

California, the Prototype State?

California policies and problems attract national attention for many reasons. It is the nation's largest state. It has been known for pioneering in public policies, such as tax limits that have been followed by many states. Its policies in some areas are being followed now, such as the vehicle emission limits recently adopted by Northeastern states. Its well-staffed, full-time, comparatively well-paid legislature is, or was, viewed by some as a model to which other states should aspire. Its young population and high tech image suggested to political analysts and marketing specialists that its trends were harbingers of changes to come in other states. But there have always been clouds behind the silver lining. . . .

The Tax and Expenditure Limits. Many state laws restricting local revenue growth are clones of California's Proposition 13 passed in 1978. Less restrictive measures in other states were designed to forestall more restrictive ones in what was reviewed as the tax revolt of the late 1970s. When the voter-initiated California measure passed, there were dire predictions of local layoffs, deterioration of public services, and other evils. To summarize many studies in one sentence, such dire effects generally didn't appear in major ways in the early 1980s. The interpretation of

why not is controversial. Tax revolt proponents say it simply proved that local governments had been overspending and overgrowing. Public spending proponents suggest that the state was able to offset the effects by using its massive budget surpluses to increase local aid.

With considerably less notice, California voters also adopted what is known as the Gann Amendment. Its effect has been to restrict state spending growth to the sum of growth in California population and inflation as measured by the Consumer Price Index. It seemed obvious that this couldn't cut back services. For example, if the state had one highway patrol officer for every 10,000 citizens at the beginning, it could hire new officers to maintain the ratio and adjust the officers' pay to cover inflation—all within the limit. New pressing needs could be covered by reducing low priority programs and economy and efficiency measures. Two potential problems were recognized when the limit passed. The first was that as wages in the private sector grew faster than inflation, public salaries would have to lag

Reprinted from *State Policy Reports* 7:18 (September 1989): 12-14.

behind private ones. This was solved by an alternative method of calculating the limit that, for technical reasons too complex to detail, prevent per capita income from being a proxy for real wage growth. The second was unanticipated contingencies, which could be solved by the safety valve of voter approval of spending beyond the limits.

The Gann limit was unnoticed in the early 1980s because it wasn't a factor affecting state policy. The sharp run up of prices in the late 1970s and early 1980s and the effect of early 1980s recession on state revenues from existing taxes caused California decisionmakers to tax and spend well below the limit. But as the decade wore on, prices remained under control and real growth in the economy swelled state revenues, causing a potential problem.

The Subtle Effects of the Limits. The local limit encouraged alternatives for raising revenues that didn't constitute tax increases that had to be submitted to voters. More state aid was the preferred local alternative along with borrowing, in which California local governments pioneered with new instruments such as certificates of participation. But much of the pressure was relieved by use of fees such as impact fees for developers and ingenious use of fees for existing services, such as streetlights.

The state level impact also fell on fees where they were an alternative, principally higher education. But fees couldn't be used for income-tested programs like Medicaid and for free public education, which together constitute a large portion of the state's budget. This turned attention to borrowing which, like taxes, requires a vote of the people, but not necessarily new taxes. Bond issues became the policy of choice, put on the ballot both by the legislature and interest groups using the initiative process and generally winning voter approval. This process had already made the constraining factor on issuing bonds an assessment of what the market will absorb without jeopardizing the state's credit rating, not the authority to issue more bonds. As might be imagined, the resulting rationing is upsetting to those interested in the spending.

Decisionmakers have flirted with state tax increases, but rejected the idea for various reasons, not the least of which has been the consistent opposition of the governor. As a result, California was unable to participate in the tax increases that have proven popular in other states, particularly increases in taxes on cigarettes, alcoholic beverages, and highway user charges. Voters took matters into their own hands last year by authorizing a 25-cent increase in the cigarette tax by initiative. . . .

Colorado Citizens Rewrite Legislative Rules

by Fred Brown

Colorado voters once again have changed the rules for their state legislature. As they did in 1972, when they approved one of the nation's first sunshine laws, the state's independent-minded electorate has insisted that public business should be conducted fully in the open.

The 1988 amendment to the constitution is called GAVEL, an acronym for Give A Vote to Every Legislator. It passed by an impressive 72 percent, sending a clear message to the General Assembly that the people wanted binding caucuses outlawed and every bill heard. It's not that Coloradans are particularly unhappy with their lawmakers; it's just that they don't see why the operations of government shouldn't be held to high standards.

In the 1989 session, things went smoothly under the new rules until late in the session when the spending packages were assembled. The Republican majority, especially in the House, retreated to familiar ground—the party caucus—to sift through the 200-plus pages of the state budget.

The majority party wouldn't let the annual budget bill go to the floor without tying up enough votes in caucus to ensure passage of specific provisions. But GAVEL still inhibited

discussion, say House leaders.

"It took us longer to arrive at what we thought was consensus," says House Speaker Carl "Bev" Bledsoe.

"It created less chance for cooperation and not more," says House Majority Leader Chris Paulson. "Part of the hard feelings that occurred on the tough issues stemmed from the fact that people couldn't go to a caucus and communicate with each other."

Besides giving a vote to every legislator, GAVEL gave a hearing to every bill. It has three major provisions:

- It requires consideration "on its merits" of every measure referred to a legislative committee of reference and specifies that a motion to report a bill to the full chamber "shall always be in order"—what Bledsoe calls the "super motion."

- It requires that bills appear on the House or Senate calendar in the order in which they were reported out of committee.

- It outlaws the binding caucus, saying that legislators cannot "commit themselves or

Fred Brown is political editor for the *Denver Post*. This article is reprinted with permission from *State Legislatures* 15:7 (August 1989): 15-17. © 1989 by the National Conference of State Legislatures.

any other member or members, through a vote in a party caucus or any other similar procedure, to vote in favor of or against any bill . . . or other measure. . . ."

Some legislators were offended by the insinuation that they were subverting the process and would continue to do so unless rigid rules were locked into the constitution. "I think it really put a taint on the interpersonal relationships among members," says House Majority Leader Paulson.

Paulson, a Republican from the Denver suburb of Englewood, the bluntest of the amendment's critics, called it "very vague, disjointed, and now it's part of the constitution. It just adds to the innuendo that the legislative process is somehow not to be trusted," Paulson says.

Nonetheless, even GAVEL's critics concede it did some good. Perhaps its biggest success was in doing away with the pocket veto by committee chairman. Its earliest victim was the House Rules Committee, once a "killing ground" for legislation the House leadership didn't like.

GAVEL's automatic calendar provision, the one requiring all committee approved bills to be scheduled for debate in the order in which they were reported out, is the system the Senate has used for years. But the House has resisted.

With the amendment in place, Speaker Bledsoe, a plain-speaking cattle rancher from eastern Colorado's prairie, simply decided not to appoint a Rules Committee before the legislature's 1989 session. "It wouldn't have any power at all," Bledsoe said. . . .

III. POLITICS: PARTIES, INTEREST GROUPS, AND PACS

Divide and Conquer

Politics in the American states is changing. Political parties, once the backbone of the U.S. political system and the chief force in state government, are becoming less influential, or so say many observers. As Malcolm Jewell and David Olson point out, "It has become a truism that party organizations are declining in importance, and there is no reason to anticipate a reversal of that trend." [1]

But what are political parties? This question must be addressed before the reasons for their "decline" can be understood. Are they the organizations from precinct to national convention—*the party in organization?* Are they the individuals who run, win, and control government under a party label—*the party in office?* Or are they the voters themselves, who identify more with a particular party and vote accordingly—*the party in the electorate?* Political parties are all three, diverse in definition, and ever changing in their impact on state government.

Perhaps the clearest signal that parties sway voters less than they once did is the rise of split-ticket voting. In state and local elections in 1956, only 28 percent of the voters who identified themselves as either Democrats or Republicans did not vote the straight party line but split their ticket by voting for candidates of both parties; in 1980, 51 percent split their ticket. [2] In 1986, 20 percent of those identifying themselves as Democrats and 17 percent of those identifying themselves as Republicans voted for the U.S. Senate candidate of the opposing party. [3] This divided party voting and its impact is discussed in further detail in the introduction to Part I.

What's Happened to the Parties?

Various explanations have been offered for the decline of political parties. Direct primaries—the means by which party voters can participate directly in the nomination process rather than have party leaders select candidates—certainly have curtailed the influence of party organizations. By 1920 most of the states had adopted the direct primary. [4] No longer could party organizations or party bosses rule the nominating process with an iron hand, dominate the election campaign, and distribute patronage positions and benefits at will. The ability to circumvent official party channels and appeal directly to the electorate greatly increased the power of individual candidates. A candidate's personality has taken on new importance as party affiliation becomes less influential in determining voting behavior.

In the political environment of the 1990s, parties are challenged by the mass media, interest groups, independent political consultants, and political action committees—vehicles that perform many of the historic functions of the political party. Public opinion polls, rather than party ward and precinct organizations, survey the "faithful." Today,

> . . . [P]olitical consultants, answerable only to their client candidates and independent of the political parties, have inflicted severe damage upon the party system and masterminded the modern triumph of personality cults over party politics in the United States. [5]

One analyst argues, however, that the rise of the political consultant has opened up the political process through the use of polls and other techniques. Now candidates can talk about the issues voters are concerned about without the "party communications filter." [6]

Changes in government itself are another explanation for party decline. Social welfare programs at the federal, state, and local levels of government have replaced the welfare role once played by party organizations. Those in need now turn to government agencies rather than to ward and precinct party leaders, even though domestic cutbacks during the Reagan years, and projected into the future, have reduced the ability of government agencies at all levels to meet those needs.

To most citizens, parties are important only during the election season. Our system is unlike most European countries where there are rigid election schedules in which campaigning is limited to a specific time period. The American state and local government election season is generally conceded to start around Labor Day in early September and run until Election Day in early November. Cynics believe this is too long, and that in most voters' minds, the season really begins at the end of the World Series in late October. Of course, the candidates have been at work for months, even years, getting ready for this unofficial election season, but the impact of other events, such as the World Series, often conspires to keep their efforts off the minds of the electorate.[7]

Alan Ehrenhalt of *Governing* makes another intriguing observation on the fate of the major political parties in the minds of the citizens. He argues that "solutionists" have become our new majority party. Those with "fuzzy optimism" promise that we can solve any of our problems and that "everything is possible" if we set our minds on a solution. "Voters, who are routinely informed by candidates that their problems can and will be solved have a right to turn cynical when the same problems are still on the table ... years later."[8] Such cynicism quickly turns to apathy and nonparticipation in politics, regardless of party affiliation.

Signs of Party Resurgence

Yet not everyone is ready to declare the parties moribund. The party process is still the means of selecting candidates for national, state, and, in some cases, local office. Control of state legislatures is determined by which

party has the majority, with the sole exception of Nebraska. Appointments to state government positions usually go to the party colleagues of state legislators or of the governor.

Although party in organization and party in the electorate are weaker than they once were, party in office may be gaining strength, argues Alan Rosenthal of the Eagleton Institute of Politics at Rutgers University. Legislators are increasingly preoccupied with winning reelection. The "art of politicking" may be superseding the "art of legislating."[9] Party caucuses have begun to play an important role in selecting legislative leadership, assigning committee and other responsibilities, and establishing positions on issues. In fact, the party in organization may not be as weak as many think. Since the 1960s, budgets and staffs have grown in size, staffs have become more professional, party services and activities have increased, and elected leaders may be even more involved in party affairs.[10]

Regional Differences in Party Politics

Of course, party politics differ in each state. As Samuel C. Patterson writes, "In some places parties are strong and vigorous; in other places, they are sluggish; in yet others, moribund. But, on balance, the state parties appear remarkably vibrant."[11]

New York appears to be content with its four-party structure of Conservative, Republican, Democratic, and Liberal parties; Nebraska operates on a nonpartisan basis for many of its elections; Wisconsin still has deep ties to populism; and California, once represented by a liberal northern half and conservative southern half, is expanding to include the strengthening Hispanic and Asian minorities. The political growth and impact of these minorities are increasing as they learn how to play the game of politics by American rules.

Today, few states are consistently dominated by one party. This is true even in the

South, which for many years was the Democrats' stronghold. Southern states now see growth around urban centers shaking up old party lines as "yuppies," northern corporate executives, and retirees join the "Bubbas" and presidential Republicans of old to create more competitive two-party systems.

At one time, being a Democrat was practically a necessity to vote and hold office in southern states. Party primaries decided who would be elected; general elections were simply ratifying events. But the old one-party dominance is fast eroding as is the role of the primary in determining who will govern.

For example, between 1986 and 1989, when the last full round of state elections was held in the southern states, Republicans won the governorship in eight states, Democrats in nine.[12] After the 1988 state legislative elections, 23 percent of the state senators and 27 percent of the state house representatives were Republican, continuing a trend of increasing Republican party strength in these bodies.[13] While Republicans continued to control only one of the thirty-four houses in the seventeen states (Delaware's House of Representatives by five votes), they gained sufficient strength in the North Carolina House of Representatives (46 out of 120 members) to be able to join with twenty dissident Democrats to replace the four-term Democratic speaker of the House with a more friendly dissident Democrat.

While still a political minority, the Republicans' winning trend is causing southern Democrats to question the political "sanity" of continuing to hold divisive party primaries in which Democrats battle with each other when seeking the party nomination, only to have their Republican challengers use these same arguments to defeat them in the general election. In effect, the primaries expose weaknesses in the Democratic candidates that the Republicans exploit. In fact, the North Carolina legislature recently reduced the percent of the vote needed to win in the first primary from 50 percent to 40 percent in an attempt to forestall divisive second primaries.

Not all of these Republican wins are beneficial to the party: in February 1989, the former grand wizard of the Ku Klux Klan and organizer of the National Association for the Advancement of White People, David Duke ("the Duke"), won a seat in the Louisiana legislature as a Republican. In a bitter and often racist campaign, Duke defeated John Treen, a longtime Republican party functionary and brother of the first Republican governor of Louisiana in this century. Treen had the strong support of newly elected president George Bush and former president Ronald Reagan—an unprecedented national-level intrusion into a local race. Within three months, the Duke not only had become a folk hero for many Louisianans, but his "avowed racism in an area that's racially polarized" intensified the state's problems.[14]

Interest Group Politics

Are interest groups an evil that must be endured or are they a necessary part of the governing process? Is their impact on state government primarily beneficial or harmful? Perhaps most importantly, are the interests that groups seek to advance or protect in the interest of the whole state or only of the lobbies themselves? State officials, pressured by a myriad of interest groups, wrestle with these questions and reach different answers.

From state to state, interest groups' influence on the political process varies. Business groups are by far the most predominant; the influence of labor groups pales in comparison. Thus, the bias in the interest group structure of most states is business oriented and conservative. Lately, however, groups representing government employees, local government officials, and the public interest (for example, Common Cause and environmental protection groups) have increased their visibility and effectiveness in state politics. According to Sarah Morehouse, there are twenty-two states in which interest groups are very strong, eighteen in which they are moderately strong, and ten in which they are weak.[15]

An interest group's effectiveness depends on the representatives it sends to the state legislature and executive branch agencies—the so-called professional lobbyists. Who are these people? Usually they have served in government and are already known to those they seek to influence. Their ranks include agency heads, former legislators, and even former governors in private law practice who have clients with special interests. Some of the most effective lobbyists represent several interests.

The relationship between political parties and interest groups in the states tends to follow a discernible pattern: the more competitive the party system, the weaker the interest group system. As of the early 1980s, of the twenty-two states in which interest groups were classified as strong, sixteen are one-party or modified one-party states; of the eighteen states in which interest groups were classified as moderately strong, thirteen were competitive two-party states.[16]

This apparently symbiotic relationship between parties and interest groups largely determines who controls state government. Theoretically, in a competitive, two-party state, the stakes are more likely to be out in the open as one party fights the other for control. Conversely, in the noncompetitive, one-party state, the stakes are less easy to see as interest groups do battle with each other to maintain or change the status quo. Again, in theory, the power of the party flows from the voters through their elected representatives; the power of interest groups is derived from their numbers, money, and lobbying skill. But in practice the relationship is not as clear as this explanation would suggest. In fact, once the

parties organize state government, state politics usually become the special quarry of interest groups—except, of course, on distinctive, party-line issues (such as selecting the leadership).

The Role of State Governments

State governments have two main roles in relationship to the other actors in state politics: they set the "rules of the game" in which parties and interest groups operate, and then they regulate their financial activities. The rules govern the nomination and election processes and the ways in which interests are allowed to press their demands. However, the rules change at a glacial pace because those who know how to play the game fear that change will upset the balance of power—or at least their spot in the power system. In fact, it often takes a lawsuit by someone outside that power system to change the rules or a scandal to tighten financial reporting requirements.

For example, the federal courts continue to support challenges to at-large voting schemes on the grounds that they dilute a minority group's voting strength.[17] At-large voting schemes allow voters to select several representatives at one time from a larger geographical area rather than just one representative from a smaller geographical area. For example, the Maryland U.S. congressional delegation consists of six Democrats and two Republicans selected from eight individual districts. Had that delegation been selected by a statewide (at-large) vote in 1988, the Democratic candidates, who had just under one million votes, would hold all eight congressional seats since the Republican candidates garnered only 624,021 votes.

Recently, portions of Mississippi's electoral laws were successfully challenged in federal courts. In 1987, a federal district court ruled that Mississippi's dual registration voting laws were in violation of the federal Voting

Rights Act. The Mississippi laws required voters to register twice: once in the county courthouse for federal, state, and county elections and again at the local courthouse for local elections.[18] In 1988, a federal district court ruled that the state's judicial election procedures were discriminatory under the Voting Rights Act. This ruling led to changes to concentrate minority voting power. The numbers proved the case: although blacks made up 35 percent of the state's population, of 111 judges in the state, only three were black (less than 3 percent).[19]

Laws regulating campaign finance have been on the books for almost 100 years. In 1892, New York and Massachusetts adopted laws requiring candidates to report how they spent their campaign money in reaction to the corruption of the day. Other states followed with a variety of "publicity laws" and restrictions on corporate contributions and limits on campaign expenditures. By 1925, a majority of states had some restrictions on their books, but these often were not enforced.[20]

Recently, the states have adopted policies that increase their regulatory role regarding political parties. Public disclosure and campaign finance laws are more strict, and political action committees (PACs) are monitored with a more watchful eye due to their increased activity.

The number of PACs has grown rapidly in the American political scene. At the national level, they increased from 608 in December 1974 to 4,165 in December 1987, a 685 percent increase.[21] The number of PACs in New York nearly quadrupled from 84 in 1978 to 325 in 1984. Special interests financed 60 percent of the campaign costs for an assembly seat in the 1984 contests in California, and they contributed 40 percent of the money raised by Illinois legislators in 1984-85, leading one observer to protest, "What we have now is government of the PACs, by the PACs,

and for the PACs." [22] In the 1987 elections in Louisiana, more than 600 PACs registered with the state's campaign finance office.[23] PAC spending for statewide offices and state legislatures across the country was $95 million in 1972, $120 million in 1976, $265 million in 1980, and a whopping $400 million in 1984.[24]

Part III provides some insight into politics at the state level. Rob Gurwitt of *Governing* takes a look at the Christian Right and its influence on Republican Party politics in the states. Kay Lawson reviews the impact of a U.S. Supreme Court decision on internal party politics in California and how that decision affects party politics in all states. Ken Goldfarb in the *Empire State Report* shows how important union politics can be in one state—New York—especially when the unions consist of government employees. Finally, Frank Kuznik in *Common Cause Magazine* discusses how redistricting will affect state legislatures and, in some cases, the state's congressional delegation.

Notes

1. Malcolm Jewell and David Olson, *American State Political Parties and Elections* (Homewood, Ill.: Dorsey Press, 1982), 280.
2. David E. Price, *Bringing Back the Parties* (Washington, D.C.: CQ Press, 1984), 15.
3. Survey by ABC News, November 4, 1986, reported in *Public Opinion* 9:4 (January-February 1987): 34.
4. Price, *Bringing Back the Parties*, 32.
5. Larry Sabato, *The Rise of Political Consultants: New Ways of Winning Elections* (New York: Basic Books, 1981), 3.
6. Walter DeVries, "American Campaign Consulting: Trends and Concerns," *PS: Political Science and Politics* 12:1 (March 1989): 24.
7. Rick Sinding, "Politics," *New Jersey Reporter* 17:3 (September 1987): 300.
8. Alan Ehrenhalt, " 'Solutionists': America's Majority Party," *Congressional Quarterly Weekly Report,* September 20, 1986, 2251.

9. Alan Rosenthal, "If the Party's Over, Where's All That Noise Coming From?" *State Government* 57:2 (Summer 1984): 50, 54.

10. Timothy Conlan, Ann Martino, and Robert Dilger, "State Parties in the 1980s: Adaptation, Resurgence, and Continuing Constraints," *Intergovernmental Perspective* 20:4 (Fall 1984): 23.

11. Samuel C. Patterson, "The Persistence of State Parties," in *State of the States,* ed. Carl E. Van Horn, (Washington, D.C.: CQ Press, 1989), 169.

12. The Republicans won Alabama, Florida, Oklahoma, South Carolina, and Texas in 1986, and Delaware, Missouri, and North Carolina in 1988. The Democrats won Arkansas, Georgia, Maryland, and Tennessee in 1986, Kentucky, Louisiana, and Mississippi in 1987, West Virginia in 1988, and Virginia in 1989.

13. "1988 Election Results," *State Legislatures* 14:10 (November/December 1988): 25.

14. Associated Press, "Former KKK Head Wins La. Election," [Raleigh] *News and Observer,* February 19, 1989, 1A. Jason Berry, "In Louisiana, the Hazards of Duke," *Washington Post National Weekly Edition,* May 22-28, 1989, 25.

15. Sarah McCally Morehouse, *State Politics, Parties, and Policy* (New York: Holt, Rinehart & Winston, 1981), 107-112.

16. L. Harmon Zeigler, "Interest Groups in the States," in *Politics in the American States: A Comparative Analysis,* 4th ed., ed. Virginia Gray, Herbert Jacob, and Kenneth N. Vines (Boston: Little, Brown, 1983), 116.

17. "Newsbriefs: At-Large Voting under Attack," *Governing* 1:2 (November 1987): 8.

18. "Justice: Mississippi Voter Registration Laws Struck Down," *State Government News* 31:2 (February 1988): 29.

19. Ronald Smothers, "Ruling Spurs Change in Racial Makeup of Mississippi Judiciary," New York Times News Service, in [Raleigh] *News and Observer,* June 3, 1989, 4A.

20. Kim Kebschull, et al., *Campaign Disclosure Laws* (Raleigh, N.C.: North Carolina Center for Public Policy Research, 1990), 20.

21. Findings of Citizen's Research Foundation as reported by Jeffrey Stinson in "PAC Money Follows Power to the States," *USA Today* March 26, 1986, 8A.

22. Harold W. Stanley and Richard G. Niemi, *Vital Statistics on American Politics* (Washington, D.C.: CQ Press, 1988), 143.

23. Citizen's Research Foundation, "PAC Money Follows Power," 8A.

24. "PAR Analysis: Campaign Finances in the 1987 Governor's Race" (Baton Rouge, La.: Public Affairs Research Council of Louisiana, May 1988), 7.

The Christian Right Has Gained Political Power. Now What Does It Do?

by Rob Gurwitt

Every once in a while, passionate ideology barges in on American politics.

Old-guard Republicans had to struggle to live with the true-believing Goldwater conservatives of 1964; eight years later, regular Democrats felt no less threatened by anti-war McGovernites. It all can be hard on the system, which runs on pragmatism and compromise and gets befuddled by undiluted conviction.

These days, in a diverse collection of states, the system is being tested by the Christian Right. After pounding on the door of American politics for a decade or more, religious conservatives finally kicked it in [in 1988] with the Reverend Pat Robertson's presidential campaign; although that effort came up short in the end, it did so only after mobilizing thousands of new local activists. Now newcomers and more politically experienced conservative Christians alike are demanding real political influence.

And, unnoticed by most of the national media, they are beginning to get it. Conservative evangelical Christians either run or help run the Republican Party in at least half a dozen states, are campaigning for and winning council seats and school board posts from Oregon to Georgia, and—largely through Robertson's campaign—have developed a group of experienced political strategists who now are surfacing in the campaigns and organizations of mainstream candidates and political groups. The Christian Right is no longer a political innocent. Its leaders have learned how to reach for power.

But they have yet to show that they understand what to do with it. Or that they know how to exercise their influence without alienating the potential allies they need to succeed at setting public policy.

While religious conservatives have become an unquestioned force in Republican Party politics, their passage into the GOP has in many places been ridden with conflict, leaving lasting and possibly debilitating scars. Some of these problems will go away; time and experience are already smoothing the rough political edges displayed by many of these religious newcomers. But others seem destined to encounter long-term difficulty. Recent experience suggests that the Christian Right's greatest challenge lies not in bringing the political world to heel but in accommodating itself to the elements of strategy and compro-

Rob Gurwitt is a staff writer for *Governing*. This article appeared in *Governing* 2:11 (August 1989): 16.

mise that [the] world demands.

If the Christian Right first came to the country's attention with the Reverend Jerry Falwell and his Moral Majority, it came of age with Pat Robertson. For much of its first decade, it was a movement defined by its leaders; it took Robertson's 1988 presidential campaign to develop a truly politicized base. . . .

. . . Robertson mobilized and organized Christian conservatives to a degree unmatched by any of the conservative religious groups that had dominated the field in earlier years. "The Robertson effort, perhaps more than any other effort, brought people out of their pews," says Anne Kincaid, who ran the Virginia preacher's campaign in his home state.

Robertson supporters flooded Republican nominating caucuses and conventions around the country. They were especially dominant in the South, where the GOP apparatus is still fragile and thus vulnerable to a wash of newcomers. But even in states with a strong traditional Republican organization—most notably Michigan—they proved the tactical equals of their opponents in other presidential camps. And wherever they were, they learned the intricacies of caucus and convention maneuvering and political battle.

Some of those who learned best have been snatched up by the Republican mainstream. R. Marc Nuttle, who ran Robertson's national effort, is now executive director of the GOP's congressional campaign committee. Kincaid [advised] Virginia's [1990] Republican gubernatorial nominee, Marshall Coleman. Other Robertson alumni have taken leadership posts in [several] state Republican Party organizations. . . . "We should be seen as a shot of vitamin B-12 to add new blood," says Kincaid.

There are states, though, where the newcomers seem less a revitalizing booster than a graft the body is fighting to reject. "They have the attitude," complains John Stuckey, Georgia's former GOP chairman, "that brought

you the burning of Joan of Arc, the Salem witch trials and the Ayatollah Khomeini."

Stuckey has reason to be outspoken. He spent most of last year locked in harsh combat with the Robertson forces after they took over a good number of his state's precinct and county Republican meetings and seemed poised to take over the state party itself. Neither side was very gentlemanly, and Stuckey, says a sympathetic GOP county chairman, "bore the brunt of the hate and the obscene phone calls."

Stuckey minces no words in saying why he thinks the Christian Right has no place in the GOP. "You're dealing with a philosophy that says, when you have a divinely dictated end to achieve, the means to achieving it are always uncompromising and sometimes totally overweening and fanatical," he says. "It damn sure ain't a New England town meeting."

Some of the hostility of 1988 . . . has to be blamed on the regulars and their hostility to the evangelicals. But there was also an element of unreasoned suspicion on the part of the evangelicals themselves; even when establishment leaders tried to run their meetings fairly, they were sometimes treated with contempt. In a number of states and counties, the encounter between Robertson's forces and the GOP establishment had more in common with the Crusades than with the reasoned workings of democracy.

In Georgia and North Carolina, establishment figures were shouted down or simply snubbed and ignored. In Snohomish County, Washington, party Chairman John Thomas found his way to the podium at his county convention blocked by a group of Robertson supporters standing with their arms behind their backs. "There was some pushing and shoving," he says, "but we were finally able to wrap up the convention with no violence." Religious conservatives later ejected him from his post.

Virginia's Anne Kincaid says that evangelicals' motivations were understandable, even if the results were counterproductive. "There's been this sense of frustration on conservative Christians' part, a sense of impatience and a little bit of arrogance—that we know better than these people, that they haven't been able to change things quickly enough." But it's a mistake to act on that, she says. "I tell people, operating out of impatience only creates bitterness. All it's done is create battle lines."

Some of the battle lines have come down in the months since then; some have not. In Michigan, the scene of angry skirmishing before the 1988 caucuses, GOP Chairman Spencer Abraham says that life is calmer. Some Robertson supporters who had won party posts have left the scene, while others are moving into the GOP mainstream.

In Washington state, feelings are still a little raw. There, Robertson's backers were able to dominate the 1988 caucuses, but GOP regulars regained control this year and have little desire to share it with the Christian Right. "Their leadership handled their perceived power rather crudely," says an aide to one Republican official, speaking of the Robertson forces. "When it became clear that there was no organized mass following beyond Robertson, people weren't very tolerant of their prior behavior." Even so, Dick Derham, a former Reagan administration official who headed Jack Kemp's presidential campaign in Washington state, believes evangelicals will one day blend in. "Some of the Robertson leaders who have remained active continue to have a very narrow focus," he says. "But in the main, of the ones I work with, five years from now you won't know they came out of the Robertson campaign."

Even in Georgia, there are voices calling for a rapprochement. Eric Johnson, chairman of the Chatham County (Savannah) GOP,

was one of the few Republican regulars who counseled patience ... in the heat of the 1988 campaign. He acknowledges that there is still considerable distrust between the two factions but also believes that, given time, relations between them will improve. The Republican Party in his state is, he points out, still completely overshadowed by the Democrats. The religious newcomers could, in the end, be a boon. "We need their forces, their networks, their energy," he says, "and they need us to help train them to run for office. Right now, they remind me of the way we used to be: They're so used to being in the minority, they don't care how to become a majority—they just want to make their views known, throw their rocks and go home."

But even if the internal Republican tensions caused by the Robertson enthusiasm do start to fade, conservative evangelical Christians have yet to settle the question of how suited they are to the day-by-day political routine. Leaders as well as critics of the Christian Right worry that many conservative evangelicals get drawn into politics by one candidate and then drop out once that contest is over—they don't participate in party building or other organizing efforts. And as long as they don't lick stamps, stump door to door for candidates with whom they're not entirely comfortable and show their support for the party in other ways, their welcome is likely to be restrained. "We're finding in our direct mail appeals that the evangelicals are not even coming up with the $10 or $15 contributions we need," says Johnson.

Kincaid, a one-time liberal and advocate of the Equal Rights Amendment who was born again, lectures Christian Right newcomers on the importance of sticking with politics. "This has to be a generational commitment," she says. "This in-and-out on personalities is what has given the Christian Right a bad name."

The movement has, in fact, attracted some very dedicated, patient people. Wendy

Flint is one of them. She was a young mother in pigtails in 1985 when she attended a school board meeting in Vancouver, Washington, to ask that the school library rid its shelves of a book she thought was too sexually explicit. Upset at the thought of such a book "in the hands of 12- and 13-year-olds," she spoke up. "We were treated rudely," she says; the board voted to keep the book.

Flint and like-minded parents banded together to challenge the incumbent board, and she and one other Christian conservative won seats. Now she's president of the board.... [I]n the years since her election, with help from the organization Christian Voice, she has taken her political experience on the road to advise other conservative parents on how they, too, can win school board seats.

"I went in jeans to that original meeting," Flint says. "When I got into politics, everything had to change. I had to look sophisticated and educated. Now here I am in these nice suits with my short, sophisticated haircut. I've come a long way—politics has got a hold of me. I don't think I'll ever leave."

That is the sort of "generational commitment" Kincaid and other Christian Right strategists are looking for. But it is not the only quality that the Christian Right still has to develop. Its enthusiasts not only have to stick with the job, but they have to learn to practice the art of coalition politics—even if that sometimes means submerging some of their strongest values and working alongside people they thought of as the enemy not so long ago.

Oregon is one state where they have been unable to do that very well. Conservative Christians have shown persistence there, playing a role in Republican Party affairs for much of the 1980s, and they now dominate the GOP organization in most parts of the state. But they have relatively little to show for it. Pursuing an agenda dominated by moral and religious issues and working at a distance from the state's moderate Republican officeholders, the party's Christian Right leadership has found it difficult to compete effectively against a unified Democratic opposition.

The divisions in the GOP have been "disastrous," says Republican Representative Kelly Clark, a conservative and an evangelical who has parted company with the organized Christian Right in the state. "In the last election, Democrats had a well-oiled, well-run machine. They killed us with their machinery; our party was out pursuing an initiative on gay rights while the Democrats were unseating six Republicans in the House."

Minnesota presents a similar picture. There, too, conservative evangelicals got an early start, moving into politics a decade ago on the strength of the anti-abortion issue. They control about half of the local Republican committees in the state and have been instrumental in selecting the last two GOP gubernatorial nominees. But they have never been able to patch up their differences with the moderate Republican regulars, who nowadays give the state party little financial or organizational support. Both the 1982 and 1986 gubernatorial campaigns resulted in Democratic landslides, and the state House, after turning Republican in 1984, went back to the Democrats overwhelmingly in 1986 and remained that way two years later.

Meanwhile, the intraparty GOP feuding continues. "The hard feelings that have been carried along for the past four or five years have an effect on the decision making," says David Jennings, who has been both the House speaker and state party chairman. "Anytime there's a crisis situation, there's an opportunity to settle old scores."

Some of the evangelicals who have been involved in Minnesota politics contend that they are much more flexible than they are usually given credit for being. "It is better that we have a moderate Republican in the legislature than a Democrat any day," insists Mike Cavanaugh, a religious activist from the Minneapolis suburbs. "We need the votes for the speaker, the majority leader."

But Lucy Hahn, past president of Minnesota's Republican Feminist Caucus and a moderate GOP leader, argues that religious conservatives in the state have shown no interest in any candidates other than their own. "They tell us that we don't work hard enough for their candidates," she complains, "but they won't work for ours. They don't consider moderates to be Republicans. . . ."

. . . [T]hese struggles go to the heart of conservative Christians' prospects for national political influence, because they make clear that grasping power and using it are two different things.

There are members of the Christian Right who are aware of that. "It's one thing to try to seize the reins of power, and quite another to deal with the day-to-day headaches of governing," says David Holland, executive director of the American Freedom Coalition in Oklahoma, a group affiliated with Christian Voice. "We have to overcome problems with lack of preparation and training, with a lack of willingness to work in the trenches and pay your dues and work your way up, and especially with people's unrealistic expectations about what can be accomplished through bureaucracy and legislation."

There is, however, one convincing example of the way political pragmatism can successfully be wedded to conservative evangelical beliefs. In South Carolina, a conservative religious faction of the GOP, after a rocky start, is not only playing a crucial role in party politics but gaining legislative influence as well.

One reason evangelicals are so effective in South Carolina politics is that they draw on continuing support from the community that surrounds fundamentalist Bob Jones University in Greenville. But they have also been

involved in politics for well over a decade and have become a notably pragmatic group of politicians.

That attitude is what distinguishes Terry Haskins from some of his conservative evangelical brethren in other legislatures. Haskins is a Bob Jones graduate who was recently elected minority leader of the South Carolina House of Representatives. He made it to the legislature in 1986 after a three-year stint on the Greenville city council, which he spent immersed in such issues as zoning, emergency preparedness and sidewalk repair. "I became involved in all aspects of city government," he says. "Then, when a moral issue came up, I could speak with some credibility, because they knew I cared about the community."

The mistake that some conservative Christian legislators make, Haskins argues, is to limit themselves to issues important to conservative Christians. That hurts them on two counts. He says, "It's a very small portion of your district that will elect you solely on religious issues. . . . A politician who only gets involved in abortion, home schooling, blue laws, pornography or other issues that are social-moral, and does not get involved in helping decide where highway money goes or in insurance law reform, that politician is going to be totally ineffective on the moral issues, because he has no influence in the areas that other legislators are interested in."

As more religious conservatives are exposed to the political world, more are certain to adopt Haskins' political style: respect for others' views, a willingness to work on a broad array of issues and an understanding of when and how to strike political compromises without forsaking moral beliefs. But many others may well reject that approach. Those values are not intrinsic to the conservative evangelical view of the world.

"We tend to view things in strictly ironclad terms," says Jack Buttram, a fundamentalist and political consultant in South Carolina. "You talk compromise to most fundamentalists and they'll immediately get their backs up. To them, the word initially means theological compromise. And truth diluted with error is no longer the truth."

That is what Oregon's Kelly Clark is discovering. Earlier this year, a bill came up in the Oregon House stiffening criminal penalties for intimidating people because of race, with an amendment extending the sanctions to cover people who harass others because of their sexual orientation. Clark, though a conservative Christian, voted for the amendment.

"I did not view it as a gay rights bill, which I still oppose," he says. But skinheads and other young neo-Nazis in Portland had been preying on people they took to be gay, and the authorities wanted more teeth to use in clamping down on the violence. "The main witness for it was Portland's chief prosecutor, and he's not a gay-coddler," says Clark. After studying the measure to be sure it was not opening the door to full gay rights legislation, he decided to back it. The Christian Right was enraged.

They had initially backed Clark's run for office, in large part because, as a lawyer, he had worked with them on several cases involving church-state issues. But in his campaign, Clark played down the connection, saying that although he sided with them on issues such as abortion and euthanasia, he would probably part company on others. "I've tended to shy away from ideological litmus tests," he says.

Clark's pragmatic attitude toward legislating has impressed others in the Oregon capital, and he is counted among the most effective of his class in the House. Religious conservatives, on the other hand, are looking for someone to oppose him in next year's GOP primary.

An onlooker steeped in politics might wonder whether that is a wise course, figuring that having a generally sympathetic ally already in the legislature is better than alienating him, especially since the Christian Right's electoral record in Oregon is dismal. But Clark's departure from doctrine on legislation involving sexual orientation and his refusal to focus primarily on moral issues have cost him the support of conservative Christian activists.

Some Christian Right activists around the country are convinced that their less experienced brethren will eventually grasp the difference between political and theological compromise. . . . It is worth remembering that politics is still a very new pursuit to most evangelical Christians. For decades, they saw their priority as saving individual souls; politics, their ministers preached, was a worldly business that could sully good Christians.

That began to change by the early 1970s, pushed by the Supreme Court's *Roe v. Wade* abortion decision, social turmoil and the growing visibility of the homosexual rights movement. An increasing number of conservative Christian ministers are taking the Bob Jones approach, spreading an ideology that gives political involvement a biblical basis, charging their followers to be "the salt of the earth" and "a light to the world"—preserving society from decay and guiding it out of darkness.

It is from such preachings that people like Wendy Flint and Terry Haskins draw their inspiration. Still, despite their activism, profound ambivalences continue to exist within the conservative evangelical movement.

"Fundamentalists and charismatics still lack a contemporary philosophy or theology of political involvement," says James Guth, a political scientist at Furman University in South Carolina who has made religious conservatives his area of study. "They've made adjustments and exceptions, but they have not, as mainline Protestants have, come up with a philosophy that says that the Christian is to be politically active and is to create a better world. They're activists who feel guilty about being activists."

Eu, Secretary of State of California, et al. v. San Francisco County Democratic Central Committee et al.

by Kay Lawson

In February of 1989 the U.S. Supreme Court issued its ruling in the case of *Eu, Secretary of State of California, et al., versus San Francisco County Democratic Central Committee et al.* By a vote of 8-0, in a decision with far-reaching national implications, the court declared that several provisions of the California Elections Code were invalid, because they "burden the First Amendment rights of political parties and their members without serving a compelling state interest." [1]

In particular, the court ruled that a ban on primary endorsements was invalid as were restrictions on the organization and composition of the official governing bodies of political parties, provisions limiting the term of office for state central committee chairs and the requirement that such chairs rotate between residents of northern and southern California. The court asserted that the ban on primary endorsements (which included a ban on repudiating as well as on endorsing putative candidates, and had in the past compelled the Democratic party to accept without demurral the candidacy of a leader of the Ku Klux Klan) violated the rights of parties and their members to free political speech and freedom of association. Freedom of association was construed to include the right to

"identify the people who constitute the association and to select a standard bearer who best represents the party's ideology and preferences" as well as to promote candidates "at the crucial primary election juncture." The court ruled that the laws imposing restrictions on the internal rules and regulations of the parties served to "burden the associational rights of a party and its members by limiting the party's discretion in how to organize itself, conduct its affairs and select its leaders." [2]

The case, originally organized by the California Committee for Party Renewal, a multipartisan organization composed of political scientists, attorneys and party politicians, and brought to court by the law firm of Morrison and Forester under the direction of Attorney James Brosnahan, establishes important national precedents. Although the only other state still preventing primary endorsements prior to the ruling was New Jersey, almost every state has laws regulating the internal affairs of their political parties (the

Kay Lawson is professor of political science at San Francisco State University. This article is reprinted from *Comparative State Politics Newsletter* 10:3 (June 1989): 19-21.

Indiana Curbs Party Payroll Deductions

There are states that allow strong political parties and states that throw roadblocks in their way. And then there's Indiana.

For years, partisanship was essentially demanded of Hoosier state employees, who were required—informally—to have contributions to the party of their choice deducted from their paychecks. That came to an end in the late 1970s, but many employees still had their party contributions deducted.

Late in April [1989], however, Evan Bayh, the state's new Democratic governor, put a stop to the practice for most of Indiana's 36,000 state employees. Bayh's executive order affects an estimated 32,000 people who work in agencies that are under the control of his appointees or of two other Democratic elected officials, the lieutenant governor and the secretary of state. Republican officeholders in charge of the auditor's, treasurer's and attorney general's offices say they will allow the practice to continue.

Bayh's move was in line with a Democratic theme of ending "politics as usual"—a reference to the two-decade hold that the GOP had on the governorship before his inauguration [in] January [1989].

But if Bayh's action has a good-government air to it, there are also some purely political benefits. Not surprisingly, given the Republicans' long tenure in control of the state, their partisans far outnumbered Democrats in the ranks of the state bureaucracy. So, according to Devin Anderson, administrative assistant to the state auditor, the GOP was getting about $11,000 every two weeks from paycheck deductions at the time of Bayh's executive order. The Democrats were getting $300.

This is the second blow in three years to that sort of institutionalized party fund raising in Indiana. Until 1986, motor vehicle licensing branches were under the control of the county chairmen of whichever party held the governorship. They, or their managers, could do what they wanted with the "profits" from license plate fees; much of the money found its way into state party coffers. In 1986, however, Bayh's Republican predecessor, Robert D. Orr, ended the practice.

Source: Rob Gurwitt, "Indiana Curbs Party Payroll Deductions," *Governing* 2:11 (August 1989): 16.

exceptions are Alaska, Delaware, Hawaii, Kentucky and North Carolina).

Thirty-six states regulate the way parties select their state central committees' members (and of these, all except Pennsylvania and South Carolina also regulate who may choose members of local party committees). Thirty-two states regulate the composition of the parties' state central committees (and of these, all except Pennsylvania also regulate who may be members of local party committees, as do an additional three states—Connecticut, New York and Rhode Island—that have nothing to say regarding the composition of state central committees). Twenty-eight states include rules

for state party committees in their electoral codes, regulating such matters as when and where the committee must meet, how it shall fill vacancies, whether proxies may be used, how members must be notified in advance of meetings, what constitutes a quorum, how and whether executive committees may be formed and what shall be the powers and duties of both officers and members. Similar regulations apply to local party committees.[3]

The unanimous decision and the broad language of the court in *Eu v. S.F. County Democrats*, firmly asserting the First and Fourteenth Amendment rights of political parties and their members, call these laws into question. The court says that barring a compelling interest "to ensure that elections are fair and honest," a state may not interfere with the right of a political party to conduct its internal affairs and choose its leaders as it alone sees fit. "A state cannot," says the court, "substitute its judgment for that of the party as to the desirability of a particular internal party structure, any more than it can tell a party that its proposed communication to party members is unwise . . . a state cannot justify regulating a party's internal affairs without showing that such regulation is necessary to ensure an election that is orderly and fair." [4]

Notes

1. *Eu, Secretary of State of California, et al. v. San Francisco County Democratic Central Committee et al.* (henceforward *Eu v. S.F. Democrats*), 87-1269 U.S. Sup. Ct., syllabus, p. i.
2. *Eu v. S.F Democrats*, 87-1269 U.S. Sup. Ct., syllabus, p. ii.
3. Timothy Conlan, "State and Local Parties in Contemporary Politics: Decline, Adaptation and Continuing Legal Constraints," in *Advisory Commission on Intergovernmental Relations: The Transformation in American Politics* (Washington, D.C.: ACIR, 1986), pp. 95-162.
4. *Eu v. S.F. Democrats*, 87-1269, U.S. Sup. Ct., pp. 15-18.

Look for the Union Label When You Are Running for Statewide Election

by Ken Goldfarb

Just over seven years ago Mario M. Cuomo, the underdog, eked out a Democratic primary victory on his way to become governor.

Some of the credit for Cuomo's success has often been given to a group of supporters who now must sit on the opposite side of the bargaining table from the governor. The Civil Service Employees Association (CSEA), in an unusual move before a primary, was the first major union representing state workers to endorse Cuomo over New York City Mayor Ed Koch.

After that primary victory, into his election as governor and right on through his first reelection campaign in 1986, Cuomo has enjoyed not only the endorsement and help of CSEA, but that of other public employee unions [and] nearly all of the rest of organized labor as well.

But as Cuomo and state Democrats look ahead to an expected second reelection campaign [in 1990,] a small crack has appeared in that wall of support from labor. Some disillusionment with Cuomo has developed as a result of a belt tightening budget that meant the layoffs of state workers.

Looking back at 1982, CSEA's current president says the choice was easy when faced with the prospect of Koch as governor. "We had a real problem with his long standing attitude towards the Civil Service system," says CSEA President Joseph McDermott. At the same time, Cuomo was "saying things we liked to hear," says McDermott.

So CSEA, more than 200,000 strong, not only endorsed Cuomo against Koch, but contributed large amounts of manpower and telephone banks to help get out the vote for Cuomo. It worked.

Cuomo, given little chance in the primary, pulled off an upset, and he followed that with another surprising, although extraordinarily narrow victory over the extremely well financed campaign of millionaire Republican Lewis Lehrman. CSEA certainly made its muscles felt.

When it came time for Cuomo to run for reelection in 1986, virtually all the public employee unions and, for that matter, most of labor fell into line behind the now powerful governor. That year, Cuomo set incredible election records, even besting Franklin Roose-

Ken Goldfarb is a reporter with the *Schenectady Gazette*. This article is reprinted from *Empire State Report* 15:10 (October 1989): 31-33.

velt's gubernatorial landslides. With another likely reelection campaign about a year away [in 1990], Cuomo is again expected to get support from the same unions whose members work in state government on a daily basis, but not everyone is expected to fall in line quite as easily as they did four years earlier.

A growing faction within the second largest union of state workers, the Public Employees Federation (PEF) is none too happy with Cuomo over his last budget proposal. Hundreds of state workers, most of them PEF members, faced possible layoffs because of Cuomo's budget proposal in January [1989].

In the end, negotiations with the Legislature to restore some of the budget cuts and some maneuvering of jobs and people considerably reduced the total number of state workers who actually faced unemployment. But the whole process left a bad taste in the mouth of a number of state workers, left in the lurch, wondering about their future.

"There's going to be a battle royale," . . . according to one PEF official about any union endorsement for governor [in 1990]. William DeMartino, chairman of PEF's political action committee, says the union would hate to make an enemy of Cuomo, boss to PEF's 57,000 members. But he says there are a number of union activists who are "very, very nervous about the governor, and frankly, rather hostile."

The sticking point is job security, DeMartino says, pointing to the hundreds of PEF members whose state jobs were in jeopardy as a result of Cuomo's last budget proposal. He also pointed to a Cuomo suggestion that the state might begin the next contract talks offering just a two percent hike for its employees.

As a result, there is a "sizeable faction that feels the governor should not be endorsed," DeMartino says. While he used graphic language to describe their feelings,

DeMartino made it clear that he was not necessarily subscribing to that kind of thinking. He believes the political action committee "has a more pragmatic approach." In his view, Cuomo generally takes positions in favor of working class people and state workers, and the PEF PAC is probably going to support Cuomo, even if there is a fight over that endorsement.

"We share a common goal," Cuomo says. "I want what they want." Taking care of the sick and needy are objectives he says he shares with many of these workers who serve in the state's hospitals, psychiatric centers, welfare offices and elsewhere. But he adds, "I can't do what I want to do." He points to budget limitations that force what Cuomo often refers to as the "hard decisions. . . ."

But Cuomo poses the question, would state workers get more out of a Republican administration [?] He says he would demonstrate that another Cuomo administration will provide these workers with more than what any opponent may offer. "I'll stand on my record."

While McDermott says he senses some disillusionment with Cuomo among CSEA's membership, he also says his union cannot base its evaluation on that one budget battle, even though he called it a "horrendous situation. . . ."

. . . McDermott says he also is encouraged that Cuomo is taking a more serious look at the possible delay of . . . [a] scheduled income tax cut [in 1990]. A strong campaign was launched [in 1988] by CSEA, most of labor, local governments and a number of groups seeking state help for the jobless, the homeless, and the hungry, hoping to see the tax cut deferred so that money could be put to use for a variety of social services and local assistance.

Cuomo's push to reform the state employee pension system impressed McDermott, who says the administration is working closely with CSEA to resolve some of their other problems.

On top of everything else, while CSEA represents more state workers than anyone else, it also represents a huge number of local government workers. About half of its membership works for cities, villages, towns and counties, and not for the state. "CSEA may have a much broader view," McDermott says. "We're not just endorsing or not endorsing a boss," as is the case with PEF.

PEF President Rand Condell says his members have had a tough time facing state layoffs over the past few years at budget time.... Many PEF members remain disillusioned even when a layoff doesn't happen, says Condell. Just the prospect of being laid off "has a devastating effect," he says, while strains of union anthems play on his office cassette deck.

As one of the more active and certainly vocal state employee unions, PEF hasn't hesitated to take on the Cuomo administration at every turn. Condell talked about PEF's battle with Cuomo over what they claim is a move to replace many jobs filled by the Civil Services merit system with more patronage positions. He complains about the "privatization" of jobs, whereby the state hires non-union contractors to fulfill state functions. Promotional opportunities are dissolving, he says, with a debilitating effect on his members....

Cuomo's popularity problems, if he has any, were also reflected statewide, in [an April 1989] poll by the Marist College Institute for Public Opinion. Cuomo registered a significant and impressive 58 percent approval rating, but those results revealed a major dip from the extraordinary 68.9 percent he scored in September [1988]. The Marist poll even gave Cuomo an unprecedented 77.1 percent in January of 1988.

Despite those figures and despite the disillusionment among some PEF members,

Condell observed that Cuomo and his managers in state government, "in a variety of subtle ways," have been reaching out to state employees unions in recent months. The PEF president says he has detected a different attitude, that there is more cooperation and a greater interest in problem solving, although some members may not see this yet, Condell conceded.

Still, DeMartino says he sees a clash between those at PEF "who feel the governor has shafted them" and the pragmatists who realize they would have to work with Cuomo for four more years. But even if the union failed to endorse Cuomo, DeMartino says it is "very, very unlikely" PEF would endorse his opponent....

In Condell's mind, it is still much too early for PEF to think about making any political endorsement. McDermott also says it is too early to think about political endorsements for a governor['s] race that is still a year away [in 1990]....

Just how important is a PEF, CSEA or other public employee union endorsement? "As a single factor it becomes less overriding after a guy's been in office a couple of terms," says Lee Miringoff, a political science professor who directs the Marist poll. Cuomo's incumbency becomes the more significant factor, says Miringoff. He also says it's too early to tell, if PEF were not to endorse Cuomo, how big an impact this would have [on] his expected reelection campaign.

In Cuomo's mind, "everybody's important," even though he trounced Westchester County Executive Andrew P. O'Rourke, pulling in about 65 percent of the vote in 1986. "Unions are important because they represent values I share," says Cuomo.

"It's important for the governor to win the overwhelming endorsement of labor," says State Democratic Chairman John Marion. "You cannot afford to lose your base."

Divide and Conquer

by Frank Kuznik

Computerized data bases. High-speed map generation. Luke Skywalker counting votes. That's how the cutthroat task of re-districting is shaping up for 1991. But just because gerrymandering has gone techno, don't expect it to be any less partisan. Or convoluted. If anything, the decennial madness unleashed by the redrawing of state and con-gressional districts should be wilder than ever this time around, thanks to some legal waffling by the Supreme Court and a giant leap the Census Bureau is taking into the space age.

Gerrymandering used to be a simple, straightforward abuse. The majority party cut up a state in a manner that would maintain its lock on state legislative and congressional seats, and the opposition had no choice but to—as they say in the Bogart movies—"take it and like it." Now there are not only high-tech tools that have transformed numbers-crunching into a specialized science, but judicial restraints in the form of strict numerical and racial quotas, and a growing number of groups poised to drag would-be gerrymanderers into court.

The result is a complex, unwieldy system that, while still manipulable, offers more pro-tection against gerrymandering—or attempts at protection, anyway—than ever before. And the trend toward more monitoring should take off like a rocket in the coming round of redistricting, thanks to the Census Bureau, which is packaging its 1990 numbers on disks that anybody with a few hundred dollars can buy, pop in a personal computer and use to draw up their own redistricting plan.

Of course, having a plan is no guarantee of a seat at the carving table in the state capitol. But open and automated access to the bureau's data marks a new era in redistricting, one with more and better-educated watch-dogs keeping an eye on how political boundaries are being redrawn. "There's going to be a lot more input this time than just from the boys in the back room," notes Michael Hess, deputy chief counsel of the Republican National Committee (RNC).

None of which has kept Republicans and Democrats from drawing up blatantly partisan districts. Indeed, both parties have been in major legal battles defending egregious re-districting plans they created after the last census and reapportionment in 1980. Predict-ably, pros on both sides of the aisle discovered

Frank Kuznik is a Washington, D.C., writer. This article is reprinted from *Common Cause Magazine* 10:3 (May/June 1989): 13-16. © 1989 by *Common Cause Magazine,* Washington, D.C.

that carving up a state to one's advantage while maintaining statistical quotas is by no means an impossible task.

Conventional wisdom holds that whoever controls redistricting can control the political balance in a state for the next decade, which is why the process engenders such epic battles. The coming round already has an Armageddon-like cast to it, with strategists in both parties convinced that it represents nothing short of—in the words of one Democrat—"control of everything from the Congress down to school boards into the 21st century."

Were there an obvious solution to political gerrymandering, it might well be in place by now. But there isn't. Every 10 years, the country has to be reapportioned—that is, have congressional and state districts reconfigured based on population changes. The federal government runs the head count and hands out new numbers, but the process of redrawing district boundaries is constitutionally the province of state government.

As long as there is more than one party fielding candidates for office, there are going to be arguments about how those boundaries get drawn. Even third-party commissions or review boards are no guarantee of objectivity, according to Kimball Brace, president of Election Data Services, a redistricting consulting firm headquartered on downtown Washington's power corridor, K Street. He says his experience working for commissions led him to believe that they can be just as political as the parties.

"Any way you draw a district has a political impact," he says. "One side or the other is going to be angry at you because you ended up drawing a line down Elm Street instead of Main Street. Whether it's gerrymandering is really up to whomever you're talking to's viewpoint. Maybe the best thing is that both sides are angry at you."

The redistricting process has become so

intricate that, like the presidential election, it gears down but never completely stops. Brace has been working full time on redistricting since 1979, helping states such as Michigan, Rhode Island and Kansas create redistricting plans; serving as an expert witness in court cases; and compiling election data for the 1991 redistricting. He now has a staff of eight in D.C., and a similar-sized sister firm, Contemporary Technology Corp., in Houston.

States that can afford to are building their own operations. New York invested more than $1 million in a data collection and computer system for redistricting 10 years ago and has spent another $1 million since to keep it current. Texas has had eight people working full time on redistricting since 1986.

For all this, gerrymandering is still an ingrained part of the American political process. But next to gerrymanders of the past, today's don't seem nearly so outrageous.

The term "gerrymander" dates from 1812, when the Massachusetts legislature carved a district out of Essex County vaguely resembling a salamander (the creature of myth, not the lizardlike habitué of ponds and streams). Legend holds that painter Gilbert Stuart, then with the *Boston Centinel,* added heads, wings and claws to a drawing of the district and handed it to his editor with the pronouncement, "That will do for a salamander." Eager to hand the blame for the district's shape on Democratic Governor Elbridge Gerry, the editor rechristened it a "Gerrymander"—a term that has stuck.

In 1842 Congress passed the first of a number of strictures designed to discourage gerrymandering, but those were allowed to lapse in 1929. There were virtually no restraints on the redistricting process in place again until 1964, leaving the door open for all kinds of shenanigans. Some of the highlights from 1931, the first year of wideopen redistricting:

● A federal panel of three judges voided Kentucky's redistricting plan, citing in particular an "outrageous" district with a "shape very much resembling a French style of telephone. . . ."

● A plan that would have given rural Republicans in Minnesota an advantage was also thrown out. It included one district that nearly cut the state in half, beginning at the South Dakota border and meandering eastward nearly 175 miles to pull in a single ward in Minneapolis.

● Michigan, still in the grip of prohibitionists, fell victim to the Anti-Saloon League, which *The New York Times* credited with "taking so much Wet territory from the districts of two Wet representatives, and adding so many dry votes, that the anti-prohibitionists have little chance of re-election."

The sixties gave birth to the "one man, one vote" ruling—a Supreme Court decree that the population of congressional districts within a state be as equal as practicable. It has been the starting point for redistricting plans ever since.

"The one thing the courts will absolutely hold the legislatures to in congressional redistricting is minimum population deviation," says Jeffrey Wice, counsel to the Democratic State Legislative Leaders Association. "You're allowed no more than a minute difference. If there's a one percent variation, it's no compliance. Even with only a .5 percent variation, the courts may rule against you if there's an alternative plan somebody develops with smaller deviation."

As a result of the Voting Rights Act, congressional redistricting plans are now also vulnerable to legal challenge if they clearly dilute a minority group's ability to elect a minority representative. "Moreover," says Wice, "any state or local government which has had a form of discrimination in terms of access to the polls, literacy tests or low minor-

Redistricting and State Politics

. . . Redistricting . . . lends insight into a state's politics. In Illinois, remapping is fiercely partisan; the Democratic plan for the 1980s merged four suburban Republican districts into two, while preserving all the Democratic districts in Chicago. But across the Mississippi River in Iowa, a state with strong "reform" tendencies, the Legislature defers responsibility for redrawing the lines to its nonpartisan bill-drafting agency.

Legislatures do not, of course, have total control over redistricting. In most states, the governor can veto remap plans; therefore, the 38 gubernatorial elections being held [in 1989 and 1990] will have a strong bearing on redistricting. In addition, the federal courts play a significant role in redistricting. In the last round of line-drawing, courts ordered changes in several congressional maps, finding in favor of the "out" political party or a racial or ethnic minority group that said its rights had been violated by a gerrymandered remap. In the same vein, 16 states must obtain U.S. Justice Department approval of their redistricting plans under the Voting Rights Act.

Still, it is the legislatures that begin, set the tone for and often dominate redistricting. The partisan composition of the legislatures and their peculiar personalities will decisively shape the Democratic-Republican division in the U.S. House during the 1990s. . . .

Source: Bob Benenson, "Redistricting: House of the Future at Stake in 1990 Legislative Contests," *Congressional Quarterly Weekly Report,* November 4, 1989, 2972.

ity turnout in the past must now go to the Justice Department's Voting Rights Division to preclear any change in voting election laws—which includes changing boundaries."

The burning legal question after the 1981 redistricting was whether a political party could be the victim of discrimination; that is, in a clear gerrymandering situation, could the losing party go to court and plead the same kind of violation of rights that, say, a black or Hispanic group can? The Democrats tried in 1982, challenging a Republican redistricting of Indiana which—even though the state was losing a congressional seat—packed most of the state's Democratic vote into three districts and set up a Republican majority in the remainder, which included a brand-new district with no incumbent.

The U.S. District Court in Indiana ruled the plan unconstitutional. In 1986 the U.S. Supreme Court overturned that decision— more or less. It decided that the Republican majority had indeed discriminated against the Democratic minority, but that the plan would stay in place because the Democrats were unable to show any serious damages resulting from Republican gerrymandering. In other words, the court decided that political gerrymandering is wrong, but refused to provide a remedy—unless, as Wice notes, "you can show that your party has been wiped off the face of the state's political landscape."

That decision came back to haunt the Republicans in early 1989, when the Supreme Court let stand a California court's ruling upholding a brilliant exercise in gerrymandering crafted almost single-handedly by the late Democratic Rep. Phil Burton. A figure of near-legendary influence, Burton reportedly redrew the entire state's political boundaries without any electronic help. According to one observer, "he had all the information in his head." His initial effort was killed in a referendum after Republicans collected more

than one million signatures to get it on the ballot. The plan was so egregious that even in a state with a Democratic majority of registered voters it was rejected by nearly two-thirds of the electorate.

Undaunted, Burton drew up a second plan, which differed only slightly from the first, and rammed it through in the closing minutes of the 1982 legislative session. [In 1988] a three-judge District Court panel in San Francisco dismissed a Republican suit against the plan, and [in 1989] the Supreme Court chose not to hear an appeal of that decision.

Where does all this leave mapdrawers going into 1991? In the muddiest waters imaginable. The RNC's Hess sums up the thinking in both parties when he says, "What the Supreme Court has not addressed is the real potential for political shenanigans." In essence, the court has cast itself as a referee in what was essentially a political sport, but without saying what the new rules are. And it's guaranteed that there will be more cases like the Indiana and California lawsuits winding their way through the judicial labyrinth.

Lawyers aren't the only ones who will be making money off the 1991 redistricting. At the National Conference of State Legislatures annual meeting held in New Orleans in March [1989], no less than eight vendors were demonstrating redistricting software packages—some costing upwards of $250,000. States without the hardware to run such packages will have to spend additional thousands to get on the redistricting fast track, according to Ronda Tentarelli, director of Southern operations for Denver-based Public Systems Associates [PSA]. PSA's hardware, for example, sells for $125,000.

PSA helped Louisiana and Colorado with redistricting in 1981, when all computers did was store and spit out numbers. "This time we have a graphics-driven package," Tentarelli

The Legal Realm in Redistricting

... The [U.S. Supreme C]ourt entered the arena of population equality in the 1964 *Wesberry v. Sanders* decision, which ruled that congressional districts had to be "substantially equal" in population. Since then, a series of rulings has significantly tightened the standard, so that now virtually no variance in population is allowed among districts within a state. Critics argue that the court's obsession with the exactness of the numbers actually encourages gerrymandering, since it is often difficult to devise equal-sized districts without dividing communities or drawing the lines into tortured shapes. "It was good as originally intended," says Bernard Grofman, "but it's been carried to absurdity."

A second major area of litigation in the redistricting process involves minority representation. Blacks and Hispanics represent many districts that are losing population, but they are probably in a stronger legal position than they have ever been to protect their districts, and perhaps to carve out new ones. The 1982 amendments to the Voting Rights Act changed the criteria for proving racial gerrymandering. No longer does a plaintiff have to establish that there was an "intent" to dilute the clout of a particular voting bloc; the plaintiff merely has to show that was the "effect" of the remap.

With the greater threat of a lawsuit, legislatures are unlikely to eliminate a minority district. This could create some touchy problems during the redistricting process, particularly for urban Democrats. If they are forced to eliminate a district represented by a black or Hispanic, or one represented by a white, the one held by the white is likely to go.

For Republicans, the big legal question these days is where the court stands on the issue of partisan gerrymandering. The Supreme Court has not been shy about overturning redistricting plans that discriminate against racial minorities. But it is relatively new to the question of partisan gerrymandering—cases where the aggrieved is a political party rather than an individual.

The court entered the picture in 1986, when it declared in *Davis v. Bandemer,* a case involving a Republican legislative redistricting plan in Indiana, that partisan gerrymanders could be unconstitutional. However, the court upheld the Indiana remap, and failed to outline clear standards that the political parties could use in challenging a plan on the grounds that it is a partisan gerrymander.

Republicans had hoped to get a better definition of such standards when they filed suit against the map drawn by the California Democrats. But in deciding *Badham v. Eu* in January 1989, the Supreme Court ruled without comment that the map did not constitute an unconstitutional partisan gerrymander.

Even a favorable ruling for the GOP in *Badham v. Eu* would have had little practical effect, since the lines will be redrawn in two or three years anyway. But the decision clearly disappointed many Republicans, who had hoped to enlist the Supreme Court as an ally in the upcoming redistricting battle. Many Republicans felt that the California case was about as clear an example of partisan gerrymandering as they would get....

Source: Rhodes Cook, "The Legal Realm in Redistricting," *Congressional Quarterly Weekly Report,* August 12, 1989, 2142-2143.

says. "You can have your data and a map on the screen at the same time, and using either a mouse or menu [a pointer or the keyboard], select a precinct and have it added or taken away from a district."

Sounds like gerrymandering heaven. Or used properly, the ultimate tool for fair redistricting. What's certain is that all but a handful of states will be doing redistricting on computer screens in 1991. Why?

The major impetus for that comes from the Census Bureau, with its new packaging that includes everything but Star Wars stickers. "For the first time the bureau will produce census information not only on paper and mainframe computer tape, but on compact laser disks—which means that anyone with a microcomputer and a disk drive can very easily access the census statistics down to precinct block level," says Marshall Turner, chief of the Census Bureau's 1990 Redistricting Data Office. "In fact, on one CD [compact disc] one could have the entire nation."

Given that, how can one afford not to automate? Especially since the bureau is letting each state lay out its own census grid for 1990. In the past, the bureau counted warm bodies in blocks defined by visible features like streets, rivers and railroad tracks; henceforth the states get to define their own blocks. That means, according to Turner, "that when they get data in a state like New Jersey, whose legislature has to adjourn at the end of February—but still get a plan enacted before it does—they don't have to spend hours and days and nights and whatever trying to fit census data into election precincts. It will already be done."

As for new players taking a seat at the redistricting table—or more accurately, computer screen—Turner expects to see plenty. "We've already heard from groups like the NAACP and Southwest Voter Registration Project, just to name a couple," he says. "What I'm also starting to see around the country is many individual legislators developing their own data base, even within the same political party. Just because the party has plans, it doesn't mean that they as incumbents will like the districts they're given."

This, then, is what the march of technology portends for 1991: A more open redistrict-

ing process. And a lot messier one.

"In 1980 we had maybe 20, 30 different plans to contend with in a state," says redistricting consultant Brace. "In 1990, because it will be easier to draw plans, you'll have 200, 300 plans—even 2,000 or 3,000 plans. The problem is going to be trying to put all those 3,000 different versions of a state together and make some sense out of it."

It's important to remember that underneath the layers of technology and legal reform, the mechanics of redistricting remain in the hands of the same people who have always held it—state legislators. That's why both the Republicans and Democrats are funneling millions of dollars into state races [in 1988] and [in 1990], trying to win legislative seats and governorships that will tip control of state redistricting into their camp. Indeed, one of the first goals Republican National Committee Chairman Lee Atwater set publicly after taking office was influencing redistricting by winning state races.

The current [257-176] Democratic majority in the U.S. House of Representatives reflects the lead that Democrats have held at the state level for nearly three decades. However, the 1990 census will show a population shift from the Northeast and upper Midwest to the South and Southwest that is expected to work in the Republicans' favor. And barnburner races for governorships (in a projected 11 states), state houses (in 10 states) and state senates (in nine states) could change the political landscape significantly by 1991.

As the redistricting process heats up, this is what you can expect to hear from the parties: The Republicans will use what happened in California to support their contention that the Democrats gerrymandered their way to an unfair advantage in 1981, and call righteously for "a level playing field." The Republicans will also pound away at the "vote-to-seats ratio"—a numbers exercise which argues that if your party receives, say, 53 percent of the popular vote in a state, you're entitled to a similar ratio of offices. The courts have specifically rejected that line of reasoning.

The Democrats—who have Brace on board for 1991—will counter that the Republicans are as guilty of gerrymandering as anyone, and talk at great length about the need to preserve and create minority districts. They'll argue that protecting incumbents is not necessarily evil ("They must be doing something right if they keep getting re-elected") and perhaps raise the issue of "statistical adjustment," which argues that minorities in densely populated urban areas are perennially undercounted by as much as 11 percent and deserving of an automatic markup.

One thing is certain: With so many new elements in play, this redistricting battle will go on long after the lines are actually drawn in 1991. As Brace predicted in a think piece he wrote for *The Wall Street Journal* after the Supreme Court's 1986 equivocation on what constitutes an illegal gerrymander, "If you think political campaigns are already too long and costly, just wait until you see the 'campaigns' to change the redistricting lines drawn after the next census in 1990."

And he should know.

IV. MEDIA AND
THE STATES

The media—in all forms—have become important actors in state politics and government. This is especially true with the changes that have been occurring in politics, such as the decline of political parties and the rise of individual, media-oriented campaigns. Every candidate for statewide office, and many candidates for other state and local offices, now have to count a media consultant among the consultants they must hire. The rapidly increasing costs of political campaigns in the states are, in great part, tied to the rapidly escalating costs of running media-oriented campaigns.

But this is only part of the story in understanding why the media are important in the states. With the demise of the old political organizations and machines, the means of government-citizen communication have changed. Some of this communication is now in the hands of those who work in the agencies of state government—the bureaucracy. Increasingly, these individuals are professionally trained and usually are nonpolitical personnel whose goals are to make government agencies and programs work. However, in many cases, it is the media that carry the messages between government and citizens.

The media have no formal powers per se, but they are protected by the First Amendment's free speech clause. This allows a certain freedom of action for the media; they cannot be constrained by governmental action. However, part of the media is regulated by the federal government through the licensing of radio and television stations. Among the components of granting a license are the equal time and public service provisions.

The equal time provision protects an individual or a group by providing them with an opportunity to respond to attacks or critiques by others; it is sort of a "letters to the editor" space required for radio and television. This provision is especially important for political campaigns because it may affect what will be allowed on the air. The public service provision calls on the licensee to provide a certain amount of air time to public affairs because they are licensed by a public agency and have a monopoly right.

Types of Media

"The media" is a broad term that needs to be broken into its components for us to better understand how the media operate in the states. There are the print media, the daily and weekly newspapers we read; the television stations, which provide local and national news; the radio stations, which offer a large variety of formats; and the wire services, which provide the backbone of news stories and other information for the other media.

In fact, it is the wire services and the daily newspapers that set the agenda for television and radio, although TV and radio stations pick and choose what they want to cover. Look at your state's or city's major morning paper and compare the main stories on the front page with what you hear on the early morning radio news. Go into any radio or television station and watch how closely they follow and use the information coming over the AP or UPI wire services.

There are assets and liabilities to each type of media. For example, the print media can cover a broad range of items and concerns to make a paper attractive to many readers. In fact, some critics argue that the print media may be covering too many types of stories and may be losing its focus and concern over larger public issues. Television is a "hot" medium because stories are expressed through pictures, which is an easier way for most people to absorb the news. However, TV is limited by its own technology since it depends on pictures to carry the message; how does one take a picture of taxes? A study conducted in the mid-1970s of forty-four newspapers and television stations in ten cities found that newspapers allocated more space to stories on state government than did television stations. Newspapers also gave stories on state government greater prominence (front page location) than did the television stations (lead story status).[1] But Bill Gormley, the study's author, argued that even with this newspaper coverage, "few give it the kind of coverage it needs."[2]

Gormley cited the comments of others who had misgivings about the media's coverage of the states. Political scientist V. O. Key, Jr. argued in 1961 that the media "may dig to find the facts about individual acts of corruption but the grand problems of the political system by and large escape their critical attention."[3] Former North Carolina governor Terry Sanford (D, 1961-65) questioned, "Who, in some 40 states or more, can say he begins to understand state government by what he reads in the newspapers?"[4]

State Media Structures

There is great variety in the media structures across the states just as there is great variety in population size, population centers, and economic complexity. For example, New Jersey sits within two major media markets— the northern part of the state receives broadcasts from the New York City metropolitan area, and the southern part receives broadcasts from the greater Philadelphia metropolitan area. Radio, TV, and cable stations emanating from those major markets dominate what is seen or heard in New Jersey, and there are no strong New Jersey-based media outlets to combat this. News about New Jersey must fight for a spot in these media outlets.

West Virginia also faces this problem: much of the state is served by media markets in Cincinnati, Pittsburgh, and Washington, D.C. West Virginia lacks its own major media outlet because its terrain makes it impossible for any station to reach all parts of the state. In his 1980 reelection bid, Governor John D. "Jay" Rockefeller IV (D, 1977-85) spent a lot of money on outlets in these large cities in order to reach potential voters in remote areas of the state. There were stories of voters in Washington, D.C., going to the polls to vote for Rockefeller because they had seen his ads on TV so often.

Then there are states that have many media markets within the state's own boundaries. California clearly is the leader in media markets because there are so many large communities to be served in the state, ranging from San Francisco and Sacramento in the northern part of the state to Los Angeles and San Diego in the southern part. And there are many other markets in between. Texas also has a large range of media markets, as does Florida, New York, and North Carolina.

At the other extreme are states with only one major media market that dominates the state. Examples are Colorado with the Denver media market, Georgia with Atlanta, and Massachusetts with Boston. In fact, the Boston media market spreads well into Rhode Island, southern New Hampshire and southwestern Maine, making it difficult for residents there to get a clear understanding of what is happening in their own states. When one such market or major city dominates the state, there is little chance for those in the remainder of the state to voice their own particular interests. A rural-urban or rural-suburban rift in the state's media coverage is the rule.

Some comparative figures also make the point about the wide variation between the states in media markets. In 1987, there were 1,645 daily newspapers in the United States, or an average of thirty-three per state, if they were distributed equally. They aren't. There were 118 daily newspapers in California, but only three in Delaware. Texas had 108, whereas Hawaii and Utah had six each. The other states ranged between these extremes.[5]

This means some states' residents have a greater opportunity to read newspapers than do residents of other states. In 1987, the daily newspaper circulation per 100 residents was forty-four in New York and forty-two in Virginia, compared to fifteen each in Maryland and Mississippi. The rate was thirty-six in Massachusetts and thirty in both Nebraska and Rhode Island, compared to seventeen in Utah and eighteen each in Alabama, Georgia, Kentucky, and Louisiana.[6]

The number of television stations also varies by state, although with the expansion of cable systems across the United States, the actual number of stations available to a household through cable may be in the twenty-five to forty range. But even within those cable systems and their many channels, there is considerable variation in the number of local stations available. In 1985, there were 1,167 television stations in the United States, or an average of twenty-three per state if they were distributed equally. Again, they aren't. Texas had seventy-nine and California had seventy-six stations, compared with Delaware with two and Rhode Island with four. Florida had fifty-two stations and Ohio had forty-five, Utah and Vermont had seven each, and New Hampshire and Wyoming had eight each.[7]

Radio is a considerably more ubiquitous form of media; there are 9,521 stations in the United States. If the stations were distributed equally across the states, there would be an average of 190 stations per state. In actuality, there are 594 radio stations in Texas and 564 in California, compared with twenty in Delaware and twenty-eight in Rhode Island. Pennsylvania has 384, New York has 376, and Florida has 366, whereas Hawaii has forty-one, Vermont has forty-nine, and Nevada has fifty.[8]

Much of the variation in the data noted above is tied to the size of the state in terms of land area and population. But some of the variation is related to population diversity: some newspapers and radio stations target specific populations.

How the Media Work in the States

There is almost a definite pattern in how the media cover state politics and state government. During political campaigns, when candidates are vying for nominations and election to office, the media are involved selectively. Being involved can mean several things. First, the media cover some of the campaigns on a day-to-day or week-to-week basis, especially those campaigns with the greatest "sex" appeal in terms of what the media feel will sell papers or draw listeners and viewers.

Second, the media have become the major vehicle for political messages—the paid campaign ads lasting fifteen or thirty seconds that we see on TV and hear on the radio and the printed advertisements we see in newspapers.

Third, some of the media become part of campaigns when they conduct public opinion polls, which delineate the issues important in the race and show which candidate is ahead. The media also become part of campaigns when they sponsor debates between the candidates and endorse candidates through editorials.

For their part, candidates and their campaign organizations develop ways to obtain "unpaid media"—getting candidates and their names on TV or in print to increase their name recognition. Knowing when the major TV stations must have their tapes "in the can" for the nightly news can determine when a candidate makes an appearance or holds a press conference.

Fourth, some parts of the media become a part of the calculus by which decisions are made and actions are taken in politics and government. The best example of this is the pervasive influence that the *Manchester Union Leader* has on New Hampshire government and politics. This newspaper runs very conservative editorials on the front page for all to see. An observer of the state wrote in the 1960s that "[m]any state officials said they feared personal and vindictive editorial reprisal on the front page if they took exception to one of the paper's policies." [9] These officials felt "the paper has created an emotionally charged, reactionary atmosphere where new ideas are frequently not only rejected but fail to appear in print for public discussion." [10] This may be an exception to how most papers operate, but maybe not. Sometimes such an atmosphere or situation can be created in more subtle ways than front page editorial attacks, but exist nonetheless.

However, there are other media organizations that have acted in a more responsible manner over the years. These organizations have worked with those in government and politics to help their readers understand what is happening. For years, the *Louisville Courier-Journal* did this for Kentucky and for parts of adjoining states. [11] As one newsman argued, "Publishers have a responsibility to the public to do more. Call it public service, if you will . . . but the press has the responsibility to enlighten and serve." [12]

A second pattern to media coverage and activity in the states has to do with the timing of state legislative sessions. There is an adage that when the legislature is in town, no one is safe. More to the point is when the legislature is in town, so are the media of the state. Not only do the capital press and media corps regulars cover general legislative activity, but specific newspapers and TV stations send reporters to cover the representatives from their city or county. Also, if there is some legislation that will have an impact on a particular section of the state, there most certainly will be media from that section to monitor what is happening.

This leads to some interesting observations by those who have watched this "cover-the-legislature-at-all-costs" phenomenon. First, coverage of other state government activities, programs, and individuals often is neglected as a result. Why? "[I]t's a lot easier to cover the legislature. . . . Stories are easy to get. Legislators seek out reporters, doling out juicy quotes and swapping hot rumors." Plus, editors want their reporters to be there. "When reporters aren't there, editors want to know why not." [13]

Second, there have been changes in the nature of the capital press corps. There tends to be fewer gray beards than in the past and more younger reporters. The tradeoff seems to be youth, vigor, and inexperience versus age and experience; hence the coverage may not be as good as in the past even though there may be more media folk involved. For example, the capital press corps in one state capital once operated under the following set of rules for new reporters: "(1) Don't fall down; (2) Don't get sick; and (3) Don't *ever* look like you don't know what you are doing." [14] No one knows what the rules might be now.

Another major factor in how state governments and politics are covered by the media is the location and size of the state capital. In some states, the capital city is not the largest city; instead, it seems to be a "compromise" city between two large urban centers. Examples of this include Springfield, Illinois, located about two-thirds of the way from Chicago toward St. Louis, Missouri; Jefferson City, Missouri, located midway between St. Louis and Kansas City; and Trenton, New Jersey, located closer to the Philadelphia metropolitan area than to the New York area.

Some other state capitals are near the geographic center of the state, such as Little Rock, Arkansas; Des Moines, Iowa; Oklahoma City, Oklahoma; and Columbia, South

Carolina. However, several capitals are in what seems to be out-of-the-way locations, including Sacramento, California; Annapolis, Maryland; Albany, New York; and Carson City, Nevada. The decisions in locating these capitals seem to have been made in order to keep the capital away from large urban areas. Still other states put their capital in the largest city, where most of the action takes place. Some examples of this are Denver, Colorado; Atlanta, Georgia; Boston, Massachusetts; and Providence, Rhode Island.

When the state capital is in an out-of-the-way location, the media may find it more difficult to cover events since the government may be the only game in town. When there is not much action—or when the legislature adjourns—many in the press return to their home cities, leaving state government uncovered. When the state capital is located in the state's largest and most active city, there may be better coverage of state government, but that may be drowned out by the coverage of all the other activities in the city.

The National Media and the States

How does the national media treat what goes on in the states? One quick answer is that the national media doesn't cover the states unless a disaster occurs. Media specialist Doris Graber calls the level of state interest at the national media level "flashlight coverage." [15] She argues that there are basically two types of news in the eyes of the national media: high priority news and low priority news. The former is news that "has been judged in the past as intrinsically interesting to the audience by the usual news criteria. . . . [It is news that is] exciting, current, close to home, about familiar people, and audiences are likely to deem it relevant to their life." On the other side of the coin is low priority news, which "has been judged intrinsically uninteresting although it may be important." [16]

Graber argues that state news traditionally has been in the low priority news category, with only an occasional "entertainment or convenience item" receiving "a brief spotlight" in the news. However, when state news can be tied to high priority news, such as national elections, coverage increases. [17]

A recent study of the media coverage of the 1989 Virginia gubernatorial election is instructive of another aspect of what national coverage can mean during a state-level election. [18] This race was in an off-presidential year, which meant there wasn't too much political news. In addition, the Democratic candidate, L. Douglas Wilder, was vying to become the nation's first elected black governor. The study showed how two "local" papers covered the race (the *Richmond Times-Dispatch* and the "Metro" section of the *Washington Post*), and how the national media covered it (included were articles from the *Christian Science Monitor, Los Angeles Times, New York Times, Wall Street Journal, Newsweek, Time,* and *U.S. News and World Report*).

The results are revealing. The national coverage focused narrowly on the historical aspect of the race, and on the fact that Wilder was prochoice on the abortion issue while his opponent was prolife. The local papers focused more broadly on the substantive issues, and provided candidate and voting group profiles. The national media obviously concentrates on the aspects of a story that appeal to a broad audience; however, this treatment does not ensure coverage of the whole story—or even the correct story.

Working with the Press

There is another side to the media-government relationship: how those who serve in state government react to the role of the media. Most governors, some state agencies and a growing number of legislatures have established press offices to work with—and even cater to—the media and its needs. This means each governor has a press secretary or communications director. Recently, state legislators have realized the need for a media liaison who works either for a party caucus or the party leadership. Many agencies in state government also are developing offices that work with the press.

For press offices, working with the media on a daily basis usually entails distributing press releases and answering queries. But press offices are also responsible for making sure their bosses handle themselves properly with the media corps. At the 1982 New Governors Seminar sponsored by the National Governors' Association, newly elected governors were given the following advice on dealing with the media:[19]

● Good press relations cannot save a poor administration, but poor press relations can destroy a good one.

● Never screw up on a slow news day.

● If you don't correct an error immediately, in the future you'll be forced to live with it as fact.

● Never argue with a person who buys ink by the barrel.

● When you hold a press conference and are going to face the lions, have some red meat to throw them or they'll chew on you. It should be something of substance, as long as the governor isn't the Christian.

● Never make policy at press conferences.

The articles in part IV are from a symposium issue of *State Government News*. Charles Wolfe looks at the state government-media relationship from the perspective of the news judgments the press must make. P. Michael Saint provides some simple rules for public officials to consider when relating to the press.

Linda Wagar explores what public officials have done, and might do in the future, when there is a crisis in their state.

Notes

1. William T. Gormley, Jr., "Coverage of State Government in the Mass Media," *State Government* 52:2 (Spring 1979): 46-47.
2. Ibid., 47.
3. V. O. Key, Jr., *Public Opinion and American Democracy* (New York: Alfred Knopf, 1966), 381.
4. Terry Sanford, *Storm Over the States* (New York: McGraw-Hill, 1967), 51.
5. Table A-39, "Number of Daily Newspapers, 1987," *State Policy Data Book, 1989* (Alexandria, Va.: State Policy Research Inc., 1989).
6. Table A-40, "Daily Newspaper Circulation per 100 Residents, 1987," *State Policy Data Book, 1989.*
7. Table A-41, "Number of Television Stations, January 1985," *State Policy Data Book, 1989.*
8. Table A-42, "Number of Radio Stations, January 1985," *State Policy Data Book, 1989.*
9. Sanford, 50.
10. Ibid.
11. Ibid., 51.
12. Ibid., 52.
13. Jack Betts, "When the Legislature's in Session, Does Other News Take a Back Seat?" *North Carolina Insight* 12:1 (December 1989): 63.
14. Jack Betts, "The Capital Press Corps: When Being There Isn't Enough," *North Carolina Insight* 9:2 (September 1986): 48.
15. Doris A. Graber, "Flashlight Coverage: State News on National Broadcasts," *American Politics Quarterly* 17:3 (July 1989): 278.
16. Ibid., 288.
17. Ibid., 288-289.
18. This study was reviewed by the editor prior to its publication.
19. Thad L. Beyle and Robert Huefner, "Quips and Quotes from Old Governors to New," *Public Administration Review* 43:3 (May/June 1983): 268.

Press Row View: News Judgments

by Charles Wolfe

A television reporter I know has developed, through his years of statehouse coverage, a personal acid test for judging the newsworthiness of events.

He usually applies the test during the grand announcement of a task force's creation, a blue-ribbon commission's empanelment, an omnibus bill's introduction and the like. Turning his mind's eye toward one of the more socially circumscribed of his state's numerous rural nooks, he asks: "Will it mean a damned thing in Owsley County, Kentucky?"

The Owsley County test is one that reporters often don't take seriously enough. It's one that forces the media to acknowledge a basic fact: Most readers—or listeners or viewers—do not follow with rapt attention the daily occurrences at the seat of government.

The longer one pounds the state government beat, the easier it becomes to assume that everyone has been following the action in the statehouse and knows precisely what's going on.

News that House Bill 99 has cleared a Senate committee and is headed for a potentially final vote on the floor might be meaningful to the lobbyist who has faithfully tracked it. But it doesn't mean a thing to the rest of the public, including the good citizens of Owsley County—who don't give a fig about the bill's number, but only want to know how it will affect them.

A tendency to attach unwarranted importance to bill numbers and other institutional terms or titles is but one of many teeth in the trap for the capital press corps. Others include jargon, preoccupation with personalities and inattention to the less glamorous, albeit important, inner workings of government.

It is doubtful that any part of the governmental process gets more coverage than the state budget—from its formulation through its enactment—and the periodic tabulations of income and outgo as the administration tries to make the books balance at the end of the fiscal year. The media often do a poor job, however, of reporting budget news. Their stories can be superficial, nothing more than a collection of numbers unconnected in any meaningful way to the circumstances of the public that coughs up the money on which the numbers are based.

Charles Wolfe is a statehouse reporter for the Associated Press in Frankfort, Kentucky. This article is reprinted with permission from *State Government News* 32:5 (May 1989): 10-11. © 1990 by the Council of State Governments.

Figures of millions and billions of dollars get tossed casually about in government and the danger of equally casual reporting always exists.

The late U.S. Sen. Everett Dirksen from Illinois was right in saying, "A million here and a million there and pretty soon you're talking about real money." We *are* talking about a lot of money; we're just numb to it.

It is a challenge for a reporter to follow the legislative odyssey of a budget bill, to cover its mark-ups, amendments, perhaps even its veto and to total up the relative winners and losers. But there is another challenge—to make that budget and its billions of dollars mean something to the average wage earner in Owsley County. Reporters need to find out what lies beneath the surface numbers. If a tax increase or rollback is at issue, they need to ask what the tab is per capita, not just the total dollar amount.

A part of state government that gets generally short shrift from the press corps is the process by which administrative regulations are written to implement new laws. It is tedious business to say the least, but many believe it is where the real lawmaking takes place.

Critics of the process contend a legislative mandate can be turned on its ear with a regulation or a lengthy delay in promulgating that regulation after the legislature has left town. Yet, so arcane is the process that the public rarely hears about it.

It became such a sore point with the Kentucky General Assembly, however, that legislation was passed to require that the state's mountains of administrative regulations be codified in statute, ostensibly giving the legislative branch greater control of its handiwork.

Reporting the story required an explanation of the Kentucky Administrative Regulations, the Kentucky Revised Statutes, the dif-

ferences between them and why it was important. It was a story that was difficult to explain in paper and on the air and therefore it didn't get the coverage that many state officials thought it deserved.

Another common complaint about the media is that they tend to interview the same officials over and over again. Reporters quickly learn which legislators, lobbyists and state officials are knowledgeable, influential and can be counted on for reliable, unbiased information or reaction. But there is a natural tendency of reporters to gravitate to those known to be the most articulate, or provocative, or to hold the seats of greatest power.

There is a corresponding desire on the other side to have all events portrayed in the most favorable light. Attempts to manage the news are ongoing in state government. Such attempts, however, often backfire.

Some techniques will cause reporters reflexively to question the legitimacy of a news event. One is the standing room only news conference, in which the official making the announcement is accompanied by a crowd of associates. The idea seems to be that sheer force of numbers will compel press coverage. But it at times has had the opposite effect on capital press corps, which have developed their own irreverent rule of thumb: The amount of news to be generated at a governor's news conference is inversely proportional to the number of people standing behind the governor.

The press is frequently accused of overplaying the frictions and conflicts of government—a governor fighting with the legislature; legislators fighting with each other—but the process does not take place in a vacuum. If the executive and legislative branches are at a stalemate, that's serious news for the public.

It probably means crippling inaction on several fronts—education, tax reform, infrastructure, to name a few. The public needs to know the ramifications as well as the personalities.

The same thing holds in legislative leadership races. If there is factionalism, reporters need to know what is behind it and how is it likely to be translated into legislation.

Finally, woe to the reporter who slips into the habit of writing in the contrived style of the bureaucratic language.

Government officials are unlikely ever to talk about raising taxes to get more money to meet rising program costs. Instead, they will "dialogue about impacting a shortfall with revenue enhancements." Technocrats are wont to "prioritize." They are mindful of "opportunity windows." They might even "interface." They talk about people or things being "impacted"—an adjective, commonly describing a painful condition of the wisdom teeth, which has somehow been tortured into a verb.

If the capital press corps does its job, it will cut through the verbal clutter, all the way to Owsley County.

Polishing Political Teflon

by P. Michael Saint

Every government official's worst nightmare is saying the wrong thing in a press interview, giving an innocent answer to a "harmless" question, only to have it taken out of context and blown up into a political crisis.

For many politicians and officials, particularly those new to the experience, dealing with the statehouse press corps is at best a traumatic event and at worst a disaster.

Yet in every state, there are officials who seem made of Teflon, or are born lucky. They, unlike their less fortunate colleagues, are forever being favorably quoted in the press, on radio and television. They not only stay out of trouble; they are treated as if they can do no wrong.

So what separates the victims from the heroes, at least when it comes to press coverage?

From my experience as a statehouse reporter, statehouse press secretary and public relations consultant, it's understanding the following rules and living by them.

● **Never lie to a reporter.** That doesn't mean you can't answer only what you are asked, give less information than asked or respond with a "no comment." But *NEVER, EVER LIE.* A reporter who catches you in a lie will bash you in print, this time, next time

and every time thereafter. Most press coverage assumes that those quoted are telling the truth. When that assumption proves false, it is the reporter who looks bad. And once burned, a reporter generally will neither forgive nor trust a "lying politician."

● **Answer the calls of the press.** Reporters will put up with "no comment" or "you will have to check with my boss (or, with my staff)," or with "I don't know, let me find out for you." But they hate news makers who do not take or return phone calls. Reporters do not believe officials have meetings or anything more important to do than wait around to take press calls. They assume that if you don't return their call, especially when it's a big story and they are on deadline, then you must be deliberately ducking them. Consequently, they will go out of their way to indicate their displeasure in print.

P. Michael Saint is president of Saint Communications, a public relations agency in Hingham, Massachusetts. He is a former reporter for *The Patriot Ledger* (Quincy, Massachusetts) and former press secretary to Massachusetts Lt. Governor Thomas P. O'Neill III. This article is reprinted with permission from *State Government News* 32:5 (May 1989): 12-13, 16. © 1990 by the Council of State Governments.

● **Stay on the record.** Reporters assume that everything they see or hear can be reported in the paper. Never say to the press after telling them something, "That's off the record." If what you said is news, they will print it anyway. Even when you warn them beforehand that something is off the record, you are still putting them in an awkward position. Assume everything is on the record and act accordingly. Also, assume they will quote you by name. Under certain circumstances, if you know and trust the reporter, you can ask the reporter not to quote you by name. But it is safer to only say what you want to see in print.

● **Think before you speak.** Whatever you say in response to a question may be quoted. So always take your time and think over your response before opening your mouth. The only time a reporter won't give you the chance to think is on live television or radio, where they can't allow "dead air."

● **Always have an agenda.** Every interview, under good or bad circumstances, is a chance to make points for your department or office. So before taking or returning a call or walking into an interview, decide what you hope to achieve. Figure out the message or messages that you want to communicate and make a conscious effort during the interview to get your points across—several times. (Remember how well President Reagan could turn a hostile question on budget deficits into a fervent appeal for aid to the contras?)

● **Always prepare for an interview.** In most cases, a reporter will have done some research, attended a public meeting, interviewed someone else or gathered some kind of information before calling you. So take some time to prepare yourself. What are the facts? What, exactly, is your position? What tough questions are likely to be asked, and how should you answer them? What pithy, quotable line can you use that will almost demand

direct quotation in the paper?

● **Never be argumentative, nasty or yell at the reporter.** While it's sometimes difficult, never lose your cool in an interview. Reporters will ask stupid questions. They will ask insulting questions. They will ask personal questions. They will make accusations, in the form of questions, simply to see how you react. They will probe to see if you are defensive, lying or hiding something. Don't fall into their trap. If you lose your cool, you are the one who will look bad in the paper (or, even worse, on television), not them. If you lose your temper, you will say something quotable that you won't want to read in the paper.

● **Don't accept their definitions.** If a reporter asks a loaded question, such as "This tax hike, which makes our state the most heavily taxed in the nation, is the third hike in six months, is it not?" If you answer yes, they will say you agreed to the assertion that you are the most taxed state. If you say "no" they will read back to you the dates of the last two tax hikes and portray you as someone who denies the truth about commonly known facts. Take each component separately and make you own points ("Our overall tax burden is lower than two-thirds of the states. Unlike most states, we tax according to a person's ability to pay.")

● **Only be ambiguous when you want to be.** If you answer a question ambiguously, a reporter is free to make it sound like you agreed with whatever side of a question makes for a better story. Only be ambiguous or vague when it suits your purpose.

● **Don't be offended by reportorial ignorance.** No reporter will know as much about your department, office or issue as you do. As the expert, you have the advantage, so don't be afraid to show your knowledge. However, try not to lose patience with the reporter who may know nothing about the subject of the interview. Every day reporters are sent to report and write stories on subjects about which they have absolutely no knowledge. Most end up with fairly accurate, if somewhat simplistic, stories.

● **Avoid jargon.** Avoid bureaucratic jargon and industry terms. Most reporters, and most who read their articles, do not use or understand language associated with human services, engineering, taxation or other specialized areas. If you can speak in common English, without being technical, your message stands a much better chance of being successfully communicated.

● **Know what you're getting into.** When reporters begin shooting questions at you, stop them and ask why they are doing so. What has happened that they need to get [a] comment from you? Ask what the nature of the story is that they are working on. You are operating at a distinct disadvantage when the reporters know what they are looking for, but you don't. You'll be better able to evaluate their questions and frame your response if you know, for example, that they're doing a trend story on new tax laws and not a story on your legislative record in support of new taxes.

● **Announce your own news first.** Your news is yours to announce, until some-one does it for you. If someone tips the press off to some development involving you, it will be their spin, their context or their perspective that will set the tone of the story. This means if someone beats you to announcing the federal grant, you may not be mentioned, even though you did all the work. This principle is even more important in bad or controversial news. If you announce it first, you can at least put it in perspective and present some explanation. If the press gets wind of it elsewhere, they won't have your explanation, and they may have the views of your critics or opponents.

That about covers what I feel are the most important rules for dealing with reporters. There are other rules, of course, like those that deal with cultivating close friendships with reporters and rules on the finer points of journalistic ethics.

But by and large, these rules will help most officials stay out of trouble and get the most from their chances at press coverage.

In summary, tell the truth, be accessible, prepare, stay calm, choose you words carefully, get your message across and be the first to announce anything that is news—good or bad.

Good Press at Bad Times

by Linda Wagar

When former California Gov. Jerry Brown turned a Mediterranean fruit fly [Medfly] infestation into a political disaster, press secretaries across the country took note.

The 1980-82 incident was viewed by many as a textbook example of a botched handling of a crisis. Brown was criticized for making a dramatic flipflop when he decided to use the insecticide malathion to end the infestation threatening California's multibillion dollar agricultural industry, despite his earlier concerns over environmental problems the insecticide might cause. He also was blasted for turning the infestation into a media event to further his political career.

"It was a media feeding frenzy," recalled Dan Walters, a columnist with the *Sacramento Bee*. "I think it attracted such heavy coverage because Jerry framed it in such dramatic terms. It began as environmentalists' last stand, but within 48 hours Jerry had made a dramatic turn around."

The Medfly attack exemplified how media coverage of a politician's management of a crisis can help make or break a political career. For Brown, the Medfly marked the second time he had changed his stand on a major state issue (the first being Proposition 13, which he decided to support after it was approved by voters). His Medfly flipflop also was preceded by two unsuccessful attempts for the presidency. In sum, Brown was ripe for criticism, and the Medfly provided an oversupply of ammunition.

While Brown's case was well publicized, it was not a typical example of how state leaders manage crises. Other state leaders received high marks from reporters for their adroit handling of harried situations.

Reporters in cities such as Des Moines and Seattle said they found most state officials to be honest, accessible, well organized and accurate in crises. From prison riots to forest fires and even in the face of personal attacks many state officials showed a lot of savvy in their dealings with the media.

But there were exceptions.

The media named several cases where they believed government officials made an already bad situation worse by the adversarial manner in which the media were handled.

Mecham and the Media

One example is the case of former Ari-

Linda Wagar is a staff writer for *State Government News*. This article is reprinted with permission from *State Government News* 32:5 (May 1989): 18-21. © 1990 by the Council of State Governments.

Talking Too Much

The following is an excerpt from the book Silence Cannot Be Misquoted *by Ronald J. Bellus, the former press secretary to former Arizona Gov. Evan Mecham, who was impeached [in 1988].*

I have had scores of people ask me how I was able to keep my sanity and a sense of humor through all this turmoil. As press secretary, I had to face the media after each comment Mecham made. It was getting frustrating. I often felt the best client a press secretary could have is Marcel Marceau.

As a press secretary, it was my responsibility to work on "damage control." Many reporters were sensitive to the situation; others (including) just about every columnist in Phoenix and Tucson used the ammunition provided by Mecham and shot him with it.

He kept loading their guns.

As I viewed it then and still do now, Mecham's fall from grace and what would have been nearly a decade of true fiscal conservatism in Arizona government came about for two reasons. First, certain members of the "Establishment" didn't like his independence—their inability to influence him. Second, Mecham's own proclivity to speak off the cuff provided the ammunition to his critics to turn enough public opinion against him.

It wasn't the substance of Mecham's policies that irritated people as much as it was his way of presenting those policies. It was his style—his often blunt and candid manner—that bothered many people.

Source: Linda Wagar, "Good Press at Bad Times," *State Government News* 32:5 (May 1989): 19. Used with permission. © 1990 by the Council of State Governments.

zona Gov. Evan Mecham who in 1988 became the first U.S. governor in 59 years to be impeached. As troubles began reaching the boiling point for Mecham shortly before his second year in office, wire service and print reporters found their access to the governor drastically reduced, according to Statehouse Reporter Sam Stanton of the *Arizona Republic.*

Stanton blames Mecham's decision to deal as little as possible with the local print media for contributing to the governor's downfall.

"We weren't able to print the governor's side of the story, just his denials of anything we did uncover," Stanton said. "His unwillingness to talk to us had to have made his situation even worse."

Mecham maintained that the local print media were out to destroy him. While Mecham's former press secretary Ron Bellus agrees that media coverage was unfair, he also acknowledges that the former governor did not provide a model example of how to deal with the press when under fire.

Bellus described Mecham as a governor who did not know when to shut up. Mecham, he said, was overly concerned about negative press and would hold numerous news conferences to denounce coverage with which he disagreed.

"He, at the drop of the hat, would call a press conference if there was a story he didn't like," Bellus said. "He would turn what should have been a one- or two-day story into a week's worth of coverage. It was completely the wrong way to handle it."

In addition, Mecham made his distaste for several influential members of the press readily apparent by refusing to grant them interviews and ridiculing them in public.

"You don't start a fight with someone [who] buys ink by the barrel," Bellus noted.

Other governors who have come under

fire while in office have dealt with the press more gracefully. Often the governors who were most adept and comfortable with the media relied little on their press secretaries to intervene during sticky situations.

Bayou Savvy

One executive branch member lauded for his savvy with the media is former Louisiana Gov. Edwin Edwards who in 1985 was charged and acquitted of fraud and racketeering.

"Edwards was very glib and very smooth and brushed (the charges) off as the creation of some Republican," said Ed Anderson, a statehouse reporter with *The Times-Picayune* in New Orleans. "He could have run and hid from the press, but he didn't."

Justine Weeks, who as a television reporter covered Edwards' trial and later became his press secretary, agreed that the governor was adept in dealing with the press.

"The governor was of the feeling that if you don't talk to the press and don't provide information then the press begins to feel you are trying to hide something," Weeks said. "The governor always wanted to maintain easy accessibility."

Weeks noted in particular a 1987 incident involving the indictment of a legislator and the pardon board chairman in a pardon-for-sale scandal. The legislator was later acquitted of the charges, while the pardon board chairman pleaded guilty. Weeks said there was concern in the governor's office that the media would try to connect the governor to some of the charges filed against the legislator because he was a close friend and political ally of the governor's.

Edwards, Weeks said, was not surprised with the indictment of the pardon board chairman, but legitimately was "more shocked than he had ever been" by the legislator's indictment.

"The governor's emotions regarding the indictment of his close friend really came through in the press conference and that was the best way he could have handled it," Weeks said. "If the governor had been more standoffish, the press would have remained suspicious of the governor's knowledge of the situation. But it was obvious from the governor's face that he was shocked to hear about the indictment."

Weeks said the governor did as much as possible to improve his public image, given the accusations leveled against him.

"He responded to their (the press) questions as quickly as possible and he gave them as much information as he could," Weeks said. "In hindsight, that is really all he could have done. He was his own best press secretary."

Learning from Mistakes

When examining the government's handling of major crises beyond the executive branch, one that comes readily to mind is the February 1980 prison riot in Santa Fe that left 33 inmates dead. It was an unusual crisis from the media standpoint because Ernie Mills, a syndicated New Mexico broadcast commentator, was pushed into action by state officials to negotiate with the inmates. The inmates had taken over the prison, were killing prisoners who had acted as informants and were threatening the lives of 12 guards taken hostage.

The inmates had asked for Mills because many of them were Vietnam veterans and they trusted Mills because of his work as a war correspondent in Vietnam.

Mills said one of the things that distresses him is that state officials appear to have learned little from the gruesome tragedy about dealing with the media during crises.

"I personally feel that in state government very seldom do officials look down the road to what they would do in the case of a crisis," Mills said. "I think that when something like this occurs there is a lot of embarrassment and people don't want to go back and find out exactly what went wrong."

For example, Mills noted, that choosing him as negotiator could have been a fatal mistake if he had not decided to put his role as negotiator before his responsibility to the media.

"At one point I learned that prisoners were hiding three prison guards to protect them from other inmates," Mills said. "If I told the media the whole prison would have learned about it because they were monitoring television and radio broadcasts."

Mills said it bothers him that a policy still does not exist in state government regarding the use of the media in such roles.

Corrections Department spokesman Kevin Jackson said no strict policy had been adopted because the department believes that the best strategy to follow in a crisis is to be flexible.

"If you have a hard and fast policy sometimes it can work against you," Jackson said.

But Jackson said the department has learned from the Santa Fe riot how better to react during a crisis. Jackson said that during the 1980 riot wrong information was released because of confusion over who should be talking to the media. In addition, corrections officials were slow in giving out information as it became available.

Such problems have been corrected, Jackson said, noting that the department's current policy is to release press updates—good or bad—as soon as possible and to maintain a central control over who makes announcements to the press.

Prison Riot Coverage

One state to receive high marks for its handling of the media during a prison riot was Iowa. *Des Moines Register* reporter Bill

Petroski said he was impressed with how quickly he was given information when inmates took over a cell house and took seven people hostage Jan. 6, 1986.

"They (corrections officials) told me what was happening as it was going on," Petroski said, noting that by the time the crisis had been quelled the Department of Corrections had provided him with a minute-by-minute breakdown of events that occurred inside the cell block.

Petroski said that type of response was important not only to him and his paper, but to the Department of Corrections as well.

"When you have a prison uprising there are all sorts of rumors that immediately begin circulating within the prison," Petroski said. "Inmates are a great font of information— whether it is accurate or inaccurate—so any information the corrections people can come out with accurately will diffuse a lot of the misinformation being fed by inmates to the press."

Corrections Department Director Paul Grossheim agreed, but noted that sometimes the press wants information before it's feasible.

"We don't want the press learning about plans to retake a cell block," Grossheim said. "That wouldn't make much sense."

Grossheim said his department can't always answer every question and that's something that some reporters fail to understand.

"The media always want to know who is to blame," Grossheim said. "In some cases we can't immediately jump to a conclusion that an inmate did something or instigated something. Who did it is something for the grand jury to decide. I don't want to have a trial by media."

WPPSS' Woops

One of the bigger crises to hit Washington state in the last 20 years was Washington Public Power Supply System's [WPPSS] attempt to enter the nuclear age. Instead of becoming a successful nuclear pioneer in the region, WPPSS defaulted in 1983 on $2.25 billion in bonds—the largest default on record by a public utility.

Gary Petersen, director of administration, said that when the crisis first became apparent in January 1981, WPPSS handled the press poorly. Phone calls went unanswered as did requests for public records and interviews. Petersen, who was hired as deputy director of public affairs to help solve WPPSS' poor image, said that by not talking to the media, those heading the agency were adding fuel to the already raging fire of distrust surrounding WPPSS.

"WPPSS had lost its credibility with the public and with the Legislature," Petersen said. "We had to rebuild that credibility. And as a public agency we had a legal and moral obligation to let people know what was going on."

Petersen said a strategy for dealing with the press was established and a conscious decision was made to make available all information. He noted that press coverage of the crisis was exhaustive. "At one point we were handling 600 media calls a week."

The openness of WPPSS officials toward the press allowed Peyton Whitely of the *Seattle Times* to learn enough about WPPSS officials to view them as victims of the financial disaster, instead of perpetrators.

"I like to compare (WPPSS) to a famous cartoon of missionaries being boiled by cannibals," Whitely said. "The temperature went up so slowly in the pot they did not realize they were being cooked."

Peyton said the WPPSS disaster was as much the making of the federal government as it was the blame of state officials.

"(President) Kennedy was pushing for the development of a nuclear reactor," Whitely said. "For the people running WPPSS to stand up to that kind of pressure was impossi-

---

Crisis Pointers

California's Tom Mullins, whose state Office of Emergency Services has been applauded for its smooth handling of natural crises, said he tries to keep several basic points in mind when dealing with the press.

● **Shoot Straight.** "There is a natural tendency to try not to reveal all the information you have. But the fact of the matter is that the press will find out eventually," Mullins said.

● **Never Speculate.** Information should only be released when the provider knows it's accurate. The primary concern should be for the safety of the public.

● **Coordinate Press Information.** A central office always should be aware of what information is being released.

● **Stay Calm.** The [calmer] you appear, the quicker people will realize that everything is under control.

Source: Linda Wagar, "Good Press at Bad Times," *State Government News* 32:5 (May 1989): 18. Used with permission. © 1990 by the Council of State Governments.

---

ble. They enthusiastically accepted what they were being told by high-level people."

Peyton said the problem also lay in the hands of WPPSS administrators who had little expertise in the construction of nuclear power plants and in forecasters who erroneously predicted huge increases in energy demand for the 1980s.

Avoiding Backlash

As Petersen acknowledges, WPPSS might have gotten off to a faulty start with the press, but officials quickly learned from their mistakes and rectified media relations. Others, such as former Govs. Brown and Mecham, never were given a chance to recover from their press follies. Brown's heavy-handed "I'm in charge" attitude contributed to his immediate downfall after his gubernatorial term expired, as did Mecham's antagonistic relationship with the press.

Brown's successor, George Deukmejian, proved that natural crises don't always have to lead to political backlash. Deukmejian's strategy during several major forest fires and earthquakes that swept his state was to stay out of the picture as much as possible and let the professionals do their job.

"Deukmejian does not portray himself as a general on the frontline and it has been to his credit with the media," said Walters with the *Sacramento Bee*. "He has not shamelessly exploited natural disasters for cheap media attention."

Tom Mullins, director of information in California's Office of Emergency Services, agreed that Deukmejian has never tried to force his way into the forefront. "It's not a problem with Deukmejian."

Officials might well follow Deukmejian's example in keeping a low profile in natural disasters. But when the politician is the story, then openness, accessibility and organization win media confidence and might prevent a crisis from turning into a political disaster.

V. STATE LEGISLATURES

In theory, state legislatures fulfill the representative democracy function in state government. Each legislator represents a particular district with particular interests. Legislators then meet in the state capital to meld the interests of the districts they represent with the interests of the state as a whole. The result of this tugging and hauling is the state budget, state policies, and occasionally a constitutional amendment.

In practice, however, state governments operate somewhat less democratically. Subject-area specialists both within and outside the legislatures have an inordinate amount of legislative power. This is especially true for those legislators who chair or are on money committees: finance or revenue, and appropriations. Because of their heavy workload, individual legislators increasingly must rely on these experts—their peers and lobbyists—for guidance on how to vote. Once the legislation has been signed into law, administrators of state agencies and programs are largely on their own to interpret and implement the laws.

One Man, One Vote

Until the 1960s, everyone in a state was not equally represented in the legislature. State legislatures determined how district lines were drawn and thus who would be represented in the legislature and to what extent. Legislatures used various devices such as the gerrymander (excessive manipulation of the shape of a legislative district to benefit a certain incumbent or party) or silent gerrymander (district lines were left intact despite major shifts in population).[1] Both types of legislative legerdemain resulted in underrepresentation of minorities and those living in the cities.

As a result of this misrepresentation, the U.S. Supreme Court ruled in the landmark decision *Baker v. Carr* (1962) that federal courts had the power to review legislative apportionment in the states. Two years later, in *Reynolds v. Sims,* the Court ruled that both houses of a state legislature must be apportioned on the basis of population—that is, "one man, one vote." And in the *Davis v. Bandemer* case (1986), the Court gave political parties standing in court suits over apportionment if a particular political party felt gerrymandered unfairly. And which party won't feel treated unfairly if they do not get the legislative apportionment plan that helps them out the most? In *Colgrove v. Green* (1946), the Court indicated that it wanted to stay out of the "political thicket" of apportionment; forty years later it jumped squarely into that thicket.

We are now in the midst of the 1990 Census and we soon will find out how many people live in each state, and where in each state they live. Once the Census results are tabulated, most state legislatures will need to reallocate and redraw congressional and state legislative districts. The party controlling the governorships and the houses of the state legislatures will be able to draw lines to its own benefit in the 1991 legislative sessions—albeit under the the various court constraints already noted. Redistricting may be one of the most politically charged items the states will find on their 1991 agenda since it directly affects the legislators themselves.

Currently, Democrats control twenty-nine of the fifty governor's chairs and sixty-nine of the ninety-nine partisan legislative chambers (Nebraska has a one house, nonpartisan legislature). Democrats control both houses in twenty-nine states, and split control with the Republicans in eleven states; the remaining nine are controlled by Republicans. But party numbers do not always add up to party control since several state legislatures are run by informal, bipartisan coalitions. These coalitions may be the result of deep divisions in the majority party over the choice of house speaker. Other coalitions are due to divisions over ideology or specific issues. Still others occur when the minority party grows in strength and seeks to redress what they see as an abridgment of their rights by joining in a coalition with dissidents from the majority party in seeking new leadership.[2]

A unique problem in party control occurred in the Indiana house, where a 50-50 member party tie led to a dual leadership system of "speakers *du jour*" or "stereo speakers," which led to a difficult 1989 legislative session. One solution adopted by the legislature was to increase the membership in the House from 100 to 101 to preclude the possibility of a tie in the future.[3] But the problem was resolved when, near the end of the 1989 session, one Democratic member switched his party affiliation to Republican.

Each state-level election from now on will have great impact on just who wins and who loses in this high-stakes redistricting game, since both legislatures and governors must agree on a bill to carry out the changes. Only the governor of North Carolina is constitutionally outside of this political fight since he has no veto to challenge what the legislature may decide, although the legislature currently is debating placing a constitutional amendment on the 1990 general election ballot to give the veto to the governor. Interestingly, one of the sticking points is whether the governor should be able to veto any legislative and congressional redistricting bills.[4]

How important are the stakes involved? U.S. representative Lynn Martin (R-Ill.) argues: "We're talking about changing the face of America. That's how important this is."[5] But, unlike such struggles in previous decades, there is now a third actor in the redistricting game: the federal courts. The U.S. Supreme Court, in *Davis v. Bandemer,*

for the first time agreed that such mapping of districts is subject to court challenge if discrimination against *identifiable political groups* can be proved. The definition of such groups, however, is not entirely clear in the Court's opinion.[6]

Legislative Reforms

These reapportionment decisions coincided with a general revival of state government during the mid- to late 1960s. The revival came at a time when the states sorely needed a new, more positive image. Television news programs pictured southern governors blocking school doorways to keep minority students out. Numerous publications described the apparent failures, unrepresentativeness, and corruption of state governments.[7] It took national legislation such as the Civil Rights Act of 1964 and the Voting Rights Act of 1965 and U.S. Supreme Court decisions to force state governments to fulfill their responsibilities to those they represented.

In the 1970s and 1980s, state after state passed laws that drastically reformed state legislatures and improved their public image. The following examples illustrate the kinds of laws passed:

● tighter deadlines and improved scheduling procedures for considering legislation

● automated bill status and statute retrieval systems

● computerized systems for the state budget process

● relaxation of constitutional restrictions on what issues legislators can consider

● more flexible and rewarding systems of legislative compensation

● greater staff capability in bill drafting, legal services, budgeting, and postaudit and program evaluation

● longer sessions, and the replacement of biennial sessions with annual ones

● longer terms for legislators, and individual offices for each legislator

● expanded personal staffs

Separation of Powers

Other parts of state government, not just the legislatures, were reformed in response to the "indictment" of the states in the 1960s. Gubernatorial powers were strengthened to make governors the chief executives of the states in fact, rather than just in theory. However, these reforms did little to reduce the natural conflict between the executive and legislative branches that is built into state constitutions.

The U.S. Constitution and state constitutions share a fundamental principle: separation of powers. Consider, for example, this article from the Colorado Constitution that clearly separates legislative, executive, and judicial authority:

> Article III. Distribution of Powers. The powers of the government of this state are divided into three distinct departments, the legislative, executive and judicial; and no person or collection of persons charged with the exercise of powers properly belonging to one of these departments shall exercise any power properly belonging to either of the others, except as in this constitution expressly directed or permitted.

The principle of separation of powers is expressly adopted in the constitutions of thirty-eight states. Twenty-nine of these states include some exceptions to a strict interpretation of the principle. (The last clause of Article III above is an example of such an exception.) Nine states require strict separation with no exceptions allowed. But twelve state constitutions do not include any separation of powers provisions.[8]

Executive Branch Appointments. Appointments are perhaps the area of greatest tension between the executive and legislative branches of state government. Legislatures often have a constitutionally mandated power to confirm gubernatorial appointments. They can cause the governor problems with this authority, as Republican governor George Deukmejian of California found out in 1988 when he tried to appoint Republican U.S. representative Dan Lungren as state treasurer. In the Democratically-controlled legislature, the House approved the appointment by a 43-32 vote, but the Senate voted against the appointment 19-21. This split vote raised an interesting constitutional question: Deukmejian argued that a nomination is confirmed unless rejected by both houses, but the legislative counsel argued that either house could veto an appointee. The state's attorney general, John Van de Kamp, a Democrat, agreed with the legislative counsel. Part of the politics of this situation was Lungren's ambition to run for governor in 1990 and the Democrats' view that Lungren's appointment would strengthen his future candidacy.[9] (Van de Kamp was a leading contender for the Democratic party nomination in the 1990 governor's race.)

In some states, legislatures have the statutory or constitutional authority to make appointments to boards and commissions; they even can appoint their own members to these positions. Only four states strictly ban legislators from serving on boards and commissions. Eleven states allow legislators to serve on advisory bodies only. However, twenty states permit legislators to sit on boards and commissions that exercise management responsibilities.[10] This "legislative intrusion" into the executive branch has been challenged successfully in Kentucky, Mississippi, and North Carolina.

Legislative Veto. A second area of tension lies in the increasing use of the legislative veto—a procedure permitting state legislatures (and the U.S. Congress) "to review proposed executive branch regulations or actions and to block or modify those with which they disagree." [11] In lieu of legislative veto legislation, some states have enacted laws regarding review of administrative rule-making procedures.

Over the past decade, there has been a rapid rise in the use of the legislative veto—up to forty-one states by mid-1982. However, the tide recently has turned against this legislative bid to gain increased control over the executive branch. Courts, both state and federal, have invalidated the legislative veto as an unconstitutional violation of the separation of powers principle. [12] And voters in several states have rejected their legislature's use of a legislative veto. [13]

Legislatures and Citizens

Between 1980 and 1985, voters in at least ten states made their legislatures the target of the initiative process. Nineteen separate initiatives aimed at state legislatures ranged from redistricting and reapportioning, to regulating the size of the legislature and the amount of legislative pay, to moving to a unicameral legislature, to barring the state legislature from repealing initiatives. [14] As discussed in the introduction to Part II, voters in several states during the 1988 and 1989 elections also addressed issues concerning the legislatures, both initiated by the legislature itself and by the voters through the initiative process. [15] But legislatures were the losers as pay raises were rejected in Arizona, Massachusetts (by a 4.8-1 vote), Nevada, and Texas, where voters also rejected an increase in legislators' daily expense allowances. In addition, South Dakota voters decided that their legislature no longer may place initiatives on the ballot.

Why are voters targeting their legislatures? One reason might be the continuing decline in public esteem of state elected officials. In a 1985 national poll, only 16 percent

of the respondents rated the honesty and ethical standards of state political officeholders as high or very high—although this was better than in 1977 when only 11 percent did. At least state officials were rated three times better than car salesmen, who were at the bottom of the list at 5 percent. [16] A recent study compiled the results of state polls that asked citizens their views on the overall performance of their state legislatures. The results indicating the legislature was doing a fair or poor job outnumbered those saying it was doing a good or excellent job. [17] Comparing these results with a multistate study in the late 1960s, which asked a similar question, it is clear that citizens' views of legislative performance have declined over the past two decades. [18]

Legislative Activity

There is a rhythm to what happens in most state legislatures. Even-numbered-year sessions tend to be much quieter than those held in odd-numbered years. Why? It is tied to the electoral cycle. Most state legislators are elected in even, nonpresidential years such as 1990. Many others are elected in the even, presidential year elections, as in 1988. During election years, legislators and governors usually adopt a "play it safe" strategy and attempt to avoid taking positions on controversial issues that could cost them votes. Some states do not even convene their legislatures in election years; others have short sessions.

Policy initiatives in numerous areas—education, health care, economic development, and hazardous waste disposal, to name a few—are being undertaken by the states and their legislatures rather than by the federal government and Congress. This full agenda leads columnist Neal Peirce to argue that "it's not in Washington that the future of American politics is being written." [19] A major conservative spokesman agrees, but laments that "the Great Society may be over in Washington, but it has just begun in the states." [20]

Part V explores different aspects of state legislatures. Amy E. Young of *Common Cause Magazine* discusses the potential for conflicts of interest for state legislators who serve on a part-time basis. Linda Wagar of *State Government News* offers two articles: one on the "fear and loathing" that heads of ethics panels often face from their peers; and the other on how politicans struggle to balance the demands of single-issue voters with the rest of their responsibilities. Robert X. Browning discusses that unique situation in Indiana with "speakers *du jour*," and Alan Rosenthal reviews the status of state legislative leadership and how it has been changing. Alan Ehrenhalt of *Governing* magazine takes a detailed look at the Wisconsin state legislature and how the liberal Democrats have been able to maintain control of that body.

Notes

1. The name "gerrymander" originated in 1812, the year the Massachusetts legislature carved a district out of Essex County that historian John Fiske said had a "dragonlike contour." When the painter Gilbert Stuart saw the misshapen district, he penciled in a head, wings, and claws and exclaimed: "That will do for a salamander!"—to which editor Benjamin Russell replied: "Better say a Gerrymander"—after Elbridge Gerry, the governor of Massachusetts. Congressional Quarterly's *Guide to U.S. Elections,* 2d ed. (Washington, D.C.: Congressional Quarterly, 1985), 691.
2. Malcolm E. Jewell, "The Durability of Leadership," *State Legislatures* 15:10 (November/December 1989): 11, 21.
3. James Grass, "Legislative Deadlock Makes for Full House," *USA Today,* April 19, 1989, 6A.
4. Rob Christensen, "Side Issues Slowing Momentum for Veto," [Raleigh] *News and Observer,* April 25, 1989, 2C.
5. Tom Watson, "Drawing the Line(s) in 1990: A High-Stakes Game to Control the Legislatures," *Governing* 1:8 (May 1988): 20.
6. Ibid., 20-21.
7. See, for example, Frank Trippet, *The States— United They Fell* (New York: World Publishing, 1967).
8. Jody George and Lacy Maddox, "Separation of Powers Provisions in State Constitutions," in *Boards, Commissions, and Councils in the Executive Branch of North Carolina State Government* (Raleigh, N.C.: North Carolina Center for Public Policy Research, 1984), 51.
9. "Politics: Split Vote Leaves Rep. Lungren Dangling," *Congressional Quarterly Weekly Report,* February 27, 1988, 549.
10. "Legislators Serving on Boards and Commissions," *State Legislative Report* (Denver: National Conference of State Legislatures, 1983), as reported in George and Maddox, "Separation of Powers Provisions," 52.
11. Walter J. Oleszek, *Congressional Procedures and the Policy Process,* 3d ed. (Washington, D.C.: CQ Press, 1988), 297.
12. The U.S. Supreme Court case was *Immigration and Naturalization Service v. Jagdish Rai Chadha* (1983).
13. New Jersey in 1985, Alaska and Michigan in 1986, Nevada in 1988.
14. David B. Magleby, "Legislatures and the Initiative: The Politics of Direct Democracy," *The Journal of State Government* 59:1 (Spring 1986): 35-36. Some of these initiatives failed, some passed, some are still in circulation seeking the requisite number of signatures to be placed on the ballot, and one was disallowed.
15. Sandra Singer, "Voters Dabble with Legislative Details," *State Legislatures* 15:1 (January 1989): 30.
16. "An Erosion of Ethics?" *Public Opinion* 9:4 (November-December 1986): 21.
17. Patrick Cotter, "Legislatures and Public Opinion," *The Journal of State Government* 59:1 (Spring 1986): 47-50.
18. Merle Black, David M. Kovenock, and William C. Reynolds, *Political Attitudes in the Nation and the States* (Chapel Hill, N.C.: Institute for Research in Social Science, 1974).
19. Neal R. Peirce, "Conservatives Agony: The States Turn Left," *State Government News* 30:11 (November 1987): 14.
20. Ibid.

Dual Careers Mean Potential Conflicts for State Legislators

by Amy E. Young

Because most state legislators serve on a part-time basis, they are likely to have second jobs. Typically they work as lawyers or in business or education, according to a 1986 study by the National Conference of State Legislatures. Professional expertise in fact can give citizen lawmakers useful background and perspective on pending legislation—farmers who serve on agricultural committees, for example, may have valuable firsthand knowledge of farming issues. At the same time, however, potential conflicts of interest can arise when these same legislators are making farm policy that affects their own pocketbooks.

Such scenarios are common in state legislatures. In Virginia, for example, only three of 20 members of Virginia's House Corporations, Insurance and Banking Committee reported no direct interest in corporations or the insurance or banking industries on their financial disclosure forms. Common Cause of Virginia Executive Director Julie Lapham says it came as no surprise when the committee rejected a bill that would have capped rates on bank credit cards—without its members even discussing their possible conflicts of interest.

Common Cause (CC) state leaders, using a CC model ethics law, are pushing for strong measures that define a legislator's "interest" in legislation, require detailed financial disclosure of legislators' outside interests and create independent commissions that can provide guidance and investigate potential conflicts.

In Virginia's case, there is a financial disclosure requirement for investments or income over $10,000, but the law doesn't compel members to reveal the name of the companies in which they have an interest; they need only name the *type* of business. "Virginia actively advocates putting people on a committee for their background and experience," says ... Lapham. "But without accurate disclosure, it's very hard for the public to decide who has a conflict of interest."

Louisiana has a conflict of interest statute but it does not require any financial disclosure. "Unless [the conflict] is a matter of public record or someone else knows, it is up to the legislator's conscience to file," says Peter Wright, deputy general counsel for the investigative arm of the state's Board of Ethics for Elected Officials. If a legislator does choose to file a statement in conjunction with a particu-

Amy E. Young is an editorial assistant for *Common Cause Magazine*. This article is reprinted from *Common Cause Magazine* 15:5 (September/October 1989): 40. © 1989 *Common Cause Magazine*, Washington, D.C.

lar piece of legislation, the law prohibits that member from discussing or introducing a bill, says Wright, but not from voting on it.

"When you have that kind of system," he notes, "it makes it easier to inadvertently or purposefully advance a position [that leads to personal gain]."

In some legislatures it is up to a colleague to decide how to handle a potential conflict. New Hampshire state Senate President William Bartlett Jr. gave the okay on the Senate floor to Majority Whip Sheila Roberge to cast a vote raising the salaries of 20 state employees, one of whom was her husband. Bartlett reasoned that the conflict was not that serious, according to local newspaper accounts.

"Generally we have ... an honor system," Ramsay McLaughlan, executive director of the state Democratic Committee, told one reporter. "If you feel you have a conflict, you don't vote on that issue." According to statehouse records, however, Rule 16 (abstention for conflict of interest) was used only 24 times in 28,012 votes cast in 1988.

New Hampshire has two conflict of interest laws but they "fail to define what an 'interest' is," says Common Cause of New Hampshire Executive Director Susan Clay. The state also has no ethics commission. Clay says she has been lobbying for ethics reforms for seven years but the effort has met with strong resistance.

Oregon has a Government Ethics Commission, but it is hampered by its lack of independence. Betty Reynolds, executive direc-

tor of the commission, points to a current investigation involving state Sen. Paul Philips, the associate director of N. W. Strategies, a political consulting firm. According to Reynolds, the commission is looking into charges that the senator may have violated six conflict of interest statutes, including the use of his official position to obtain confidential information for a client and to influence public agencies to benefit a client.

Philips refused the commission's request for information, forcing it to subpoena documents. And soon after the investigation began, he cosponsored a bill to abolish the commission. Although that bill failed, the legislature did pass a bill to cut the commission's budget by 25 percent and restrict its ability to conduct investigations.

"The commission has to constantly fight to do their job since it's under the legislature's control," says Common Cause of Oregon Executive Director Terry Nelson, who supports measures to establish the commission as a separate entity with provisions for funding and legal assistance independent of the legislature.

A number of state organizations are using CC's model ethics law as a starting point in developing legislation. In West Virginia, where a landmark law was enacted this year, the effort has already prompted two requests for advisory opinions on conflict of interest and raised the general awareness of the issue, according to Common Cause of West Virginia Executive Director Bob Hall.

Fear and Loathing of Ethics Taskmasters

by Linda Wagar

In the chummy atmosphere of the legislature, those that ride herd over unethical behavior often find themselves in awkward positions.

The heads of ethics panels are at once feared and loathed by colleagues.

"It is absolutely the most difficult job and the least rewarding," said New Jersey Senate Assistant Majority Leader Paul Contillo, D-Bergen County. "Your colleagues see you as an antagonizer and the public sees you as Tom Sawyer the whitewasher."

Contillo said he stepped down after four years at the helm of the Joint Legislative Committee on Ethical Standards in part because he had grown tired of being viewed as an antagonist.

The chairman of another state's ethics committee said he felt much the same way and has tried to resign several times.

"Every time I ask someone to take the job, I just get laughed at," said Kentucky Sen. Ed O'Daniel, D-Springfield.

Lawmakers said ethical violations are going to occur as long as part-time legislators rely on practicing law, selling cars or running a bank for the majority of their income.

Legislators often must bend over backwards to ensure that they, their families or their business colleagues don't profit from their political positions.

"The nature of a part-time legislature creates a conflict of interest and makes the issue of ethics more important," said Tennessee Sen. James Kyle, D-Memphis.

An inherent problem with ethics commissions is that determining whether behavior is unethical is a judgment call in an already gray area.

"You have to determine things such as whether a legislator knew his brother-in-law owned part interest in something he was voting on," said New Jersey's Contillo. "I really felt my credibility was on the line with some of the decisions I made. I'd go home and not be sure I'd done the right thing."

O'Daniel said his colleagues were not shy about making their feelings known regarding the actions of Kentucky's Board of Ethics. He has been asked by fellow lawmakers to stop investigating the alleged ethical violations of a Kentucky House member charged with profiting from state contracts.

"People have asked me 'Why don't you

Linda Wagar is a contributing editor of *State Government News*. This article is reprinted with permission from *State Government News* 32:6 (June 1989): 30. © 1990 by the Council of State Governments.

let the criminal proceedings take their course and forget the ethical violations?' " O'Daniel said.

"I feel that unless the legislative ethics committee does what it is required to do statutorily, we might as well repeal the law of ethics and revert to laws saying that unless you're convicted of a crime anything goes."

Kentucky's Board of Ethics is headed by O'Daniel, but five of its nine members are not in state government, including two who are members of the press.

Some lawmakers said a board similar to Kentucky's was needed in other states because a mix of public and private sector members makes it easier to lodge criticism against a lawmaker.

"It's difficult to criticize a fellow legislator unless he is so far off base that it's making everyone look bad," Contillo said, noting that his ideal ethics commission would be composed of a former legislator and private citizens.

Contillo said most lawmakers would not approve a state ethics board unless it had at least one legislative member.

"If you had a board made up of people from Common Cause and the League of Women Voters, most legislators would complain that they were lunatics who don't understand government," Contillo said. "I think the problem is that they understand government too well."

Tennessee's method for ruling on ethical violations is through a Senate Ethics Committee, comprised only of senators. No such body exists in the House. Douglas Henry Jr., who chairs the Senate committee, said he has never had a complaint from legislators or the public about unethical behavior regarding a member of the Senate since he took charge of the committee four years ago.

Henry, a Nashville Democrat, said the committee spent most of its time giving opinions to legislators on conflict of interest inquiries.

Oklahoma Sen. Bernest Cain, D-Oklahoma City, said few allegations of unethical behavior were lodged against lawmakers in his state either. Cain said lawmakers are fearful of making enemies in the Legislature because it could translate into a loss of political clout.

"If I try to get someone punished and it doesn't happen, then I've made an enemy for life," Cain said. "And that enemy will have other friends in the Legislature who are also going to be my enemies."

"I didn't get involved in politics not to have influence and accomplish something. I handle areas that deal with mental health and appropriations. I don't want to be in the back of the room unable to speak out when something important is happening. I'm willing to make compromises to keep my position."

Balancing the Demands of Single-Issue Voters

by Linda Wagar

Legions of single-issue voters shouting threats of political death to opponents are becoming a frustrating fact of statehouse life.

From abortion to gun control, 1990 should prove to be a year to remember as politicians struggle to balance the demands of special interests against the needs of constituents.

Nevada Sen. Sue Wagner of Reno said the frightening aspect of single-issue voters is that they know little about the overall ability of the candidates they battle to elect.

"When a candidate is elected on a single issue, that says nothing about the other 1,000 bills to be voted on," Wagner said.

But West Virginia Speaker Robert Chambers said the more disturbing aspect of single-issue voters is that lawmakers have been known to bend to their demands.

And Chambers said he is no exception. He said he once voted for a piece of "frivolous" legislation because a vote against it would have cost him his seat.

The vote was to approve a referendum for an amendment to the West Virginia Constitution guaranteeing the right to bear arms. Chambers said he was initially opposed to the measure, but when he recognized the power of the lobby in support of it he changed his mind.

"I thought it was frivolous," Chambers said. "But I don't think that taking a stand on principle against a frivolous measure was worth risking my political career."

Chambers, however, quickly regretted his decision. Shortly after the amendment was approved, the West Virginia Supreme Court ruled that the new amendment rendered unconstitutional a state law requiring a license to possess a gun.

"I hadn't foreseen the possibility of that law being overturned," Chambers said. "It made me sorry that I'd voted in favor of the amendment."

Chambers said some West Virginia lawmakers have lost re-election bids because they found themselves on the wrong side of an issue. An organization opposed to tax increases was successful in removing Chambers' predecessor in leadership from office.

But Chambers said that while he is mindful of the power of special interest groups he won't be swayed to vote in favor of an issue that would do great harm to his principles. Chambers acknowledged, however, that rec-

Linda Wagar is a contributing editor of *State Government News*. This article is reprinted with permission from *State Government News* 32:11 (November 1989): 34. © 1990 by the Council of State Governments.

ognizing when that time has come is not always clear.

"We are all willing to bend a little but it can be difficult to figure out where that line is drawn."

New Jersey Assemblyman Robert Singer of Ocean County said he has grown irate over the recent tactics of a special interest group in his state. Singer said the National Organization for Women of New Jersey asked him to sign a sworn oath pledging his support for legalized abortion.

"I resent people [who] ask me to sign an oath designed to prevent me from ever changing my mind," Singer said. "The only oath I'll take is my oath of office."

Oregon Sen. Bill Bradbury of Bandon predicted that single-issue voters will start crawling out of the woodwork because abortion is no longer an issue on which politicians can hedge their position. Bradbury recalled that lawmakers once were able to duck the issue by spouting rhetoric such as "abortion is a very personal, moral decision."

All that has changed because the issue now revolves around the question of whether a lawmaker favors spending state tax dollars on abortions. "The only answer is yes or no," Chambers said.

But placing the abortion debate aside, Alaska Sen. Jim Duncan of Juneau echoed the sentiments of all those interviewed when he noted that lawmakers who try to adjust their votes to the demands of every special interest group eventually will lose the respect of their colleagues and constituency.

"When you are elected to public office you are there to make some tough decisions," Duncan said. "I've found that the public will generally respect you if you had a rational reason for voting the way you did."

But Duncan acknowledged that exceptions to that rule occasionally occur. Such was the case a few years back when a battle was underway in Alaska to move the state capital. Duncan, who represents Juneau, said if he had voted in favor of the move (no matter how rational his reasoning) his constituents would have retired him from office.

California Assemblyman Sam Farr of Carmel said the United States is seeing a rise in special interest groups because a growing number of politicians have little direction and are susceptible to their manipulation.

"I see a lot of people coming into public office not knowing why they are here," Farr said. "They remind me of Robert Redford in 'The Candidate.' After he wins the election, he asks himself, 'What do I do now?' "

Farr said his nine years in office have taught him that over the long haul a single vote isn't all that relevant because it easily can be undermined by the next session of the legislature.

"Society changes, votes change," Farr said. "The important thing is maintaining the integrity of the process and the integrity of the individuals in that process."

Indiana Elects Democratic Governor and Equally Divided House

by Robert X. Browning

On the morning following the [1988] November election in Indiana, voters learned that they had elected the first Democratic governor in 24 years, a House of Representatives evenly divided with 50 Democrats and 50 Republicans, and a Senate with a 26 to 24 Republican majority presided over by a Democratic lieutenant governor. In the days that followed, it became even more apparent that 1989 would be a very interesting political year.

Secretary of State Evan Bayh defeated Lieutenant Governor John Mutz to become the nation's youngest governor. Bayh, son of former U.S. Senator Birch Bayh, had first won state office in 1986 when he defeated Robert Bowen, the son of another well-known Indiana politician, former governor Otis Bowen. Bayh's candidacy for governor was initially challenged by the Republican party which argued that he had not lived in the state long enough to meet state constitutional eligibility for governor. The State Supreme Court ruled in Bayh's favor prior to the May primary.

Bayh's campaign criticized the Republican party for being out of touch after 20 years in power and for increasing taxes. The state assistance to the Subaru-Isuzu plant in Lafayette was also made a campaign issue through Bayh campaign ads critical of the assistance to the Japanese firm. The successful Bayh campaign effectively appropriated the Republican position of being the party of smaller government and lower taxes.

The other big election story was the gain in House seats by the Democratic party. Through the early part of the 1980s the House Democrats were in courts arguing that Republican gerrymandering had prevented them from achieving a majority. The House Democrats held 37, 43, 39, 48, and 50 seats following the 1980, 82, 84, 86, and 88 elections respectively. In recent years, both parties have been targeting legislative races more selectively and helping candidates raise large sums in competitive and targeted districts.

Secretary of State Evan Bayh convened the evenly divided House on November 22 [, 1988]. Both parties had used the time following the election to try and woo a defector from the other party to form a majority. The day before organization day, the House Republicans obtained a restraining order preventing

Robert X. Browning is associate professor of political science and director of Public Affairs Video Archives at Purdue University in West Lafayette, Indiana. This article is reprinted from the *Comparative State Politics Newsletter* 10:2 (April 1989): 1-2.

Bayh from casting a deciding vote in the election of the speaker. Bayh announced from the podium that his role would be limited to that of a presiding officer and he would not get involved in the debate. He did, however, effectively influence the proceedings in two important ways. First, he would require the House Democratic and Republican leaders to publicly recount the progress of negotiations. Second, he indicated that he would keep the House in session throughout the Thanksgiving holiday in order to resolve the deadlock.

A number of options, including having an outside speaker, co-speakers, or a Democratic speaker with the other powers vested in Republicans were put on the table. Finally, in the early morning hours of Thanksgiving Day, a unique power sharing agreement was reached. Under the terms of this agreement, Indiana's House of Representatives will be an experiment in bipartisan cooperation which will be tested over and over in the strongly partisan environment of Indiana politics.

The power sharing compromise split all powers and positions evenly between the two parties. Two speakers were elected, each presiding on alternate days. Each committee would have co-chairs with equal numbers of Democrats and Republicans. There would be a Democratic and Republican clerk and equal staffs. A new office was built for the Democratic speaker and the office of the Ways and Means chairman was divided down the middle.

The most far-reaching reform was the removal of the speaker's power to hand down bills. Under the new agreement, every member would control his or her own bills. These and the other new rules were required to prevent the obvious stalemate of evenly divided party votes. For example, since the speaker assigns all bills to committees, if the two speakers disagree on the assignment of a particular bill, the Democratic speaker will assign Democratic bills and the Republican will assign Republican bills. Committee chairs must agree on which bills the committees will hear. In case of disagreements, each committee co-chair was given five wild cards to use. These wild cards permit a co-chair to schedule a bill for a hearing when the other co-chair objects. A divided committee vote on reporting a bill from committee means that the bill moves forward to the House calendar. Then the sponsor has the power to call it for second and third readings.

To Democrats, who have controlled the House and Senate only once in the last twenty years, the compromise gave them a chance to enact legislation. With a Democratic governor and a one vote difference in the Senate, they were optimistic about the session. Republicans found themselves in the unfamiliar role of having to share power and being critics of the administration. After a month, the strains of this compromise arrangement were beginning to show. This unique experiment will test whether the necessities of compromise can overcome longstanding partisan differences in a strong party state such as Indiana.

A Vanishing Breed

by Alan Rosenthal

In the 1960s Jesse Unruh of California spearheaded the establishment of the modern legislature and of strong leadership in the states. As speaker, Unruh professionalized the California Assembly and set the standard for state legislatures elsewhere. The few political scientists who were interested in the states considered California "number one in the nation," and a study funded by the Ford Foundation and conducted by the Citizens Conference on State Legislatures supported that opinion.

In large part, the Assembly's achievement depended upon Unruh's power, which he wielded with a heavy hand. There was no question in his mind or the minds of members of the Sacramento political community that "Big Daddy" was boss. Unruh accumulated power, provided members with various benefits, and exerted policy leadership in the state. A supporter of a unicameral legislature, Unruh used to explain: "I thought unicameral meant the man."

Jesse Unruh went on to serve as treasurer of California, and when he died in 1987 the California Legislature appeared to be in decline. Electoral politics and campaign finance, rather than policy, dominated the agenda. The initiative was being used more and more to bypass the process that Unruh had so loved. And the leadership of Speaker Willie Brown was under fire, from dissidents within his caucus and from an increasingly restive minority party. The golden age had passed.

Because of the transformation of the institution and the membership, legislative leadership throughout the nation had changed and is changing. The power of leadership is on the decline. Individual leaders are being challenged for holding office too long or behaving too dictatorially.

This is not to say that strong legislative leaders are extinct. Currently, a number of legislators are exercising muscle in their states. Speakers such as Mike Madigan of Illinois, Tom Murphy of Georgia, Gib Lewis of Texas, Vern Riffe of Ohio, and John Martin of Maine are among them. So are senate presidents like William Bulger of Massachusetts. Mel Miller, who succeeded Stanley Fink as speaker in the New York Assembly is also

Alan Rosenthal is director of the Eagleton Institute of Politics at Rutgers University in New Brunswick, New Jersey. This article is reprinted with permission from *State Legislatures* 15:10 (November/December 1989): 30-34. © 1989 by the National Conference of State Legislatures.

strong, but will his power match that of his predecessor? Or will Ralph Marino, who [recently] took over the post of majority leader in the New York Senate, wield power comparable to that of Warren Anderson who previously served in that position?

The chances are that the strong leaders of today will be followed by weaker ones tomorrow. Take the case of Ohio. If Vern Riffe runs for governor or leaves his position for whatever reason, candidates who hope to succeed him might have to agree to a reduction in the power of the speakership as a quid pro quo for support. And it may be true elsewhere as well as in Maine, where a colleague commented about John Martin, "There's nobody like him, and when he goes there will be nobody to take his place."

Because of the new climate and the newly independent member, today's leaders are less secure in their positions than their predecessors. Although a number have been serving in top positions for years, a leader's position is becoming perilous.

Some leaders leave of their own accord, often to run for another office. . . . Roger Moe, Minnesota's Senate majority leader, is considering running for governor [in 1990] even if it means taking on incumbent DFL Governor Rudy Perpich in the primary. Tom Loftus, Democratic speaker of the Assembly in Wisconsin, is preparing to run for governor against the Republican incumbent, Tommy Thompson. In his fourth term as speaker, Loftus regards 1990 as an "up or out" time for him. He may not actually feel the hot breath of his colleagues who have leadership ambitions, but Loftus has a knack for sensing when talented people are getting restless.

Restlessness is a greater problem today than before, because professional politicians want to move ahead in their careers. An assistant leader in Pennsylvania characterized the new breed: "They have a lust for power,

even during their first term." But movement has slowed down, due to the many contestants and the few opportunities for higher office. With few voluntarily leaving and the reelection rates of incumbents running over 97 percent in the U.S. House and 80 percent to 90 percent in many state senates, the prospects for a member of a state house advancing are not very promising.

Some leaders, such as New York's Stanley Fink and Warren Anderson, step down and return to private life, unable or uninterested in making a run for another position. Fink, the Assembly speaker, aspired to the governorship but his path was blocked. Anderson, the Senate majority leader, left when the Republican caucus had become particularly demanding and divisive.

Other leaders leave, not by choice, but by decision of the voters. J. Roberts Dailey, a three-term speaker of the Indiana House, lost in 1986, after being targeted by special interest groups opposed to his position on a state lottery. A notable upset occurred a few years later in Florida. Sam Bell, an extremely powerful appropriations committee chairman, who was slated to become speaker for the 1991-1992 session, lost because his district came to see him more as a statewide legislator than as a Volusia County representative.

A leader may be re-elected to the house or senate, but his party may lose control. Changes in party control account for 12 switches in leadership in 1984, nine in 1986, and five in 1988 (including the Indiana House, which was tied). In view of the development of the Republican Party in states such as Florida and North Carolina and party competition growing in a number of places, the likelihood is that changes in party control will take an even higher leadership toll in the future.

Despite the incidence of voluntary retirement, election defeat and switches in party control, legislative leaders on average may have had longer runs lately than their predecessors did in the 1950s and 1960s. That is mainly because some, but by no means all, of the traditions for the rotation of leadership out of office after one term have been broken.

For example, it was traditional for Maine's speakers to serve only one term. David Kennedy broke tradition with three terms and John Martin, his successor, is now in his eighth term. Until 1970 leadership rotation in New Jersey was annual; then with a constitutional amendment providing for a two-year legislature, it became biennial. Now, the custom is to limit speakers and presidents to two sessions. Most recently, the Utah Senate abandoned the tradition and the Utah House may soon follow suit.

Currently, Arkansas, Florida, Nebraska, North Dakota and Wyoming still rotate presiding officers each biennium. Some states rotate leadership after two terms. Indeed, in two-thirds of the states over the past 40 years rarely has a leader served more than two sessions. And the prospect is that the tenure of future leaders in states like California, Georgia, Maine, New York, Ohio and Virginia will diminish somewhat.

During [the 1980s], a number of leaders have been challenged and some have been ousted by their own caucuses or by the membership at large. One or several factors motivated the opposition—the leader's alleged arrogance, abuse of power or neglect of members' needs, or their impatience with his stay in office. In 1980, Leo McCarthy, speaker of the California Assembly, was challenged (and only with the aid of Republican support did he hang on until the end of his term) because he held a major fund raiser for a possible statewide campaign for governor instead of for the campaigns of Assembly Democrats. McCarthy's successor, Willie Brown, learned his fund-raising lessons well, but still has seldom been free from attack. . . . [In 1989]

a number of legislative leaders faced serious opposition, both from within their caucuses and from the minority party. In Florida, Democrat Carl Carpenter made a run at the speaker-designate, Tom Gustafson, by forming a coalition with the minority Republicans. The attempt failed.

Irv Stolberg, who had first served as speaker of the Connecticut House in 1983-1984, then as minority leader, and again as speaker, expected—and was expected—to be re-elected in 1989. The practice until 1971 had been one term and then it became two terms, so Stolberg's effort to win a third term was unprecedented. Owing to several factors, including Stolberg's aggressive personality, his liberal ideology and the two-term tradition, a group of Democrats joined with the Republicans in a bipartisan coalition to defeat Stolberg and replace him with Democrat Richard Balducci. The new speaker publicly pledged to serve no more than two terms.

Until recently House speakers in North Carolina had served only a single two-year term. Liston Ramsey, however, had held the speaker's office since 1981, longer than anyone in the state's history. Democrats resented Ramsey's leadership style, the concentration of power in the speaker's hands and the long tenure of Ramsey and his lieutenants who were blocking their own advancement. Furthermore, legislative Democrats were unhappy with the 1988 election results and the Republican gains from 36 to 46 members in the House. With losses at the polls, party members feel particularly threatened and leadership is more vulnerable. In any event, Democrats joined with the Republican minority, electing Josephus Mavretic speaker and replacing Ramsey. An agreement was made that the speaker henceforth would be limited to two terms; and there is the possibility that the office will return to a one-term rotation.

The last ouster of 1989 occurred in Oklahoma. Here Speaker Jim Barker was dumped one week before the legislative session ended. Dissident Democrats had a majority of votes in caucus, but they needed Republican votes—all of which they got—in order to win on the floor. The Oklahoma uprising appears to have been prompted by a combination of committee chairmen and junior members, none of whom wanted the speaker telling them what to do.

In each of these cases, minority party support was essential in order to overthrow leadership. Bipartisan coalitions are by no means unprecedented. They had been a constant feature of New Mexico politics, with its "cowboy coalition" and loyalist Democrats. They occurred in the California Assembly, the New York Assembly, the Oregon Senate, and the Vermont House, and repeatedly in the Florida Senate of the 1980s.

As state legislatures become competitive, the minority grows more frustrated in its role and more partisan as a result. In North Carolina, Republican Governor James Martin served as middleman in the deal that brought Republican legislators into a coalition with Democrats and won them greater power. In Connecticut, minority Republicans joined a coalition even though they gained no chairmanships nor rules changes. But the House minority leader saw the possibility of a little political mischief and some partisan advantage as a consequence of the Democratic rebellion. It would take a while for the breach between Stolberg's liberal Democrats and Balducci's more conservative Democrats to heal, and in the meantime the Republicans would be in a pivotal position.

Limiting the Powers of Leadership

Not only are legislators seeking to moderate the styles and control the tenure of individual leaders, but they are also trying to limit the powers of leadership to manage legislative personnel and the legislative process.

The managerial powers of leadership in most state legislatures exceed that of congressional leadership, particularly in the U.S. Senate but also in the U.S. House. Still, there is substantial variation from state to state and from house to senate. Generally, power is more centralized in houses and more dispersed in senates, because the latter are smaller, more collegial and consisting of more experienced and individualistic members.

One managerial power is that of appointing assistant leaders. In most states, the speaker and the president or president pro tem lack the authority to name the majority leader, whip or other assistants. Except in the case of 13 houses and eight senates where leadership does have such authority, the caucus or the membership at large makes these appointments. Another power is that of appointing the chairmen of standing committees. Even this power is restricted in one-third of the chambers, where chairmen are either elected by the entire chamber, chosen by the caucus, selected by a committee on committees or a rules committee, ascend by virtue of seniority or where leadership nominations must be ratified by a party caucus, a committee on committees or the entire membership.

Still another power is naming conference committee members. Here, too, leaders are limited in one-quarter of the chambers. In Wisconsin, for example, the president's appointments must be confirmed by a majority vote of the Senate. In the senates of Illinois, Minnesota and Virginia a committee on committees names conferees.

Control of the calendar is another significant power of leadership, but it too is limited in most places. Bills in many chambers are taken up automatically in the order in which they are reported by standing committees. In other chambers a rules or calendaring committee, which usually—but not always—reflects the preferences of leadership, decides on the calendar. Only in a minority of chambers does the speaker or president pro tem have absolute authority with respect to calendaring.

There is nothing new about relatively weak leadership. It has long been the norm in a number of states. In Nebraska, for instance, the speakership is rotated biennially and committee chairmen are elected by the membership. Elsewhere, too, weaker leadership seems to be the trend. . . . Recent assaults on individual leaders have also been directed at the power of their office. In Mississippi, it was not only Buddy Newman's style but also his power as speaker that disturbed many of his colleagues in the House. With Newman's overthrow, the rules were changed. Now members of the Rules Committee and the Management Committee are elected by House members, and not selected by the speaker, and seniority determines appointments to the Appropriations and Ways and Means Committees. A new position of speaker pro tem, elected by the entire membership, has been created to chair the Management Committee. The pro tem has come to be a countervailing power to the speaker. In the Rhode Island Senate, although a minority of Democrats failed to stop the election of Majority Leader David Carlin, they joined with the Republicans and stripped the position of much of its power, including that of appointing committee chairmen. Moreover, the minority leader won the right to order a bill out of committee for floor consideration.

The Growing Strength of the Minority Party

If the managerial power of leadership is under challenge, the growing strength of the minority party in a number of states is one of the reasons why. The minority is seeking to limit the power of the majority. It can do that by winning rules changes that allow the minority leader to appoint minority party mem-

bers to committees, provide proportional representation for the minority on committees and ensure that minority members' bills will be taken up on the floor.

In their coalition with Democrats, North Carolina's Republicans cut down on the speaker's authority, among other things, by gaining 20 of 50 subcommittee chairmanships. Florida's Dale Patchet tried to get Speaker-designate Tom Gustafson to agree to a rules change permitting the minority leader to appoint minority members to committees. Although Gustafson agreed to follow the practice, he would not limit the speaker's formal authority nor bind future speakers by changing the rules. Thereupon, Patchet and most of his Republicans joined in a coalition with a few Democrats who were willing to meet his conditions.

Minority Republicans in the California Assembly, sometimes in combination with Democratic dissidents in the "Gang of Five," have been taking aim at the speakership for years and pushing several measures that would weaken the office. According to the new minority leader, Ross Johnson, "The notion of a powerful speaker or a powerful legislative leader is an idea whose time has come and gone." Recently, Philip Rock, the Democratic president of the Illinois Senate, has also had his problems with the minority party and a few members of his own so-called "raucous caucus" of black and white liberals and white ethnic conservatives from Chicago and moderates and conservatives from downstate. The minority Republicans, who sought to increase their representation on major committees, preserved and managed to achieve a compromise that produced some gains for them. During the 1989 session of the Kansas House, Republican members of the majority and Democratic members of the minority managed to change several important rules, potentially reducing the power of the speakership.

In California and Colorado, where the initiative is in great vogue, it has been used to attack the power of leadership. The most notable effort was Proposition 24 in California, which was sponsored by Paul Gann and supported by conservative Assembly Republicans. It would have restricted the influence of the offices of speaker and president pro tempore by providing that the allocation of legislative resources to the parties be proportionate and requiring a two-thirds vote for important administrative decisions to be made. Proposition 24 passed, but was invalidated by the state supreme court. In Colorado a 1988 initiative, GAVEL or Give a Vote to Every Legislator, passed with 72 percent of the vote of the electorate. It amended the constitution to provide that every bill would have to be heard in committee, bills would appear on the House and Senate calendars in the order in which they were reported out of committee and members could not commit themselves to vote a certain way in a party caucus. This restricted the power of leaders to schedule business and organize their party's membership for proceedings on the floor.

The Next Generation of Leaders

If there is indeed a trend toward the diminution of leadership tenure and leadership power, will the next generation of leaders be able to lead? That is the question. In the years ahead, the need for legislative leadership will be greater than ever. Without effective leadership, not only by the governor but from within the legislature as well, the most difficult issues and the new responsibilities facing the state will be left unattended or unsettled.

Legislative leadership has a role that no one else in the legislature can perform. It is up to leadership to take a stateside perspective, deal with the other chamber and with the governor, represent the legislature to the press, serve and protect its members and help maintain the legislature as an institution. Whether or not leadership can be effective in light of its uncertain tenure and power is problematic. With less authority to manage legislative personnel and the legislative process and without the clout to exercise sanctions when necessary, leaders will have to rely more heavily on their abilities to sweet-talk and persuade. They will have to develop new resources and techniques and manage even more by consensus than they have in the past.

The next generation of legislative leaders will not possess the power of earlier generations. Thus, in order to succeed they will have to be even more talented and skillful than many of their predecessors. One thing is sure, however; their job will be tougher.

How a Party of Enthusiasts Keeps Its Hammerlock on a State Legislature

by Alan Ehrenhalt

"Gloriam spreti honoris auctam." "I shall enhance my reputation by refusing office."

So said Cincinnatus, the Roman general and hero. He was a born politician, but he hated politics. In 458 B.C., with Rome under a ferocious Aequian assault, Senate leaders were convinced the Republic was doomed unless Cincinnatus came out of retirement.

As the historian Livy tells it, they found him on his farm, plowing, and pleaded with him to return to public life. He wiped the sweat off his face, asked his wife to bring him a toga and accepted a six-month term as absolute dictator of Rome.

It took him two weeks to vanquish the enemy, crack down on corrupt public officials and bring in a reformist government. Having done those things, Cincinnatus resigned as dictator, five and a half months ahead of schedule, and resumed full-time farming. Politics, as he saw it, was a necessary evil. He had no intention of making it a career.

It was safe to say Cincinnatus would not understand the Wisconsin legislature.

He would not understand, for example, David Clarenbach, speaker pro tempore of the state Assembly. At 35, Clarenbach is now in his 18th consecutive year as an elected official. He has never held any other full-time job, either in public or in private life. He loves politics, and he is not embarrassed about admitting it. When people call him a professional politician, he dares them to run against him on that issue. No one has come close to beating him.

Clarenbach is a key member of the Democratic majority that has run the Wisconsin Assembly for nearly two decades without interruption. Republicans last elected a speaker in 1969. It is not hard to see why those things have happened. In this state, the GOP has come to be the party of Cincinnatus—the party of those who, in the final analysis, would rather be doing something else for a living. The Democrats are the party of those who believe that there isn't anything they'd rather devote their lives to.

To find the governmental consequences of two decades of Democratic legislative power, one need only look around. In the early and mid-1970s, working with Democratic Governor Patrick J. Lucey, the Wisconsin legislature expanded and centralized the state univer-

---

Alan Ehrenhalt is political editor of *Governing* magazine. He is writing a book on political change in America, from which this article was excerpted in *Governing* 2:9 (June 1989): 28-33.

sity system, rewrote tax laws to benefit poorer communities and moved out ahead of virtually the entire country in passing environmental and consumer protection laws. In the 1980s, with funds for expanded government impossible to come by, the legislature has focused on a social agenda. It has passed the nation's strongest gay-rights and sexual-privacy laws, rewritten a 150-year-old statute to guarantee marital property rights to spouses and enacted comparable-worth provisions aimed at benefiting female state employees.

It might be said that those sorts of laws are only what one would expect in Wisconsin, the nation's most frequently cited "reform" state and the one where Robert M. LaFollette first turned the progressive agenda into law more than 70 years ago.

But the reality is more interesting than that. The progressive impulse has actually been fitful in Wisconsin, operating in short bursts of enthusiasm that followed long periods of conservative Republican control. Except for the decade before World War I under LaFollette and a much shorter period in the 1930s under his son, Philip, Wisconsin has generally shied away from the politics of innovation.

The roots of modern-day liberal government in Wisconsin lie not so much in the history of the state but in the careers and values of the people who have assumed control. Their stories are not unique to the state. They will ring familiar to anyone who has been watching legislatures in numerous other places where Democrats have established what seems to be a permanent majority.

Every other year, Democrats and Republicans battle for legislative control in Wisconsin in what is advertised as a debate about which party best reflects the views of the electorate. Within the corridors of the state capitol, however, the biennial legislative elections are recognized for what they really are: a

competition to attract candidates who have the skills and energy to win and the desire and resourcefulness to stay in office.

This is the competition that Democrats keep winning. Republicans know it perfectly well. "For me to recruit a Republican to run for the state Senate is very difficult," says Michael Ellis, leader of the GOP minority. "Democrats can go out and find a whole slew of people making less than $30,000 a year [the salary for legislators is $31,236] who want to go out and change the world.

"You come in here at 8 o'clock on a Monday morning, and all the Democratic parking spaces are filled. This is their career, this is what they do with their lives. It's it. Republicans will show up at 9 o'clock on Tuesday when the session starts at 10. They leave at 4 on Thursday. They come and vote on the bills, and then they leave. The Democrats come back in on Friday to work out what they are going to do the next Tuesday and Thursday."

In an era when the legislature meets most of the year, pay is comparatively low, and campaigns are grueling, an enormous advantage goes to the party of enthusiasts. In Wisconsin, those enthusiasts are the student activists of the late 1960s, now nearing middle age and remarkably protective of institutions they once questioned.

David Travis, now 40, is one of them. Over a decade in the state Assembly, he has performed a multitude of institutional tasks: chaired the Reapportionment Committee, served on the Joint Committee on Finance and chaired the state Sentencing Commission, which exists in part because of legislation he wrote.

But David Travis did not enter politics to do any of those things. He entered politics for one reason: Vietnam. He escaped the draft by the space of four numbers in the lottery and became a full-time antiwar campaigner. When one of his candidates got elected to the state Senate, he went along as a staff aide. Later, he ran the Senate Democratic caucus. In 1978, an Assembly seat opened up right in Madison, where he lived. Travis got it and has held it ever since. He sees himself explicitly as part of a group.

"A lot of people," he says, "arrived in government here out of opposition to Vietnam. That was intertwined with civil rights, the Peace Corps, the environment. We were out to change the world."

Joe Strohl's story is a little different, but only a little. Two years older than Travis, he was just out of college in 1970, teaching eighth grade in Racine, organizing peace demonstrations and studying campaign strategy in sessions put together by the antiwar New Democratic Coalition. He met up with Les Aspin, who was running for Congress on an antiwar platform. When Aspin won, Strohl took a job running his Racine office. In 1978, Strohl was elected to the Wisconsin Senate. Now he is majority leader.

Much of the politics that engaged Strohl in the 1960s is still part of him, and has become part of Wisconsin law. He first campaigned for the state Senate as a critic of the state's utilities, and took office opposing nuclear power. He is responsible for a good part of the tough approach toward the nuclear industry taken by state statutes.

David Clarenbach is younger than Travis or Strohl, but his career reflects all the political currents that produced them, and more besides.

He grew up in a family that amounted to a workshop in political activism. His father was an antiwar delegate to the 1968 Democratic National Convention; his mother chaired the National Organization for Women. When he was 16, Clarenbach was campaigning to register black voters in Mississippi. He returned to Madison to crusade for

the rights of high school students and fought successfully to get them represented on the local school board.

His timing was perfect. Eighteen-year-olds were allowed to vote for the first time in 1972, and Clarenbach was already developing a citywide reputation in Madison as a student rights agitator. Suddenly there was a built-in constituency for a bold political move. So Clarenbach went after a position on the Dane County Board, a 41-member body that was, at the time, more conservative than liberal. He announced his candidacy in a district where 30 percent of the voters were students, 30 percent old people. He went after both. And at 18, he became a county supervisor.

At that point, he began to realize just what a marketable political commodity he was. In 1974, a vacancy came up on the Madison city council, and he ran for that and won it. But he wanted to be in the legislature and, at 20, he knew more about how to get there than almost anyone in Madison. A seat there came open later the same year, and he was an easy winner.

David Clarenbach showed up in the state Assembly in January of 1975 with shoulder-length blond hair and an agenda that featured legalization of marijuana and unconditional amnesty for draft evaders. "He came in as a liberal flake, and an immature one," says the dean of Assembly Republicans, Joseph Tregoning. Clarenbach doesn't really disagree with that. "In a much larger bowl than the city council," he admits, "I was an equally isolated fish."

That was almost 15 years ago. Today, Clarenbach's hair is short, he wears conservative suits, and he is speaker pro tempore of the Assembly. He is a parliamentarian. He presides over the Assembly more often than anyone else, and his ability to move a bill or handle a debate is unsurpassed. "If you want to roll through bills," says one colleague,

Democrat Stan Gruszynski, "Clarenbach can do it faster than anybody. He speaks so fast you can't keep up with him. It's a pride he has taken in knowing the process, knowing the rules, establishing decorum."

Clarenbach has not changed very much ideologically. He ran in 1974 as a gay-rights advocate, for example, and in 1982 he became the author of Wisconsin's landmark gay-rights law. In fact, he did not have to change his mind on any important issue to be a leader. He simply reached out for influence as the arrival of more and more Democratic activists swung the legislature closer to his point of view.

David Clarenbach's career helps to explain why the Wisconsin legislature governs as it does. But it provides little insight into why Democrats control it year after year. To understand Democratic control, it is necessary to look at a Democrat from a different sort of district: someone like John Medinger.

Medinger represents small-town and rural portions of La Crosse County. It is a Republican county and in past years has cast its presidential vote for Gerald Ford, Ronald Reagan and George Bush. But since 1976, it has elected a Democrat, John Donald Medinger, to the Wisconsin Assembly.

The Democratic legislative majorities of the past 20 years have been built in districts like this one, districts in the sparsely populated "outstate" counties north and west of the city of Madison. Wisconsin has a solid core of Democratic votes in Madison, Milwaukee and a few southeastern industrial cities, but not enough to give the Democrats control of the Assembly or Senate. To win control, they must take a respectable number of the seats outstate, where they are rarely successful in gubernatorial campaigns and almost never in the presidential vote.

Medinger's district is that sort of place. It has been a piece of the Democratic Assembly majority since he first won it. How has he held it? By spending most of his waking hours at constituent service and making sure the voters are thinking about service rather than issues. And, because he works so hard, he fends off any high-quality Republican opposition.

Nothing but elbow grease could possibly explain how Medinger won in the first place. "The year I got elected," he says, "I was 28, living in an apartment, no family, no kids, no property, long hair, hippie glasses. I was making $7,500 pumping gas and driving a school bus. My opponent was county treasurer."

Medinger outcampaigned him and won. He took office as a highly unconventional representative for La Crosse County. Today he is 41, balding and pudgy, no hippie by any means. But he is still an unconventional politician. Some of his conservative neighbors were surprised when he and his wife adopted two black children. He has voted for gay rights and, with the exception of gun control, almost all the items on the liberal Democratic agenda in Madison. In 1988, he got a rating of 100 from the Wisconsin AFL-CIO.

But all the political risks of Medinger's career in Madison have been overcome by the friendships it is possible to accumulate in a full-time legislative career. He drives the 137 miles to Madison and the 137 miles back three times a week, even when the legislature is not meeting. When he is in La Crosse, he is in perpetual motion. "If I don't have anything to do at home," he says, "I go sit in a coffee shop and shoot the breeze. I might be home two nights a week to tuck my kids in. I go to every pancake breakfast and every rummage sale. I am always looking for something to do. If there's nothing else, I go to a basketball game and mingle with the crowd." The year he got a 100 rating from the AFL-CIO, Medinger was rated at 29 by the Wisconsin Association of Manufacturers. But the La Crosse chamber of commerce endorsed him for re-election anyway.

"There are some Republicans in my district who could run against me," Medinger says, "and make my life miserable . . . . But the Republicans can't come up with candidates who will put in 100-hour weeks. So they don't make it."

What is it about being a legislator that has driven John Medinger and his Democratic cohorts to work so hard for so many years for so little money? Part of it is simple fun. But even for the most enthusiastic politician, some aspects of the work cease to be fun after a few years. Floor debate and strategy sessions maintain their allure, but fund raising and door-to-door campaigning generally do not. As they become senior legislators, nearly all the Wisconsin Democrats see the job as a trade-off between tasks they love and tasks they simply endure.

After ten years in the Assembly and six campaigns, David Travis clearly feels that way. "This is a very rough business," he says. "It's not fun to knock on doors when it's 100 degrees. I did that last summer. In campaigns, I get dry heaves in the morning. I get back spasms. It's a very high-stress occupation."

But he has been putting up with the stress for more than a decade. To a great extent, that is because he is a liberal Democrat, a believer in government. He may doubt himself, he may doubt the Wisconsin legislature, but he never doubts that government itself is an institution worthy of his participation. "To me," says Travis, "the seminal issues since World War II have been racial segregation, health care and Vietnam. Vietnam ended. Segregation has been attacked. Health care is now available to all older people in this country. It shows me that over 20 years in this country, the government did something right."

John Medinger feels the same way. "I came here to change the world," he admits, repeating a phrase that seems to turn up in conversation with nearly all the Democrats of his generation. "I think we've won more than we've lost."

For a liberal Democrat in Wisconsin in the 1970s, government was fun. It turned dozens of young academics and staff aides into active political candidates willing to invest their efforts in moving from the sidelines to the more exhilarating experience of holding office.

"You fought big fights, and you won," remembers Tom Loftus, then a legislative aide and now the House speaker. "It was heady stuff. The sky was the limit."

In the past few years, the sky has not been the limit. Fiscal realities have scaled back ambitious legislative agendas. But the generation of Democrats that came to power in the 1980s has stood guard successfully against any Republican efforts to repeal legislation that took effect in the Lucey years. "The Lucey years made a major policy shift," says John Bibby, a political scientist at the University of Wisconsin-Milwaukee, "and because these folks are here, we haven't turned back."

Nor has the legislature turned back from its increased dependence on full-time professionals as legislative leaders. Legislative activism may have slowed down in the 1980s, but the legislative activists are more numerous than ever. The legislature will never again be the province of the part-time farmers, merchants, lawyers and insurance salesmen who dominated it for so many years before 1970. And conservative Republicans who regret the change are reduced to little more than sniping at what they see as its ill effects.

Wisconsin's Republican Party has spent much of the 1980s trying to understand how it became a more-or-less permanent legislative minority and trying to see if there is any way at all to turn the situation around.

The GOP leaders who worry about that problem have found themselves in a difficult position. They don't like the idea of a legislature dominated by professional politicians, but they have finally begun to realize they are never going to be able to unseat a party of pros with a party of amateurs.

Ellis, the Senate Republican leader, reflects that ambivalence. In one breath he denounces the Democratic majority as a bunch of fuzzy-headed liberals. The next moment he is wishing he had people of similar political dedication on his side.

"If you come out of a textbook and right into this building," he complains, "you have a pure philosophy but no broad-based experience. Your view is a rehash of other people's thoughts that you have read or listened to but not experienced. It's almost a sophomoric view of the world. It's pristine, and it's unrealistic." Ellis would love a state Senate dominated by the farmers and small-business men who ran it when he first arrived at the end of the 1960s. He thinks it would make more sensible laws. It might be a Republican Senate. But he knows it is not going to happen.

The GOP was very slow to accept that in Wisconsin, as it has been in other states, and its slowness cost it dearly. Democrats have benefited not only from the natural political skills of their candidates but also from the willingness of party leaders to recruit budding politicians and nurture their careers. And the vehicle for that nurturing process has been the legislative staff.

Much has been written about how the modern expansion in staffing has changed the American legislative process, making legislatures both more competent and more prolific. Those effects have been felt in most states. But in Wisconsin, something else has happened as well: The staff has become a farm system for aspiring Democratic politicians. In the Assembly, the current speaker, speaker pro tempore and Democratic caucus chair all were legislative aides at one time or another.

The Senate majority leader, Joe Strohl, describes the system this way: "People get out of college, go to work in the capitol, back home to run for office, and then back to the capitol as legislators. They are good candidates because they have connections with the establishment up here, and they have access to finances." By the time they run, these people tend to be creatures of Madison as much as they are creatures of their home districts.

A few staff aides become candidates not out of personal ambition but out of loyalty to a leadership that [sees them] as candidate material. "If we can't find somebody to run for a seat," says Loftus, "we'll send an aide up there to do it. We shanghai them."

There is no reason why two parties can't play that game. Republicans do not get as many legislative aide positions as Democrats do, but they have more than enough to use as a political talent pool. The strategy is worth a try, and in the past few elections the Republican Party has begun trying it.

"We're finally waking up," says Brian Rude, a former GOP aide who became assistant minority leader in the Senate at the age of 33.

If Republicans are ever going to dig themselves out of minority status in Wisconsin and in other states where they have similar problems, such as Iowa, Minnesota and California, they are going to have to come up with more Brian Rudes. But in trying to do that, they are challenging some of their own strongest biases—ones that have been powerfully reinforced in recent years by their own most successful leader, Ronald Reagan.

It was during his career in state politics, as governor of California in the 1960s, that Reagan began articulating his distaste for government in ways that all but counseled his youthful admirers to avoid it. Reagan reminded his aides in Sacramento that "when we begin thinking of the government as 'we' instead of 'they,' we've been here too long."

Those are sentiments Cincinnatus would have appreciated. But they don't win many elections these days in places like Wisconsin, where another political party is happy to be thinking of the government as "us."

David Helbach, a veteran state senator and deputy leader on the Democratic side, is one of those "government is us" types Reagan and Cincinnatus wouldn't care for. Like so many of his Democratic colleagues, he went into politics to stop the Vietnam War, took a job as a legislative aide, went home to run for office and has been a full-time legislator ever since.

As far as Helbach is concerned, the politics of the Wisconsin legislature is rather simple. "The Republicans hate government," he says. "Why be here if you hate government? So they let us run it for them."

How a Bill Becomes State Law

This graphic shows the most typical way in which proposed legislation is enacted into law in the states. Bills must be passed by both houses of the state legislature in identical form before they can be sent to the governor to be signed or vetoed. Of course, the legislative process differs slightly from state to state.

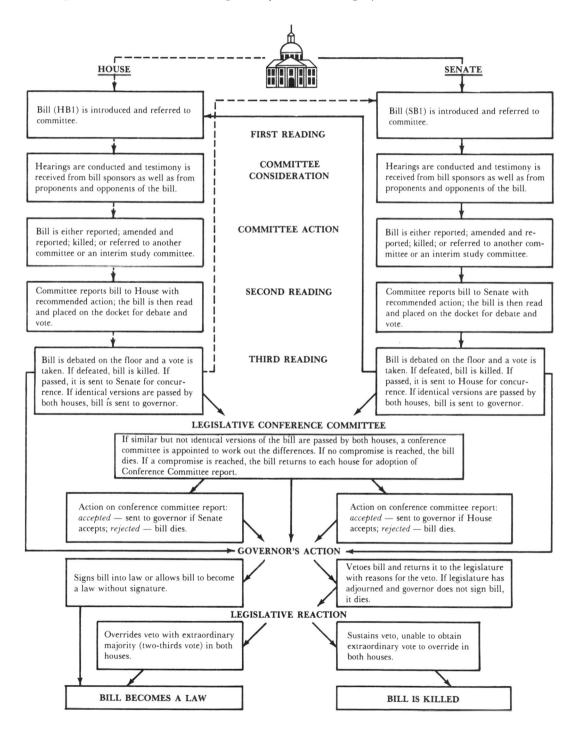

HOUSE **SENATE**

Bill (HB1) is introduced and referred to committee.

FIRST READING

Bill (SB1) is introduced and referred to committee.

Hearings are conducted and testimony is received from bill sponsors as well as from proponents and opponents of the bill.

COMMITTEE CONSIDERATION

Hearings are conducted and testimony is received from bill sponsors as well as from proponents and opponents of the bill.

Bill is either reported; amended and reported; killed; or referred to another committee or an interim study committee.

COMMITTEE ACTION

Bill is either reported; amended and re-ported; killed; or referred to another com-mittee or an interim study committee.

Committee reports bill to House with recommended action; the bill is then read and placed on the docket for debate and vote.

SECOND READING

Committee reports bill to Senate with recommended action; the bill is then read and placed on the docket for debate and vote.

Bill is debated on the floor and a vote is taken. If defeated, bill is killed. If passed, it is sent to Senate for concur-rence. If identical versions are passed by both houses, bill is sent to governor.

THIRD READING

Bill is debated on the floor and a vote is taken. If defeated, bill is killed. If passed, it is sent to House for concur-rence. If identical versions are passed by both houses, bill is sent to governor.

LEGISLATIVE CONFERENCE COMMITTEE

If similar but not identical versions of the bill are passed by both houses, a conference committee is appointed to work out the differences. If no compromise is reached, the bill dies. If a compromise is reached, the bill returns to each house for adoption of Conference Committee report.

Action on conference committee report: *accepted* — sent to governor if Senate accepts; *rejected* — bill dies.

Action on conference committee report: *accepted* — sent to governor if House accepts; *rejected* — bill dies.

GOVERNOR'S ACTION

Signs bill into law or allows bill to become a law without signature.

Vetoes bill and returns it to the legislature with reasons for the veto. If legislature has adjourned and governor does not sign bill, it dies.

LEGISLATIVE REACTION

Overrides veto with extraordinary majority (two-thirds vote) in both houses.

Sustains veto, unable to obtain extraordinary vote to override in both houses.

BILL BECOMES A LAW

BILL IS KILLED

VI. GOVERNORS AND THE EXECUTIVE BRANCH

As the head of state politics and government and the elected representative of the people, governors must perform a wide variety of duties. They greet visitors, travel to other states and even other countries to lure new businesses to their states, rush to the scene of disasters to demonstrate concern, prepare annual and biennial agendas for government activity, and, on occasion, discuss important issues with the president. From state to state the record varies on how well these and other gubernatorial responsibilities are fulfilled. Some governors are reelected to another term, others are excluded from service, and still others are elected to higher office.

Since its weak beginnings after the overthrow of colonial rule, the American governorship has grown in power and influence. The extensive reforms of the past two decades are becoming evident throughout the executive branches of the fifty states. As Larry Sabato reports, "Within the last 20 years, there has been a virtual explosion of reform in state government. In most of the states, as a result, the governor is now truly the master of his own house, not just the father figure." [1] Many of the powers that were restricted have been expanded, and governors now have new powers at their command, such as the ability to reach the people directly through the media and to serve as the key state official in the intergovernmental system of grants and programs.

Moreover, the caliber of the individuals who serve as governors has changed in recent years. Most states have been able to say "goodbye to good-time Charlie" and hello to "a thoroughly trained, well regarded, and capable new breed of state chief executive." [2] This does not mean that all governors have spotless records. There have been several cases of governors and former governors who have run afoul of the law and spent time in prison. [3] One governor, Evan Mecham (R-Ariz., 1987-88), was impeached, convicted (but did not serve time in prison), and removed from office. Now, Mecham is back and running for the 1990 Republican nomination for governor because the Arizona legislature at the time of Mecham's impeachment failed by a slim margin to adopt the so-called "Dracula clause"— an act by a state legislature that drains the lifeblood out of a politician by forbidding his return to electoral politics.

Governors Edwin Edwards (D-La., 1972-80, 1984-88) and Bill Sheffield (D-Alaska, 1983-87) had well-publicized escapes from legal and ethical problems in the mid-1980s, but were turned out of office when the voters did what the authorities could not do. More recently, former governor Arch Moore (R-W.Va., 1969-77, 1985-89) agreed to plead guilty to charges of extortion, mail fraud, tax fraud, and obstruction of justice that he committed during his last two races for governor and during his last term in office. [4]

These governors' activities, other gubernatorial missteps, and what he decried as one of the weakest group of newly elected governors in 1986 led one careful "governor-watcher" to wonder if the trend toward having better governors may be ebbing in the states. [5]

Governors and the State Ambition Ladder

An interesting aspect of the governorship is its place on the "ambition ladder" that eager politicians climb to attain higher and higher levels of success. Of the 196 governors who served between 1970 and 1990, 53 percent previously had served at some time as an elected state legislator, 28 percent as an elected state official, 27 percent as a law enforcement official, and 14 percent as an elected local official. Only 13 percent had served as a U.S. representative, and one in the U.S. Senate.

If the penultimate or last office held before winning the governor's chair is considered, fifty individuals (26 percent) moved up from a statewide elective office (usually attorney general, lieutenant governor, or even former governor). Forty-two (21 percent) moved from a legislative seat (usually a leadership position in the legislature). Ten jumped from a local elective position to the governorship (5 percent). Only twenty-four governors (12 percent) stepped directly into office from the U.S. House of Representatives, and only twelve (6 percent) never held any previous position in government.[6]

In the last full round of gubernatorial elections (1986-89), there were fifty-three contests.[7] Of the twenty-seven incumbents who sought reelection, twenty-two (81 percent) won, and three of nine former governors seeking a comeback won. Thus, governors and former governors won twenty-five of the fifty-three races. However, five governors and six former governors lost their bids, giving all governors a 69 percent success rate (twenty-five of thirty-six). Other winners who previously had held statewide office were lieutenant governors, treasurers, and auditors (two each), and a member of the executive council. With thirty-two of the fifty-three races (60 percent) being won by these current or former statewide officials, the importance of a major statewide office for winning a gubernatorial election is clear. Other successful launching positions for six of the twenty-eight new governors (21 percent) were legislative leadership positions; six switched from their congressional seat to a governor's chair (21 percent). Interestingly, for the first time in many years, four mayors of large cities became governor (14 percent of the new governors).

What do these figures tell us about making a successful climb to the governor's office?

Those who succeeded in becoming governor tended to use a "state-based" career ladder: the legislature and other state elective positions. Moving up from a local position, usually as mayor of a large city, has not been built into this ladder, although recent results suggest this might be changing in some state political systems. While moving from a federal position—representative, senator, or cabinet member—has not been part of this ladder in the past, a launching pad from the U.S. House of Representatives to the governorship appears to be developing, as evidenced in the most recent elections in New Hampshire, New Jersey, and North and South Carolina.[8] Even members and former members of the U.S. Senate are looking at this track. In 1986, former governor and U.S. senator Henry Bellmon won the Oklahoma governorship; in 1990, former U.S. senator Lawton Chiles (D-Fla.) and incumbent U.S. senator Pete Wilson (R-Calif.) are seeking to become their state's chief executive. Still, capturing the governorship from a position outside state politics appears to be difficult.

But what is the next step after the governorship? Is it a higher elective office? Two of our most recent presidents were governors—Jimmy Carter (D-Ga., 1971-75) and Ronald Reagan (R-Calif., 1967-75)—and sixteen former governors are serving as U.S. senators and one as a representative in the 101st Congress.[9] Also, the 1988 Democratic candidate for president, Michael S. Dukakis (D-Mass., 1975-79, 1983-91), was a governor. But this is the exception rather than the rule. Most governors do not attain higher elective office. Of the governors who served between 1970 and 1981, 62.5 percent had not been elected to another position by 1982.[10] Looking at just those governors who have graduated from the governorship in the 1980s, only ten of sixty-nine have run for and won another office: six have won a U.S. Senate seat, one a House seat, and three have reclaimed the governor's chair. Nine others tried to extend their political careers, but six lost in attempting to move to the U.S. Senate and three in trying to become governor again.

Most former governors enter the private sector, usually to develop a lucrative law practice. These governors must give up what former governor Lamar Alexander (R-Tenn., 1979-87) called "the very best job in the U.S.A." [11] Ronald Reagan indicated that "being governor was the best training school for this job [of being president]." [12] Is there life after being governor? The National Governors' Association (NGA) asked some former governors what had happened to them since leaving office. Yes, there was life, but the quality of that new life can be determined only by the individual. By planning early for the transition, NGA suggests, the governors "can also help ease their own adjustment to the 'good life.' " [13]

Gubernatorial Campaign Costs

Being elected governor is not as easy as it once was. One reason is the new style of campaigning that has led candidates to create their own organizations instead of relying solely on their political party. Opinion polls, political consultants, advertisements tailored to specific audiences in the major media markets, direct mailings, telephone banks, and air travel are extremely expensive, and full-time fundraisers often are needed to help gubernatorial candidates wage winning campaigns. Without the party to alert the faithful and bring in the straight-ticket votes, candidates must create what Sabato calls their own "instant organization" or "party substitute." [14]

Second, there is a growing number of wealthy individuals who aspire to the governorship and have the means to succeed. Some come from "old money" and are the descendants of those who first amassed the family

fortune: Nelson Rockefeller (R-N.Y., 1959-73); Winthrop Rockefeller (R-Ark., 1967-71); John D. "Jay" Rockefeller IV (D-W.Va., 1977-85); and Pierre S. "Pete" du Pont IV (R-Del., 1977-85). Others have "new money" and are spending it: Fob James (D-Ala., 1979-83), William P. Clements Jr. (R-Texas, 1979-83, 1987-91), Wallace G. Wilkinson (D-Ky., 1988-), and Gaston Caperton (D-W.Va., 1989-).

Third, gubernatorial races are more competitive. Awareness of the importance of state government and of the key role of the governor in state politics has increased the number of candidates for the office. In the fifty-three separate gubernatorial elections between 1986 and 1989, there were 343 candidates seeking their party's nomination for governor, for an average of 6.5 candidates per election. Of these candidates, 216 were strong enough to receive more than 10 percent of the party primary or convention vote. In 1986, fifteen candidates sought the governorship in Nebraska, fourteen in Oregon, and thirteen in Alaska. Clearly, there is no shortage of people who wish to become governor of their states.

The fourth and most obvious reason of all is inflation. Like everything else, the cost of politics rises when inflation erodes the dollar. If the 1987 dollar is used as the base point, the dollar was worth forty-three cents in 1972 and eighty-five cents in 1982.

Until the passage of state campaign spending laws in recent years, little information was available on gubernatorial campaign costs. California records go back to 1958, when the Fair Practices Commission was established, but in other states spending information was simply unobtainable, unless some scholar had studied a particular election. Even if officially reported monies raised and spent became public knowledge, unofficial funds spent on a candidate's behalf by organizations and individuals, or time and services contributed by supporters, were not recorded.

Today, more information is available. States are requiring candidates to report campaign finance information. The 163 gubernatorial contests between 1977 and 1989 cost more than $1.032 billion calculated in constant 1987 dollars.[15] This is an average of $6 million per race, although the cost of some states' races can skew this upward. (The 1986 Texas contest cost at least $35 million, the most expensive governor's race ever.) In 1986, the thirty-six races for governor cost about $260 million in 1987 dollars, the three 1987 races cost slightly more than $40 million, the twelve 1988 races cost $49 million, and the 1989 races in New Jersey ($26.2 million) and Virginia ($21.7 million) were the most expensive campaigns in those two states' political history.[16]

Looking at the gubernatorial elections in the fifty states since 1977 using 1987 dollars, there are six states in which these races have averaged more than $14 million each: Texas ($26.8 million), Louisiana ($21.7 million), New York ($20.7 million), California ($20.5 million), Kentucky ($18.4 million), and Florida ($14.0 million). Note that in addition to the largest states included in this high-cost races list, there are three southern states, suggesting that as the Democratic party declines in importance there, money politics is replacing it. At the bottom of the list are the eight states in which the average cost is still below $2 million: Montana ($1.7 million), Wyoming ($1.6 million), Idaho ($1.5 million), South Dakota ($1.4 million), New Hampshire ($1.2 million), Vermont ($.8 million), Delaware ($.7 million), and North Dakota ($.6 million).

One Among Many

The governor is not the only official in the executive branch of state government who is elected statewide. The states elect more than 500 officials, including forty-three attorneys general, forty-two lieutenant governors, thirty-eight treasurers, and thirty-six secretaries of state. There are even five land commissioners, five secretaries of labor, and one commissioner of mines elected by the voters of some states. Ten states elect their boards of education, and eleven states elect their superintendents of public instruction. The legislatures appoint some state officials, mainly in the postaudit function, and the lieutenant governors in a few states have some appointive power. This means that governors have little or no power over some parts of state government, except their own power of persuasion or the power they can create through the budget.

Fragmentation of executive branch leadership complicates the politics between the actors involved. In the early 1980s, for example, the governors and the lieutenant governors of California, Missouri, Nebraska, and New Mexico were pitted against each other over the issue of who is in charge of state government when the governor is out of state. Can the lieutenant governor make appointments to office or the bench (patronage)? Call a special session of the legislature? Issue pardons? And who receives the governor's salary while he or she is absent? More recently, some governors have had difficulties with other elected officials: in Virginia, the governor and lieutenant governor fought over the budget surplus and taxes; in Idaho, the governor and the attorney general have been squabbling over regulating the amount of timber exported from the state; in Georgia, the fight was between the governor and the attorney general, with the two officials battling over the state's open meetings law and personnel matters; and in North Carolina, the governor and attorney general fought over the governor's right to contract leases and appoint certain officials.[17]

Executive branch fragmentation has

other consequences. Perhaps most importantly, it restricts what governors can accomplish in high priority areas such as education. A gubernatorial candidate may pledge to improve primary and secondary education, but, once elected, have difficulty fulfilling this goal because other elected officials with responsibility in the education policy area may have different views on what should be done.

Recent federal court decisions have begun to restrict a chief executive's ability to remove or fire government employees, an action often needed to open up positions for appointing the executive's own team. In the 1976 *Elrod v. Burns* decision, the U.S. Supreme Court held that "patronage firings" violate the First Amendment's protection of an individual's freedom of political belief and political association.[18] In the 1980 *Branti v. Finkel* decision, the Court reaffirmed its position but did indicate "if the employee's private political beliefs would interfere with the discharge of his public duties, the First Amendment rights may be required to yield to the state's vital interest in maintaining governmental effectiveness and efficiency."[19] In its 1983 *Connick v. Myers* decision, the Court again affirmed its position but held that "the First Amendment does not protect from dismissal public employees who complain about their working conditions or their supervisor."[20] All three cases concerned local government situations but, by extension, affects governors as well.

There is a tension between the right of employees to be protected for their political beliefs and the need of an executive to put into place individuals who will seek to achieve the goals for which that executive was elected. A case currently being tried in federal district court in Raleigh, North Carolina, involves the governor of that state. Dismissed Democrats are suing Republican governor James Martin. Attorney General Lacy Thornburg, a Democrat, is defending the governor. Many inter-

ested parties are involved in the case, including the National Governors' Association on behalf of all governors.

The most significant restriction on a governor's ability to be governor is the relationship that he or she has with state legislators. There are many types of advice and counsel that governors give each other on this relationship; consider these comments by incumbents to newly elected governors in 1982:

> Don't necessarily judge your success by your legislative score card.... Avoid threatening to veto a bill. You just relieve the legislature of responsibility for sound legislation.... A governor successful in managing the selection of legislative leadership gains a Pyrrhic victory.... It's too easy to dismiss one or two legislators because there are so many. You do so at your own peril.... Legislators will complain about your spending too much time with the staff, but what they really mean is you don't spend enough time with them.... If someone urges your support on a bill by saying it's a "merely" bill, sew your pockets shut; there are no "merely" bills.... Legislators will learn that press coverage comes from opposition to the governor.[21]

Part VI provides a close-up view of the governorship in the late 1980s. In *North Carolina Insight,* Thad L. Beyle describes the powers of the governors and how these powers vary in the states. Chase Riveland discusses the various styles a governor may adopt for managing state government. Paul West shows how governors use the stump to mold public opinion, build their own popularity, and pressure their legislatures. Finally, there is a profile of the governors' long-term Washington lobbyist, Jim Martin of the National Governor's Association.

Notes

1. Larry Sabato, *Goodbye to Good-time Charlie: The American Governorship Transformed,* 2d ed. (Washington, D.C.: CQ Press, 1983), 57.

2. Ibid., xi.

3. Otto Kerner (D-Ill., 1961-68), Spiro Agnew (R-Md., 1967-69), Marvin Mandel (D-Md., 1969-77), David Hall (D-Okla., 1971-75), and Ray Blanton (D-Tenn., 1975-79).

4. "Former Governor of West Virginia to Plead Guilty," [Raleigh] *News and Observer,* April 13, 1990, 8A.

5. Query by Larry Sabato at the "State of the States" Symposium, Eagleton Institute, Rutgers University, New Brunswick, N.J., December 18, 1987.

6. Gubernatorial election data for 1970-89 may be found in Thad L. Beyle, "Governors" in *Politics in the American States: A Comparative Analysis,* 5th ed., ed. Virginia Gray, Herbert Jacob, and Robert B. Albritton (Glenview, Ill.: Scott Foresman, 1990), 203-208.

7. New Hampshire, Rhode Island, and Vermont had elections in 1986 and 1988 because their governors serve only two-year terms.

8. Judd Gregg (R-N.H.) in 1988, James J. Florio (D-N.J.) in 1989, James G. Martin (R-N.C.) in 1984, and Carroll A. Campbell Jr. (R-S.C.) in 1986.

9. The U.S. senators are: Dale Bumpers (D-Ark., 1971-75); David Pryor (D-Ark., 1975-79); Bob Graham (D-Fla., 1979-86); Wendell H. Ford (D-Ky., 1971-74); Christopher S. Bond (R-Mo., 1973-77, 1981-85); Jim Exon, D-Neb. (1971-79); Bob Kerrey (D-Neb., 1983-87); Richard H. Bryan (D-Nev., 1983-87); Terry Sanford (D-N.C., 1961-65); David L. Boren (D-Okla., 1975-79); Mark O. Hatfield (R-Ore., 1959-67); John H. Chafee (R-R.I., 1963-69); Strom Thurmond (R-S.C., 1947-51); Ernest F. Hollings (D-S.C., 1959-63); Charles S. Robb (D-Va., 1982-86); and John D. "Jay" Rockefeller IV (D-W.Va., 1977-85). The lone representative is Joseph E. Brennan (D-Maine, 1979-87).

10. Thad L. Beyle, "Governors" in *Politics in the American States,* 4th ed., ed. Virginia Gray, Herbert Jacob, and Robert B. Albritton (Boston: Little, Brown), 217.

11. Lamar Alexander, *Steps Along the Way: A Governor's Scrapbook* (Nashville: Thomas Nelson, 1986), 9.

12. "Inquiry: Being Governor Is Best Training for Presidency," *USA Today,* September 11, 1987, 11A.

13. "Is There Life after Being Governor? Yes, A Good One," *Governors' Weekly Bulletin* 86:32 (August 8, 1986): 1-2.

14. Larry Sabato, "Gubernatorial Politics and the New Campaign Technology," *State Government* 53 (Summer 1980): 149.

15. "Total Cost of Gubernatorial Elections: 1977-1989," *The Book of the States, 1990-91* (Lexington, Ky.: The Council of State Governments, forthcoming).

16. Thad Beyle, "The 1989 Gubernatorial Races," *Comparative State Politics* 11:2 (April 1990): 29-32.

17. "People: Some Governors Get No Respect," *Governing* 1:2 (November 1987): 67.

18. Elder Witt, "Patronage Firings," *Congressional Quarterly Weekly Report,* July 3, 1976, 1726.

19. Elder Witt, "Supreme Court Deals Blow to Public Employee Firings for Solely Political Reasons," *Congressional Quarterly Weekly Report,* April 5, 1980, 899-900.

20. Elder Witt, "Employee Rights," *Congressional Quarterly Weekly Report,* April 6, 1983, 791-792.

21. Thad L. Beyle and Robert Huefner, "Quips and Quotes from Old Governors to New," *Public Administration Review* 43:3 (May-June 1983): 268-269.

The Powers of the Governors

by Thad L. Beyle

... Assessing the powers accorded a governor by state constitutions and statutes provides one means of measuring the relative strength of the 50 governors in this country. The five formal institutional powers common to almost all governors are length of tenure and succession; the power to appoint key officials to various state offices; the power to remove officials; control over the budget; and veto power. In addition, the power of the legislature to change the governor's budget proposals, and whether the governor and the legislature are of the same party, are important parts of the gubernatorial power calculus. To examine and compare these seven institutional powers ... for all the states, a point system for each category and for cumulative groupings was used[1] [See Table 1]. ...

Length of Tenure and Succession

The longer a governor serves, the more likely that governor [will] achieve his goals and have an impact on the state. The length of term and ability to succeed oneself, then, are critical determinants of a governor's power. In the original 13 states, 10 governors had one-year terms, one had a two-year term, and two had a three-year term. States gradually moved to either two- or four-year terms, but one-year tenures were not phased out completely until early this century. By 1940, about the same number of states had two- and four-year terms. From 1940-1989, the number of states allowing the governor only a two-year term shrank drastically, from 24 to three (New Hampshire, Rhode Island, and Vermont). And from 1960-1989, the number prohibiting consecutive terms declined from 15 to three (Kentucky, New Mexico, and Virginia).

To rank the states according to the governor's tenure potential, more weight was given to four-year than to two-year terms, and more to unlimited re-election possibilities than to restraints on re-election. ...

The Power of Appointment

One of the first sets of decisions facing a

Thad L. Beyle is professor of political science at the University of North Carolina at Chapel Hill and was board chairman of the North Carolina Center for Public Policy Research for ten years. This article is excerpted from *North Carolina Insight* 12:2 (March 1990): 27-45, the quarterly journal of the North Carolina Center for Public Policy Research. Portions of the article are based on a study contained in Virginia Gray, Herbert Jacob, and Robert B. Albritton, eds., *Politics in the American States: A Comparative Analysis,* 5th ed. (Glenview, Ill.: Scott Foresman, 1990), 215-230.

governor-elect on the first Wednesday morning in November after the election is the appointment of personnel to key positions within the new administration. The appointive power enhances the governor's legislative role: promises of appointments to high-level executive positions, to the state judiciary, and to about 240 boards and commissions often are the coins spent for support of particular legislation.

The measure of the governor's appointive powers is the extent to which he or she is free to name the heads of the state agencies administering the six major state functions common to most states: corrections, education, health, highways, public utility regulation, and public welfare. These categories were chosen by the National Governors' Association as key indicators of a governor's appointive powers. Governors who can appoint these officials without any other body involved are more powerful than those who must have either or both houses of the legislature confirm an appointment. And governors who only approve appointments rather than initiating them have even less appointive power. The weakest states are those in which a governor neither appoints nor approves but where a separate body does so, or where separately elected officials head these agencies. . . .

The Power to Remove Officials

The reverse side of appointive power is often overlooked—the power of removal. The power to appoint officials theoretically implies the power to remove officials so that an alternative appointment can be made. Generally, this is a difficult power to exercise unless an official is accused of outright corruption or unethical behavior. In fact, the political costs of trying to remove someone are often greater than the costs of living with the problem that they create.[2]

Recently, another constraint on the gover-

nor's removal power has arisen from a series of U.S. Supreme Court decisions protecting individuals from political firings. . . . [Some of these decisions are discussed in the introduction to this chapter.]

The power of removal is strongest when lodged in the state's constitution rather than in a state statute. It is also stronger when there are few specifications or restrictions as to who might be removed, or the reasons for which removal might be warranted, or if the removal is the governor's prerogative alone and not shared with another state agency. State supreme court decisions have either provided the governor with considerable power of removal (Indiana) or a somewhat restricted power of removal (Arizona), or have hamstrung the governor (Georgia).[3]

To rank the states on the governor's removal power, more weight was given to a constitutional provision than to a statutory provision, the degree to which the governor is constrained by restrictions on the cause needed to remove an official, the scope of the removal power, or the removal process involved. . . .

Governor's Control over the Budget

An executive budget, centralized under gubernatorial control, is a 20th century response at all levels of our governmental system to the chaotic fiscal situations that existed at the turn of the century. A budget document brings together under the chief executive's control all the agency and departmental requests for legislatively appropriated funds. Sitting at the top of this process in the executive branch, a governor usually functions as chief cheerleader for the budget in the legislature as well.

A governor who has full responsibility for developing the state's budget is more powerful than those who share this responsibility with others. Most states (44) do give this power solely to the governor; in only six states do the governors have to share the control over the budget. . . .

Ability of the Legislature to Change the Governor's Budget

This is the first of two gubernatorial powers that basically are negative. In every state, the governor may propose the next state budget, but the more a legislature may change that proposed budget, the *less potential budget power* a governor has. Note the use of the word *potential;* it is applied purposely because not all legislative-gubernatorial relationships are adversarial and the governor's proposed budget most often sets the budgetary agenda for legislative consideration and decision.

There is little variation among the states on this, as only five states provide constraints on the legislature's ability to change the governor's proposals—and thus check this power. In fact, since 1965 no state has increased the governor's budget power vis-á-vis the legislature and four states actually have increased their legislature's power. . . .[4]

Veto Power

The most direct power a governor can exercise in relation to the legislature is the threat or the use of a veto. The type of veto power extended to governors ranges from the simple, all-or-nothing veto, to the item veto, to the amendatory veto, [to a partial veto,] and to no veto at all. . . . [O]nly one state has no veto power—North Carolina.[5]

In addition to giving a governor direct power in struggles with the legislature, a veto also provides the governor with some administrative powers. For example, it gives him the ability to stop agencies from attempting an end run around a governor's adverse decision—such as when agencies go directly to the legislature to seek authority or spending approval for items the governor opposes. This is especially true in the 43 states where the governor can veto

---

Lieutenant Governors

The office of lieutenant governor continues to provoke controversy, particularly as candidates line up to seek the office in 1990 elections. Eight states do without the office entirely, leading to proposals to add it in the states without it and subtract it in the states with it. Kentucky's lieutenant governor is pushing a constitutional amendment to merge his office with those of the treasurer and secretary of state. An interim legislative study committee has proposed eliminating the office in Kansas.

Problems also arise over whether the lieutenant governor and governor should be elected as a slate, which they are in 22 states. If they aren't, those elected may be of opposite parties. . . . But if they are, strong resistance often develops to the role of presiding over the Senate. Twenty-five states . . . give the office the power to break ties in Senate voting, but the occasion to use the power rarely arises. In about a dozen states, the lieutenant governor is Senate leader with power to appoint committee chairs and assign bills to committees. This seems to work in Texas, where the lieutenant governor is of the same party as the Senate majority but a different party from the governor, but has been sticky in North Carolina where the governor and lieutenant governor are Republicans but Democrats control the legislature.

Source: State Policy Reports 7:16 (August 1989): 31.

---

particular items in an agency's budget without overturning the entire bill. But like the legislature's authority to change the budget, this is also a measure of how the legislature may curtail a governor's power through its ability to override a governor's veto.

Table 1 Seven Institutional Powers of the Offices of Governor [a]

State	Tenure potential [b]	Appointment power [c]	Removal power [d]	Governor controls budget [e]	Legislature can change budget [f]	Veto power [g]	Governor & legislature of same party [h]	Total score
Alabama	4	4	3	5	1	4	1	22
Alaska	4	5	4	5	1	5	3	27
Arizona	5	3	2	5	1	5	2	23
Arkansas	4	5	3	5	1	4	5	27
California	5	4	3	5	1	5	2	25
Colorado	5	5	4	4	1	5	2	26
Connecticut	5	4	2	5	1	5	4	26
Delaware	4	5	4	5	1	5	3	27
Florida	4	4	2	5	1	5	2	23
Georgia	4	2	1	5	1	5	5	23
Hawaii	4	3	3	5	1	5	5	27
Idaho	5	3	2	5	1	5	2	23
Illinois	5	5	3	5	1	5	2	26
Indiana	4	6	5	5	1	1	3	25
Iowa	5	5	1	5	1	5	2	24
Kansas	4	5	3	5	1	5	4	27
Kentucky	3	5	3	4	1	5	4	24
Louisiana	4	4	4	4	1	2	5	27
Maine	4	5	3	5	5	2	2	22
Maryland	4	5	4	5	5	5	5	33
Massachusetts	5	6	2	5	1	5	5	29
Michigan	5	4	2	5	1	5	3	25
Minnesota	5	5	1	5	1	5	4	26
Mississippi	4	2	2	5	1	5	5	24
Missouri	4	4	3	5	1	5	2	24
Montana	5	3	5	5	1	5	3	27
Nebraska	4	3	2	5	4	2	3	26
Nevada	4	4	1	5	1	2	3	20
New Hampshire	2	4	2	5	1	2	4	20
New Jersey	4	5	3	5	1	5	4	27
New Mexico	3	4	5	4	1	5	2	24
New York	5	5	3	5	3	5	3	29
North Carolina	4	5	1	5	2	0	2	19

North Dakota	5	4	1	5	1	5	3	24
Ohio	4	5	1	5	1	5	3	24
Oklahoma	4	2	2	5	1	5	2	21
Oregon	4	5	1	5	1	5	4	25
Pennsylvania	4	5	3	5	1	5	3	26
Rhode Island	2	4	2	5	1	2	1	17
South Carolina	4	2	2	4	1	5	2	20
South Dakota	4	4	5	5	1	5	4	28
Tennessee	4	6	2	5	1	4	4	26
Texas	5	2	2	1	1	5	2	18
Utah	5	4	2	5	1	5	4	26
Vermont	2	5	2	5	1	2	3	20
Virginia	3	5	3	5	1	5	4	26
Washington	5	3	1	5	1	5	3	23
West Virginia	4	4	2	5	5	4	5	29
Wisconsin	5	4	2	5	1	5	2	24
Wyoming	5	4	2	5	1	5	2	24
Average score:	4.2	4.2	2.5	4.8	1.3	4.4	3.1	24.6

a Using a point system ranging from 0 to 5, except for appointment powers, which used a 0-to-6 point system, the states were grouped into six categories: Very Strong (VS), or 5 points; Strong (S), or 4 points; Moderate (M), or 3 points; Weak (W), or 2 points; Very Weak (VW), or 1 point; and None (N), or no points.

b Length of tenure and succession potential: These rankings are based on how long a term in office is and whether the governor may succeed to one or more successive terms.

VS-5 — 4-year term, unlimited re-election allowed
S-4 — 4-year terms, one re-election permitted (N.C. governor has no limit on number of terms he or she can serve, but must sit out at least a term after serving two successive terms)
M-3 — 4-year term, no re-election permitted
W-2 — 2-year term, unlimited re-election permitted
VW-1 — 2-year term, one-re-election permitted
N-0 — 2-year term, no re-election permitted

c Power to appoint officials to major offices. These rankings are based on a governor's ability to appoint officials in six major functions common to every state: corrections, education, health, highways, public utility regulation, and public welfare (in this category, a governor who alone can appoint all six officials can receive a score of 6, as does the governor of Massachusetts).

VS-6 — governor alone appoints all officials, or governor's cabinet appointment with governor's approval
S-5 — governor's appointment with board, council, or legislative approval
M-4 — governor's cabinet appointment without governor's approval
W-2 — board appointment with gubernatorial approval, or governor and legislative approval
N-1 — legislative appointment
N-0 — popularly elected by the people

d Power to remove officials from offices: These rankings are based on a governor's power to remove officials with or without cause, and on whether those powers are granted directly by the state constitution, through state statutes, or other avenues.

VS-5 — power based in state constitution or court decision; no specifications or restrictions as to use
S-4 — power based in state constitution or statutory elaboration of constitutional provision; specifications or restrictions in only one area (cause, scope, or process)
M-3 — power based on statutory elaboration of constitutional provision or statute; specifications or restrictions in one or two areas (cause, scope, or process)
W-2 — power based on statutory elaboration of constitutional provision or statute; specifications or restrictions in two or all three areas (cause, scope, or process)
VW-1 — power based on statute or restricted by court decision; specifications or restrictions in all three areas (cause, scope, and process)

e Governor's control over the budget: These rankings are determined by how much power the governor has to draft and propose a state's annual budget.

VS-5 — governor has full responsibility for developing budget
S-4 — governor shares responsibility with civil servant or with a person appointed by another official
M-3 — governor shares responsibility with legislature
W-2 — governor shares responsibility with another popularly elected official
VW-1 — governor shares responsibility with several others with independent sources of strength

f Ability of the legislature to change the governor's budget: These rankings are based on how restricted a legislature is in its ability to limit the budgetary powers of the governor, because the greater a legislature's power to alter a governor's budget, the less power a governor will have. The rankings above reflect a governor's power relative to the legislature's ability to alter the budget.

VS-5 — legislature may not increase the executive budget
S-4 — a special (three-fifths majority) vote is required to increase a governor's recommendation
M-3 — legislature may reduce or strike out items, but may increase and add separate items subject to a governor's line-item veto
W-2 — legislature can change budget, but must balance allocations with revenues
VW-1 — unlimited power of the legislature to change the executive budget

g Veto power: These rankings are based on the type of veto power a governor has.

VS-5 — line-item veto with at least a three-fifths majority of legislature needed to override
S-4 — item veto with simple majority of legislature elected needed to override
M-3 — item veto with majority of members of legislature present needed to override
W-2 — no item veto but special majority of legislature needed to override
VW-1 — no item veto with simple legislative majority needed to override
N-0 — no veto of any kind

h Governor and legislature of the same party: These rankings are based on the added powers that occur when the governor and legislature are of the same political party and the governor is head of the party.

VS-5 — governor's party controls both houses with substantial majority (75 percent or greater)
S-4 — governor's party has simple majority in both houses, or a simple majority in one house and a substantial majority in the other
M-3 — split party control in the legislature or non-partisan legislature
W-2 — governor's party in simple minority in both houses, or a simple minority in one and a substantial minority in the other
VW-1 — governor's party in substantial minority in both houses

Sources: The Book of the States, 1988-89 (Lexington, Ky.: Council of State Governments, 1988); Legislative Budget Procedures in the 50 States (Denver: National Conference of State Legislatures, 1988); "1988 Election Results," State Legislatures (November/December 1988), 14; and "The Institutionalized Powers of the Governorship, 1965-1985," State Services Management Notes (Washington, D.C.: National Governors' Association, 1987).

Ranking the states for veto power is based on two principal assumptions: first, that an item veto gives a governor more power than does a general veto; and second, that the larger the legislative vote needed to override a governor's veto, the stronger the veto power. . . .

Governor and Legislature of the Same Party

Textbooks and politicians always list political party chief as one of the governor's major roles. That role allows the governor to use partisanship to the utmost advantage. For example, if the governor and the majority of the members and the leadership of both houses of the legislatures are of the same party . . . the governor's power is likely to be greater than if they are of opposite parties. . . . When the leaders are of the same party, there is less chance of partisan conflicts and more chance for the governor to influence the legislature because it is dominated by the governor's own party. If they are of opposite parties, partisan conflicts can be the norm, and the governor loses power due to the inability to call on partisan loyalty for support.

In the recent past, the trend has been toward power splits where the executive and legislative branches of government are controlled by opposite parties either totally or partially. Following the 1984 elections, 16 states had such split party control; in 1989, there were 30. . . . Political scientist V. O. Key Jr. called this phenomenon a "perversion" of the separation of powers built into our system of government at the national and state levels as it allows partisan differences to create an almost intractable situation.[6] Nebraska is unique—a nonpartisan, unicameral legislature and partisan governor.

Measuring this power of party control across the states is based on the assumption that the greater the margin of control by the governor's party in either or both houses of the

legislature, the stronger the governor may be. Conversely, the weaker the governor's party in the legislature, the weaker the governor may be. Of course, this overlooks the possibility that the governor's style and personality can either surmount difficult partisan splits or make the worst of a good situation. . . .

Summary of Overall Gubernatorial Powers

To compare the powers of the 50 governors, each state was given an overall average score. For each of six categories—length of tenure and succession, the power to remove officials, control over the budget, the ability of the legislature to change the governor's budget, veto power, and the governor's party control, a zero-to-five point scoring range was used. The appointment category had a zero-to-six point range. . . . (See footnotes to Table 1 for an explanation of the scoring system for each category.) Critics may point out that each category is weighted equally and that this may obscure important differences among the powers of the 50 governors. But because such values can vary enormously from state to state, there is no simple way to weight them differently. This survey, after all, seeks to compare the powers of the various governors . . . in order to provide a perspective on the relative powers and to help policymakers and voters consider how their chief executive compares with the governors in other states. . . .

[As shown in Table 1 and Table 2, no states are in the very weak category, and only Maryland is in the very strong category. Most states fall into the moderate category (38), with some stronger (4) and some weaker (7).]

Informal Powers

These measures only tell part of the story of gubernatorial power. They emphasize the degree of control the governor has over the executive branch and his or her relationship

Table 2   Relative Power of the Offices of Governor[a]

Very weak (0)[b]				Weak (7)				Moderate (38)							Strong (4)				Very strong (1)		
13	14	15	16	17	18	19	20	21	22	23	24	25	26	27	28	29	30	31	32	33	34
					RI	TX	NC	NV	OH	AL	AZ	IA	CA	CO	SD	MA				MD	
					NH	ME		FL	KY	IN	CT	AR		AK		NY					
					SC			GA	MS	MI	IL	DE				WV					
					VT			ID	MO	OR	MN	HI									
								WA	NM		NE	KS									
									ND		PA	LA									
									OK		TN	MT									
									WI		UT	NJ									
									WY		VA										

[a] Scores are from Table 1 and power is rated on this scale: less than 17 points, Very weak; 17 to 20 points, Weak; 21 to 27 points, Moderate; 28 to 30 points, Strong; and over 31 points, Very strong. This list is shown alphabetically by group.

[b] (0) Indicates number of states in this category

with the legislature. They do not, however, measure the many informal sources of power or constraints on a governor such as supporting or opposing interest groups, a governor's ability to take advantage of the news media, access to campaign contributions, county political organizations, good looks, charisma, and overall political popularity—which itself can rise or fall with each new political brushfire. A media-wise governor can, for example, dominate a state's political and policy agenda if he or she is adept at handling the media and public appearances; by the same token, a governor's powers can decline if the governor is inept at controlling the political agenda or communicating through television cameras.

Some of the informal powers available to the governor outweigh many of the constraints of his institutional powers. A strong political base and popularity with the media [can] provide the governor with a major vehicle to command the public's attention. [If] no large urban area dominates the state's politics, there are no other highly visible political leaders with which the governor has to compete. In contrast, the mayors of New York, Chicago, Los Angeles, Atlanta, and other large cities have a political base which can vault them into a position to vie with a governor for leadership. Moreover, in [some] state[s], few other institutions provide leaders a base for political attention. . . .

And not to be overlooked is the power of a governor to reorganize the existing executive branch structure to conform with his own plans. . . . Such powers allow a governor to shift the setup of the major agencies under his control, especially when pressing state needs indicate a reorganization would be helpful. . . .

All these formal and informal powers can confer upon an individual governor considerable powers if that official knows how to take best advantage of them. . . .

Notes

1. Office of State Services, "The Institutional Powers of the Governorship, 1965-1985," *State Services Management Notes,* National Governors' Association, 1987. See also Thad L.

Beyle, "Governors" in *Politics in the American States: A Comparative Analysis,* 5th ed., ed. Virginia Gray, Herbert Jacob, and Robert B. Albritton (Glenview, Ill.: Scott Foresman, 1990), 215-230.

2. Diane Kincaid Blair, "The Gubernatorial Appointment Power: Too Much of a Good Thing?" *State Government* 55:3 (1982): 88-92.

3. See *Tucker v. State,* 218 Ind. 614 (1941); *Ahern v. Bailey,* 104 Ariz. 250, 451 P.2d 30 (1960); and *Holder v. Anderson,* 160 Ga. 433, 128 S.E. 1981 (1925).

4. Office of State Services, 7.

5. For more information on the types of vetoes in the states, see Calvin Bellamy, "Item Veto: Dangerous Constitutional Tinkering," *Public Administration Review* 49:1 (January/February 1989); Jack Betts, "The Item Veto—Partisan Advantage of Fiscal Restraint?" *North Carolina Insight* 12:2 (March 1990): 6; and Ronald C. Moe, *Prospects for the Item Veto at the Federal Level: Lessons from the States* (Washington, D.C.: National Academy of Public Administration, 1988).

6. V. O. Key Jr., *American State Politics* (New York: A. A. Knopf, 1956), 52.

1990 Occupants of the Nation's Statehouses

Listed below are the governors of the 50 states, and the year in which the next election for each office will be held. The names of governors elected in November 1989 are in **boldface.**

Alabama—Guy Hunt (R) 1990

Alaska— Steve Cowper (D) 1990

Arizona—Rose Mofford (D) 1990 [1]

Arkansas—Bill Clinton (D) 1990

California—George Deukmejian (R) 1990

Colorado—Roy Romer (D) 1990

Connecticut—William A. O'Neill (D) 1990

Delaware—Michael N. Castle (R) 1992 [2]

Florida—Bob Martinez (R) 1990

Georgia—Joe Frank Harris (D) 1990 [2]

Hawaii— John Waihee III (D) 1990

Idaho—Cecil D. Andrus (D) 1990

Illinois—James R. Thompson (R) 1990

Indiana—Evan Bayh (D) 1992

Iowa—Terry E. Branstad (R) 1990

Kansas—Mike Hayden (R) 1990

Kentucky—Wallace G. Wilkinson (D) 1991 [2]

Louisiana—Buddy Roemer (D) 1991

Maine—John R. McKernan Jr. (R) 1990

Maryland—William Donald Schaefer (D) 1990

Massachusetts—Michael S. Dukakis (D) 1990

Michigan—James J. Blanchard (D) 1990

Minnesota—Rudy Perpich (D) 1990

Mississippi—Ray Mabus (D) 1991

Missouri—John Ashcroft (R) 1992 [2]

Montana—Stan Stephens (R) 1992

Nebraska—Kay A. Orr (R) 1990

Nevada—Bob Miller (D) 1990 [3]

New Hampshire—Judd Gregg (R) 1990

New Jersey—James J. Florio (D) 1993

New Mexico—Garrey Carruthers (R) 1990 [2]

New York—Mario M. Cuomo (D) 1990

North Carolina—James G. Martin (R) 1992 [2]

North Dakota—George Sinner (D) 1992

Ohio—Richard F. Celeste (D) 1990 [2]

Oklahoma—Henry Bellmon (R) 1990

Oregon—Neil Goldschmidt (D) 1990

Pennsylvania—Robert P. Casey (D) 1990

Rhode Island—Edward DiPrete (R) 1990

South Carolina—Carroll A. Campbell Jr. (R) 1990

South Dakota—George S. Mickelson (R) 1990

Tennessee—Ned McWherter (D) 1990

Texas—William P. Clements Jr. (R) 1990

Utah—Norman H. Bangerter (R) 1992

Vermont—Madeleine M. Kunin (D) 1990

Virginia—L. Douglas Wilder (D) 1993 [2]

Washington—Booth Gardner (D) 1992

West Virginia—Gaston Caperton (D) 1992

Wisconsin—Tommy G. Thompson (R) 1990

Wyoming—Mike Sullivan (D) 1990

[1] As secretary of state, Mofford succeeded Gov. Evan Mecham (R), who was impeached and removed from office in April 1988.

[2] Barred by state law from seeking reelection.

[3] Miller succeeded as governor from lieutenant governor position when Gov. Richard H. Bryan (D) was elected to the U.S. Senate in 1988.

Source: Congressional Quarterly Weekly Report (November 12, 1988), 3298. Updated by editor.

Gubernatorial Styles: Is There a Right One?

by Chase Riveland

Leader, manager, chief executive officer, policy-maker, politician, negotiator, "keeper of the vision" and chief of ceremony are roles that must be performed by the governor of a state. A governor must fulfill these roles while keeping a wary watch on political adversaries, assuring appropriate accommodation of supporters, consuming enormous amounts of written information and digesting advice from staff, legislators, interest groups and family. The governor must set an agenda, establish priorities, manage crises, assure recognition of a range of individuals, groups and causes—all while being constantly scrutinized by the media. Governors are frequently blamed publicly for all that goes wrong in a state; yet, when something goes right, legislators and others scamper to take the credit.

The governor must manage a breadth of issues and subjects that would startle the private-sector chief executive. The typical responsibilities of the business executive—financial management, labor relations, marketing and personnel management—also are core responsibilities of the governor.

In addition to these core responsibilities, however, the governor must function under the constant surveillance of a large board of directors—legislators—many of whom inevitably are philosophically, politically and personally adversarial. Further complexity is added by the plethora of commissions, advisory groups and boards that inevitably help manage state government.

Frequently, one or both houses of the legislature are not controlled by the governor's political party, creating an environment of philosophical differences as well as political agendas that are more focused on the next election than on statesmanly development of sound public policy and law. Because elected state officials must run for office every two or four years, the next election is always near and the desire for political success omnipresent in the politically partisan mind. In these circumstances, political opposition to the governor may reflect more of a power struggle than an honest difference over policy. Indeed, the governor's basic responsibility to manage government often is questioned, challenged and threatened.

Chase Riveland is secretary of the Washington Department of Corrections. He previously served as executive director of the Colorado Department of Corrections. This article is reprinted from *The Journal of State Government* 62:4 (July/August 1989): 136-139.

Public and Private Management

In most states, the number of persons appointed by and reporting to the governor would challenge the most liberal span-of-control theories. It is not at all unusual to have more than 20 prime cabinet members and a similar number of minor cabinet positions all reporting to the governor. For example, in Colorado in the early 1980s, the cabinet included at least 16 agency heads. Washington state today includes at least 20. Executive authority often is diffused intentionally by the legislature—for example, by making an executive agency responsible to a commission rather than to the governor. Such actions, while often for good cause, mitigate the executive's ability to manage.

If to manage is to control or direct, how then does a governor ensure that his or her policies, priorities, expectations and agendas are carried out? How does a governor discourage individual agendas or agency competition for funds? Concurrently, how does a governor encourage a sense of unity or direction, create a collegial approach to priorities, and take advantage of the variety of talents, perspectives and ideas that a cabinet and staff bring to bear on developing policy and managing government? Is there a singular best style?

Management theories abound suggesting a variety of successful techniques for managing organizations, both simple and complex. Objective setting, participatory involvement, walking around, explicit mission statements, public agency business plans and matrix management are but a few of the techniques offered by trainers, textbooks and consultants. One can undoubtedly find examples where each of these techniques, as well as others, have been used successfully or have failed.

Should a newly elected governor simply adopt the most current or popular management theory in the private sector? Unless that particular technique is in keeping with the governor's personality and interests and is comfortable, the governor may not be well-served by simply borrowing private-sector strategies and styles.

For the last several years, the media, the public and politicians have chanted religiously about inept, inefficient, nonresponsive government and bureaucracy. Normally, in the same breath, they also have suggested that the simple infusion of private-sector management skills and techniques would provide obvious solutions. But before making too many campaign promises based on dedication to private-sector management, gubernatorial candidates should reassess such popular slogans. They also should discuss their practical potential with present or former governors.

The drafters of state constitutions had objectives that were different from those of the creators of corporate organizations. Although large corporations may rival the complexity of government, pure corporate organizational design generally is intended to promote accountability as measured in sales, production and profit and a crispness of management. In contrast, the writers of state constitutions ensured inevitably (if only implicitly) that governors would not be aided by crisp organizational design. Rather, state constitutions force governors to negotiate, anticipate, ameliorate, bargain, threaten, withdraw, entice, promise, reward, punish, ignore and apologize—simply to perform as the chief executive officer of the state. As if the checks and balances of its executive, legislative and judicial triumvirate were not enough, most constitutions ensure further diffusion and limitations of executive power. And then there is the electorate.

Government by its structural nature is not designed for strong executive action. It is designed to encourage negotiation, influence, input and adversarial relationships. Still, the governor operates in a public environment that

Table 1 Institutional Character in Gubernatorial Administration

	Gubernatorial staff	Budget staff	Political executives	Bureaucracy
Central purpose	To advise on governor's constituency and political sources	To advise on governor's fiscal options	To achieve consensus on multiple departmental interests	To maintain the program
Core value	Governor's tenure	Economy, efficiency	Agreement	The program
Distinctive competence	Intelligence on governor's agenda, constituency and political resources	Intelligence on fiscal options available to governor	Skills in negotiating departmental agenda	Program intelligence and expertise
Primary loyalty	Governor	Governor	Multiple	Legislative allies and clientele
Scope	Comprehensive	Comprehensive	Departmental	Bureau
Role	Advocate for governor	Advocate for governor	Broker	Program advocate
Tenure	Gubernatorial term	Short term	Temporary	Permanent
Time frame	Short term	Budget year	Short term	Long term
Method for change	Executive action	Budget cycle	Executive action	Incremental, consensual
Structure	Fluid	Mixed	Flexible	Rigid
Institutional memory	Least	More	Little	Most

Source: H. Edward Flentje, "Clarifying Purpose and Achieving Balance in Gubernatorial Administration," *The Journal of State Government* 62:4 (July/August 1989): 162.

expects crisp executive management. Consequently, a governor must attempt to perform accordingly (or at least to be perceived so) while fulfilling all other roles symbolically and politically essential to survival.

Indeed, it may be that the ability of a governor to transmit expectations, values and priorities to the staff, cabinet and public may be of great importance to the actual managing of government. The nurturing of strong allegiances and confidence may well be the best that can be expected given the complexity of governance today.

Because I have worked for two governors who had many similarities but different styles, it may be useful to briefly examine their approaches to managing government.

Richard Lamm: A Hands-On Style

Richard Lamm, governor of Colorado from 1975 to 1987, enjoyed enormous popularity among the electorate. Initially gaining office after walking the state and campaigning on a risky pro-environmental stance to keep the Winter Olympics out of Colorado, Lamm entered office as a surprising upstart and political unknown. A Democrat running for re-election during a time when most of Colorado's state and national offices were dominated by Republicans, he easily was returned to office twice, choosing in 1986 not to seek a fourth term. An attorney, certified public accountant and former legislator, Lamm was a governor whose personal characteristics and management style were integrated closely. As an individual, he is bright, inquisitive, energetic, a voracious reader and intrigued by creative solutions to problems.

As governor, Lamm was involved in the management of executive agencies to a level few governors are. He presided over monthly cabinet meetings that were attended by 15 to 20 cabinet members, key gubernatorial staff and the media. The presence of journalists not only provided the governor with a pulpit, but reinforced to all—including the public—that he was actively managing state government. Indeed, cabinet members often witnessed a new policy direction set spontaneously in the midst of whirling cameras. Cabinet members learned not to be surprised when the governor paged through a stack of correspondence and briefing memos and randomly asked for their spontaneous reaction to a question he had about the subject matter. His subsequent directives for action or follow-through dramatized to newspaper readers, television viewers and those present that he was in charge.

The cabinet also was broken down into two working subgroups, with human-service agency directors generally assigned to one group and the remainder of the cabinet to a second. Attendance at an assigned group was required; attendance at the second was optional. At monthly group meetings, the governor dealt with policy or strategy from an agenda of three to five issues. Lamm was involved in all discussions, and the others in

attendance were encouraged and expected to participate regardless of whether the subject was relevant to their responsibilities. On a given day, the agenda might contain a discussion of vouchers for K-12 education, health care cost containment, prison population projections and alternatives to the federal welfare program of Aid to Families with Dependent Children.

Lamm inevitably surprised new cabinet members with his depth of knowledge about a wide variety of topics and with his willingness to consider the opinions of everyone present. The interchange not only allowed the governor to hear a variety of opinions and to test his own views, but it also educated cabinet directors about the issues confronting other agencies. Further, these discussions built commitment among the cabinet to the governor's solutions, direction and priorities. These sessions promoted a collegial style in the administration as cabinet members worked towards cross-agency solutions. In addition, they helped cabinet members develop values on issues beyond their specific area of responsibility; many cabinet members formed their own opinions about greenways and greenbelts, sugar beet farming, the oil-shale industry and [a] variety of other topics.

Two or three times annually, Lamm held cabinet retreats at a variety of locations throughout Colorado. The governor, cabinet directors, key gubernatorial staff and advisers attended. Typically, the agenda included dinner with local officials the first evening followed by a day-and-a-half of meetings covering topical issues on legislative and agency agendas. Often, the governor focused on establishing short- and long-term direction.

Again, Lamm's involvement allowed the cabinet to participate in the development of administration policies and positions while cabinet heads learned of the governor's views on a variety of subjects. An ethos developed that generally discouraged agencies from competing against each other in policy or budget areas. The contact and interchange among the governor and the cabinet members at these retreats [were] enhanced during social time; at a Steamboat Springs retreat, Lamm cooked supper featuring his own recipe for peanut-butter-laced hamburgers.

Finally, Lamm held regular one-on-one sessions (sometimes including his chief of staff) with cabinet members. During these meetings, the governor covered the agency's problems, initiatives and successes, and developed with the agency director goals and directions. Given the number of executive agencies reporting directly to the governor and the numerous time-consuming items on his agenda, this was almost a herculean effort.

Booth Gardner: The CEO

Booth Gardner has been a state legislator, the chief executive officer of a Fortune 500 company, a county executive and a business-school dean. After a surprise primary victory in 1984, Gardner defeated the incumbent to become the chief executive of Washington [state]. As governor, Gardner has continued many of his outside activities—such as coaching a girl's soccer team—and is accurately perceived by the public as particularly sensitive to the future of the state and its residents. In 1988, Gardner was re-elected governor with 63 percent of the vote.

Known as a walk-around manager who frequently appears unannounced at agency offices around the state, Gardner possesses an unpretentious management style. His management philosophy is to hire good managers and then empower them to lead their agencies. He and his staff delegate to cabinet members authority for day-to-day agency operations and policy development. Regular cabinet meetings generally are chaired by the governor's chief of staff, as are the day-long cabinet retreats. In

addition, Gardner has created two subcabinet groups consisting of five or six of the 20 cabinet members; one deals with management issues while the other handles policy questions.

The subcabinet management group addresses issues that affect all agencies: personnel practices, efficiency initiatives, affirmative action, management development and labor relations. The subcabinet also deals with issues that it identifies itself, are assigned by the governor and are referred by cabinet members. Subgroups charged with making recommendations to the governor on particular topics may draw from other cabinet members, outside resources and the governor's staff.

The policy subcabinet committee identifies emerging or unaddressed issues that require policy decisions or direction. In the past, this policy group has handled issues such as growth management, state and local relationships and the growing underclass of people in poverty. Generally, this subcabinet develops policy or strategy recommendations for the governor. In contrast, the governor's own policy staff concentrates on the more ongoing, agency-oriented policy issues. Again, ad hoc cabinet groups are formed to address specific initiatives that cross agency lines. For example, seven cabinet directors formed a year-long working body to provide leadership for creating a state economic development plan.

Gardner enjoys larger policy and budget staffs than Lamm had in Colorado, and he uses these people to ensure consistency in state policies and continuity in state budgets. But it is Gardner who sets the tone for his administration. To cabinet members and gubernatorial staff alike, Gardner makes it clear that efficiency, effectiveness and a service-orientation are expected of every state agency. Those agency directors who assimilate and put into operation the governor's message are rewarded with greater independence, autonomy and trust.

Is There a "Correct" Model for Gubernatorial Management?

These profiles of two governors with opposite management styles suggest that there is no model to mimic, no formula to follow. Lamm and Gardner enjoyed political success and popularity; both generally are acclaimed as serious and effective managers. Yet they are different. And there is little to suggest that the style or technique of one is more likely than the other to produce success. Still, there were some important similarities in how Lamm and Gardner sought to influence the behavior and performance of their cabinet and department heads:

● Both Lamm and Gardner respected public service and imparted that view to their cabinets. Their commitment to responsible public stewardship—as well as their expectation that cabinet members live up to their commitment—was evident to staff and cabinet members.

● Both were accessible to individual cabinet members. Lamm and Gardner made it clear that the views and concerns of individual cabinet directors were important.

● Both governors articulated an expectation that public agencies should be managed well. Efficiency and effectiveness were their bywords.

● Lamm and Gardner placed a premium on appointing well-qualified leaders—rather than simply political supporters—to cabinet positions.

Indeed, the specifics of the management style selected by a governor may be of limited consequence. Much more important may be the values transmitted by the governor to the cabinet. The governor's objective is for cabinet members to put into practice the governor's values. The clarity and intensity with which a governor sets the administration's central values will have a much greater impact on managing the cabinet—and thus state government—than will any particular combination of management techniques. The process selected for developing the budget, the governor's attitude toward internal organization and support for agency directors who manage prudently are just some of the gubernatorial actions that transmit important operating values.

To state cabinet and department heads, every governor articulates—explicitly or implicitly—a set of management values. For Lamm and Gardner, important baseline values were intolerance of corruption and ethical conflicts combined with the presumption of caution in public expenditures. Yet, these were but minimal expectations. By selecting cabinet members for managerial abilities and recognizing success in achieving the stated objectives, a governor can further reinforce an administration's values.

For Lamm's administration, a key phrase was "hard choices." These words were popularized by the governor's "duty to die" speech, in which he questioned the expenditure of large sums of money to prolong life for the terminally ill or those sustained by life-support systems. (The implication was that the money might be better spent on other quality-of-life problems.) But the hard choices phrase often was bandied about in cabinet meetings, reinforcing the recognition that a finite amount of state funds existed. The message was that cabinet members needed to measure agency needs against the overall priorities—and budget—of the administration.

"Efficiency and effectiveness" is more than a slogan to the Gardner administration. The governor acted to reinforce this central value. Each year, Gardner recognizes 10 individuals for their success in promoting efficient and effective government by naming them the "Governor's Distinguished State Managers-of-the-Year." Gardner also chairs an Efficiency Commission that involves the private sector in partnership with government employees in improving public services while saving money. And he regularly rewards with cash bonuses state employees who develop innovative ways to save state money.

Lamm and Gardner publicly have articulated the core values of their administrations. Using opposing styles, they have reinforced these values to their cabinet—and through them large numbers of state employees.

Is there a right or best style for a gover-nor? Clearly not. The style that works for a governor—as is true with any leader—depends upon individual character. The governor's personality, background and interests must be blended with the gubernatorial staff and the political environment.

Public expectations run high—higher than any governor can possibly achieve. The governor who can articulate and reinforce personal values may be doing as much as can be done.

They're Everywhere!
For Today's Governors, Life Is
a Never-Ending Campaign

by Paul West

Governor-for-life would be too much. But no one doubts that Thomas H. Kean could have won a third term as governor of New Jersey last year, had the law permitted him to run. His standing as the most popular Republican chief executive in the state's history has all but obscured memories of Kean's rookie year as governor, which was such a disaster that his pollster, Robert Teeter, said privately that Kean's career might already be over. Kean turned things around by mounting a campaign: not for office, this time, but for the public's heart. He used the tools of electioneering to build support for himself and, by extension, for his policies and programs. His success was striking, but he is far from alone in what he did. So many governors are mounting campaign-style operations that state administrations these days look increasingly like government on the stump.

A tweedy patrician in New Jersey's polyester world of politics, Kean took office in 1982 by fewer than 2,000 votes out of more than 2 million cast in a disputed election. A year later, he still was a blurry image in people's minds. The legislature had opposed virtually all of his policy initiatives. Polls showed that less than half of the voters approved of the job he was doing. Few had any idea where he wanted to take the state. His tony prep school accent (St. Marks and Princeton), elitist pronunciation of his last name ("kane") and personal shyness (he was a stutterer as a child) lent an air of distance and pomposity to his manner. Although his roots stretch back to the state's beginnings, Kean didn't sound much like an American, let alone a Jerseyite. Hardly the sort to endear himself to the shot-and-a-beer guy in Bayonne.

"You can't really govern unless people have a sense of what you're about, what you stand for and what you want to do," says Greg Stevens, a former campaign aide who became chief of staff about that time.

Television was essential to building what became a love affair between Kean and the voters of his state. His first step was to stage a series of televised town meetings in each of the state's 21 counties. Since New Jersey has no commercial television station it can call its own (most of its 7.7 million people are served by New York or Philadelphia stations), Kean relied on cable television, which had wired

---

Paul West is national political correspondent for the *Baltimore Sun*. This article is reprinted from *Governing* 3:6 (March 1990): 51-55.

most of the state. He also began hosting a regular TV show that cable operators could pick up at virtually no cost.

"Even though he comes across as a patrician and not your average guy," says Stevens, "he is very likable once you get to know him. And I felt this could be communicated over the airwaves."

Eventually, Kean's voice became almost as recognizable as his face. One reason was a set of television commercials, paid for with state tourism promotion funds, that featured the governor and celebrities such as Bill Cosby and Brooke Shields. Many governors promote themselves at public expense in ads urging vacationers to see their state. The payoff was particularly high in Kean's case, because his entire home state also saw the spots, which were heavily broadcast in the neighboring New York and Philadelphia media markets. "New Jersey and you," the governor purred through the TV screen in a slogan that would become his trademark. "P-u-h-f-e-c-t together." The skillful use of electronic media to project Kean's genuine likability quickly translated into heightened personal popularity. And that, in turn, enabled him to begin asserting his will with the legislature, with ever greater success.

Throughout the nation today, governors are employing innovative methods of molding public opinion: moving the governor's office to a remote location for a few days, fielding calls on their own radio or TV talk shows, airing weekly radio addresses, holding teleconferences with business and professional elites and hooking up press conferences via satellite or phone line to every corner of the state. They're aiming to pressure state legislators on particular issues or build up their personal popularity so that legislators will think twice before opposing their initiatives.

"Governors are learning that you have to stay popular if you want to govern," says Stevens, who now works for Republican media whiz Roger Ailes. "The public is bombarded with so much information in this day and age that if you're not out there, people forget about you. If they lose sight of you for a month, they forget about you."

In most states, governors have long had the upper hand when it comes to dealing with the legislative branch. The new tools have, if anything, strengthened that advantage. "The governor has what we call the big mike," says Ted Kaplan, a Democrat who is majority leader of the North Carolina Senate. He pointed out that the executive can call upon not only the public relations apparatus in the governor's office but that of the various departments of state government as well. "I only wish we had the same," Kaplan says.

The growing link between governing and campaigning marks a significant shift. "Campaigning is not the same as governing. Don't automatically reward campaign teams with management positions" was the advice given by old governors at a 1982 National Governors' Association seminar for new governors. But fewer and fewer state executives are heeding that traditional wisdom any longer. Besides hiring campaign aides to staff their offices (as many governors have long done), some governors also seek the informal counsel of political consultants long after the votes are counted, or even keep them on retainer.

That may be one reason that television and radio advertising, direct mail, campaign-style travels around the state and other elements of running for governor are increasingly being carried over into office—making running the state look more and more like a never-ending campaign. "When does a public official ever stop campaigning?" former Colorado Governor Richard D. Lamm, a Democrat who served three terms, asks rhetorically. "In a way, you never do."

But it doesn't always work. Even though

many have scored successes with these new techniques, the overall record is mixed at best. Sometimes the public simply isn't in a persuadable mood. Or a skeptical press corps questions the propriety of using taxpayer funds. Other times governors miscalculate, forgetting to touch base with key legislators, for example, or overestimating their own standing with the voters. Sometimes a victory in the short run has soured relations with the legislature for the long run.

Among today's governors, one of the most aggressive practitioners of campaign-style governance is Democrat Richard F. Celeste of Ohio. "Dick's a campaigner, and the ways he's dealt with running the state are a quintessential product of campaigning," says Paul Costello, a former top aide. Celeste hasn't hesitated to raise funds from political contributors to defend his policy objectives with television advertisements. He did just that to beat back a 1983 referendum that would have repealed a tax increase he had advocated and to soften the political damage from the state's savings-and-loan crisis in 1985, as well as to promote his annual State of the State addresses.

Celeste has one of the most extensive communications operations of any governor, with a full-time staff of 19 that includes radio and television specialists and also draws upon workers from other state agencies to help create events and otherwise arrange the governor's "thematic travel" around the state.

Efforts to ensure maximum press and public attention are a high priority. Last November, for example, when Celeste held a teleconference on revitalizing the state's manufacturing industries that was beamed to business leaders at seven sites across the state, author David Halberstam ("The Best and the Brightest") was brought in to moderate, and paid a $5,000 fee by the state Department of Development, to draw attention to the proceedings.

"Every governor looks at himself as a mini-president," says Ohio Senate President Stanley J. Aronoff, a Republican. "If presidents can do it and have sound bites and create PR opportunities, why can't a governor of a state, especially a state as populous as 12 million. . . . There are times when I'm annoyed and times when I think that form and style supersede substance . . . but I have to admit it's effective." And Representative Jim Petro, another Republican, concedes: "It makes it tougher for legislators to oppose him, because he builds a base of support over a particular issue." In 1988, Celeste began a major campaign to increase his visibility on education issues, which national polls had identified as a top public concern. His staff was instructed to "invent" events that could be "leveraged into a wider audience" through cable hookups, satellite transmission and other techniques. A successful example: He took poor kids from inner-city schools on tours of the state-of-the-art Cleveland Clinic, to open their eyes to the possibilities of careers in health care.

Later in the year, Celeste inaugurated an hour-long radio call-in program on education issues, using a satellite hookup to some 20 stations, which not only ensured good broadcast quality but also permitted the governor to conduct the program if he happened to be out of state. Eyebrows were raised when it was disclosed that the costs, in excess of $50,000, were paid out of Ohio Lottery funds. Celeste defended the spending on the grounds that proceeds from the lottery are earmarked for education.

(The use of state funds for a governor's PR activities often draws complaints, but they rarely stick. "Generally, I think the public doesn't blame you for it, as long as it looks like you're giving them information," says Karl Struble, a Washington-based political consultant who works for Democrats.)

As part of the education crusade, Celeste has conducted a Donahue-style television program, "School Talk with Governor Celeste," that was broadcast over the state's public television stations and local cable channels. Besides responding to the local studio audience, Celeste fielded viewer calls from around the state over eight toll-free lines. It was all part of an 18-month campaign to persuade the legislature to raise taxes to support major improvements in the state's educational system. Although some extra money was found through some budget juggling, Celeste lost on the tax increase—proof, if it was needed, that there are limits to these techniques.

Any tool can be dangerous, of course, particularly if it falls into careless hands. In Florida, Republican Governor Bob Martinez learned that last summer when he tried handling the volatile issue of abortion in the full glare of the media spotlight.

In three years as governor, Martinez never had a chance to address all his constituents at once. The state's multitude of television markets and local newspapers split every message like a prism: Big news in Miami could be no news in Jacksonville or Orlando. But last summer, getting into four million living rooms at once was a snap. "It's easy," says Jon Peck, the governor's press secretary. "Call the nation's first special session on abortion, and you'll get the national networks to your door." Events, of course, failed to work out as Martinez had planned. "I wouldn't advise other people to get that opportunity quite the same way," Peck says drily, after the legislature rejected all of the governor's anti-abortion proposals.

Martinez's setback was a reminder that statehouse politics, in this instance the fact that abortion-rights advocates controlled the key committees in the legislature, cannot be overlooked in the rush to the television studio.

Martinez has attempted to recoup, portraying the abortion debacle as an example of his determination to go to the mat for what he believes. His unwavering adherence to his anti-abortion views is now firmly fixed in voters' minds, and this fall's election will test whether the electorate prizes the governor's devotion to principle above the principles themselves. His staff argues that they do.

Many political analysts think otherwise, however, and rate Martinez as perhaps the most vulnerable Republican governor seeking re-election this year. But he is an exception. With such powerful communications tools at their disposal, governors should be recording re-election rates that approach the 98 percent mark established by Congress, according to political experts. "Given the media and how a governor can use the media," says Alan Rosenthal, a Rutgers University political scientist, "it seems to me that any governor should maintain a reasonably high level of popularity, barring scandal, economic recession or incredible stupidity."

Many of the new techniques are simply updated versions of tactics that governors have used for years. The classic approach in going to the people is the one favored by Republican Governor George Deukmejian of California during his first year in office. With the state's budget running more than $1 billion in the red, the governor went on the air three times in six months, beseeching the public, in one statewide TV address, to pressure the Democratic-controlled legislature to stop "holding the state hostage." The timing of Deukmejian's live speeches was critical to their success. The governor's office was able to assemble its own TV network on 24 hours' notice, using a Sacramento station to bounce the address off a satellite to stations around the state. Deukmejian spoke at 5 p.m., just as the local news began in many of the state's media markets. Stations were forced to let the governor lead their newscast, or risk being beaten on the story.

Although Deukmejian failed to generate the hoped-for outpouring of mail and calls, he did force a compromise on the legislature. His advisers credit the public relations campaign as a crucial element in the victory.

Deukmejian also makes weekly radio addresses on Saturdays, sometimes including newsworthy announcements that the press has to report without further elaboration from him—or his critics. Like former President Ronald Reagan's Saturday radio broadcasts, Deukmejian's sometimes make the lead story for the skinny Saturday night TV and radio news programs and the Sunday papers.

Deukmejian's tactics, in fact, are consciously modeled on Reagan's. But neither was the first to go over the heads of the California legislature using electronic media. That honor fell to a liberal Democrat named Culbert L. Olson, who made a series of 15-minute radio broadcasts in the late 1930s and early 1940s (inspired, no doubt, by Franklin D. Roosevelt's fireside chats) to appeal for public support in his battles against the legislature. Olson's strategy failed, however, and he was voted out of office after one term.

When Deukmejian tried his end run around the legislature in 1983, skeptics predicted that the newly elected governor would suffer the same fate. In fact, Deukmejian was re-elected by a bigger margin than Reagan ever achieved in the state. Steve Merksamer, Deukmejian's former chief of staff, attributes much of the governor's political success to television. "Even for a noncharismatic type" like Deukmejian, he says, television has become an essential tool for building and maintaining public support on the state level.

Despite its obvious appeal to action-oriented governors, going around the legislature and making your pitch directly to the people is clearly a high-risk strategy. Even when it succeeds, it can often leave a residue of bitter feelings that can complicate future relations between the executive and the legislature. "All it does is make [legislators] mad," says California House Speaker Willie Brown, a Democrat. Former California Governor Jerry Brown, also a Democrat, agrees. "These are people you have to work with for four years. They control your budget in many cases, and confrontation with them is counterproductive." Brown learned that the hard way, by experience.

Democrat Bill Clinton of Arkansas is another governor who has seen the cost of winning by going around the legislature. He picked the fight. In 1987, after his legislature, not for the first time, rejected a proposed tax increase, he responded by creating an ethics commission to draft legislation strengthening standards of official conduct for public officials and for the first time requiring public disclosure of lobbyists' spending—a clear attempt to depict legislators in thrall to special interests. When the Senate defeated the ethics bill, too, Clinton announced a petition drive to put the initiative on the November ballot, to let the people decide.

"We ran that like a county campaign," says Betsey Wright, until recently the governor's chief of staff, who had also served as his campaign manager. Clinton personally took part in media events, standing outside a supermarket in Little Rock, for example, clipboard in hand, to gather signatures. He made a televised address. The ad campaign made heavy use of radio, still the most economical way to reach into every part of the state. In some respects, it was a rerun of the largely successful campaign for an education reform package and tax increase that Clinton had put on five years earlier, with paid television commercials and direct mail to target the message. The ethics initiative won in November, but the voters rejected an accompanying constitutional amendment that would have made it easier to raise taxes.

It all generated "a lot of resentment" for the next legislative session, says Mike Gauldin, the governor's press secretary. A proposed tax increase to fund an ambitious education and industrial development plan was shot down. The governor's failure to contact some legislators before announcing his proposals "antagonized them from the beginning," says Cal Ledbetter, a former legislator and now a political science professor at the University of Arkansas in Little Rock.

There is, however, another, less confrontational path, one that more and more governors are following. As Rutgers University's Alan Rosenthal points out, many governors now go to the public first, to build public support for one or two major programs. Only then are they taking their ideas to the legislature, making legislators feel like they are playing a key role in developing the program and, in some cases, giving them the public opinion "cover" they need to do things like raise taxes. Sometimes, it is only when the program is passed that the governor finally steps forward to claim the credit.

Vermont's Democratic governor, Madeleine M. Kunin, successfully used such an approach on the sensitive issue of private development. To draft laws that would help planners limit the state's rapid growth, she turned to that well-tested American device, the blue-ribbon panel. She named Douglas Costle, who had headed the federal Environmental Protection Agency under President Jimmy Carter, to chair a special commission that toured the state and found (surprise!) that many Vermonters felt that exploding development was destroying the state's cherished rural atmosphere. The governor herself took an active role, meeting with newspaper editors, showing up at one of 11 public hearings held around Vermont, promoting the issue on her public television call-in show and inviting leading TV, radio and newspaper executives

to her office to enlist their help. In addition, she appeared in television and radio advertisements that the state's media outlets agreed to run at no charge, as a public service. When Kunin finally unveiled her plan, in a dramatic State of the State address in January 1988, special-interest groups that were resisting the initiative were hopelessly outmaneuvered. The plan was approved by the legislature.

In 1986 in Virginia, then-Governor Gerald L. Baliles, a Democrat, launched a vigorous, campaign-style crusade designed to make it easier for legislators to vote for billions in new road construction money. Throughout most of the year, his first in office, he barnstormed, delivering speeches, broadcasting to radio audiences from a plane used for commuter traffic reports, appointing a study commission and providing recorded "sound bites" for radio from his Richmond press office.

"In terms of strategy, it had a lot of similarities to the campaign [for governor] because you wanted to get a message out," says Chris Bridge, the governor's communications director. "The issue had to strike a chord. It had to resonate with people." It resonated with the legislature, which passed a gasoline tax increase and approved the governor's plan for highway construction bonds.

As in a political campaign, keeping the message focused is crucial. When former Tennessee Governor Lamar Alexander was pushing his $1.2 billion Better Schools Program, "he drove his staff and everybody close to him absolutely nuts because he never talked about anything else," says Douglas Bailey, his media consultant. "Every speech was devoted to it. Every time he would open his mouth, the same words came out." That is, of course, a basic tenet of any political campaign. About the time the staff is saying they'll go crazy if they have to listen to the same message one more time, the public is just beginning to hear it. But the effort paid off, as the Republican governor overcame powerful opposition from the state teachers' union and persuaded the Democratic legislature to implement a sales tax increase and one of the nation's first merit pay plans for teachers.

Successful governing techniques have a way of spreading. One that is widely used now is moving the governor and other key officials to different communities around the state for a day or two. Usually, the governor will hold a press conference, deliver a speech, tour a school or other facility and meet with the editorial board of the local paper. But what is more significant, he also goes about his daily routine; many governors bring their cabinet along. The idea is to dramatize the governor's desire to stay close to the people.

Former Governor Lamm, who credits the Capitol for a Day idea to Alaska Republican Jay Hammond, sees it as a powerful tool. "You can issue a thousand press releases and send them off to the local newspaper, and it will not have the impact of going there." A day of activities in a community has far more impact than the old-fashioned civic club speech. "I would come to a town and speak to the Rotary Club, and people would never really connect with the fact that I had been there," says Lamm. "And yet when I did Capitol for a Day, they really knew that I was in the community." He is frank to call the traveling road show "a very self-interested

gimmick." (His successor, Democrat Roy Romer, has continued the device but with an inspired new name: "Dome on the Range.") But more than image-building can result. It can also give the governor a clearer idea of what people are thinking outside the parochial precincts of the capital city. It can even make a governor a better administrator. Lamm says he learned a great deal about the capabilities of his cabinet members by watching them perform at such events.

Naturally, any PR stunt is sure to produce carping from political opponents. Capitol for a Day programs are vulnerable to critics in the legislature who question the expense in time and money, which is borne by the state. But wise governors co-opt their critics by inviting the local legislators, regardless of party, to come along. "My experience was they were just tickled for you to be in their community, no matter how partisan they were," says Lamm, a Democrat who dealt successfully with a generally Republican-led legislature throughout his 12-year tenure. He also was careful, he says, to avoid overt partisan activities. He refused, for instance, the entreaties of the local party chairman to speak to the county Democratic organization while he was in town.

Lamm regards such modern communications techniques as simply another way of lobbying. "An unlobbied agenda is doomed to a small chance of success," he says.

Jim Martin: The Governors' Man

by Jacqueline Calmes

The nation's governors had spoken. Gathered in Chicago last summer for their annual meeting, they issued a resolution calling on Congress to freeze further costly mandates requiring their states to expand Medicaid coverage. Many of them probably felt that action should suffice. But Jim Martin, the National Governors' Association's [NGA] chief Washington lobbyist, knew that his job— and theirs—was just beginning.

Working with the governors' offices, Martin started by compiling state-by-state calculations of the mandates' potential impact on state budgets. Next he got a number of the governors, particularly those whose U.S. senators or representatives are members of the congressional leadership or key committees, to write, call and visit those lawmakers. Then Martin made the rounds himself.

A typical stop was the office of U.S. Senator Dave Durenberger, a Minnesota Republican who is on the Senate Finance Committee and one of its experts on Medicaid. "Durenberger has known me for years, but he asked, 'Where's Perpich on this?'" Martin recalls, referring to Minnesota's Democratic governor, Rudy Perpich. "I make sure Perpich follows through.

"Just sending a resolution to Capitol Hill is like mailing a dead letter," Martin says. "I'm constantly lobbying the governors to follow through. I treat them as the lobbyists for NGA, not myself. After all, the members of Congress aren't going to pay attention to me, but they'll pay attention to their governors."

For nearly a quarter-century, James L. Martin has tended to the states' interests in Washington, always insisting on an uncredited, supporting role. In that time, NGA's federal lobbying force has grown from one— Martin—to a dozen. But the real lobbyists, as Martin sees it, are the 50 governors.

Yet, as emphatic as Martin is about remaining behind the scenes, he is hardly unknown in official Washington. J. Thomas Cochran, executive director of the U.S. Conference of Mayors, recalls a meeting of governors and mayors with former Democratic Senator Russell Long of Louisiana about revenue sharing. The legendary Finance Committee chairman regaled the assembled officials with the legislative history of the program, and then abruptly turned aside to Martin and said,

Jacqueline Calmes is a reporter for the *Congressional Quarterly Weekly Report*. This article is reprinted from *Governing* 3:2 (November 1989): 64-68.

"*You* were there. *You* remember all of this." The red-faced Irishman, momentarily forced out of his preferred shadows, blushed scarlet.

The anecdote illustrates not only Martin's familiarity on Capitol Hill but also the institutional memory for which he is recognized after 22 years as NGA's legislative counsel. Martin was among the pioneers as state and local governments staked out a presence in Washington, first to get a share of a growing federal pie and lately to defend their interests as the pie shrinks. As such, he has become something of a model for the public-sector lobbyist.

Despite a professional lifetime in Washington, Martin has developed and retained a fierce loyalty to the state capitals. He frequently is allied with other members of the intergovernmental "family," the groups representing state, county and municipal governments. Likewise, he has figured in the family's feuds, most recently over legislation to require out-of-state mail order houses to remit state and local sales taxes. But Martin's biggest wars have been with himself; for years he struggled against alcoholism even as his commitment to his religion grew firmer. From the professional battles, he has emerged with some critics, but with his reputation and his reservoir of respect intact.

"Jim Martin really has as much of a grasp of what's happening in Washington, plus what's happening back in the states, as anyone I've ever run into," said John H. Sununu, the former Republican governor of New Hampshire who now is White House chief of staff. "He knows the way Congress works, he knows the personalities of congressmen and senators and he has good working relationships with congressional staffs. And that really has made a tremendous difference in a lot of things governors have worked on over the years."

Sununu singles out the 1988 law over-hauling welfare, an NGA priority that was tortuously hammered out between the Democratic Congress and the Reagan administration, mostly while Sununu was NGA chairman. In the end, Reagan accepted a variety of new job-training, work, education and health-care provisions to help get welfare recipients off the dole, in exchange for the first-ever federal workfare requirement on beneficiaries.

Amid the final critical maneuvering, Sununu said, Martin helped craft a strategy to extract the necessary trade-offs from both sides and enlisted Sununu as NGA's lobbyist to Sununu's fellow Republican conservative, the president.

"It got to the point where some of the give-and-take required convincing the administration that we were not caving in to liberal congressional tendencies," Sununu recalled. "I guess I had the credibility to communicate why it was good for the country to make some of the changes that we felt could work. And Jim was smart enough to identify which issues had to be worked on in order to get congressional concessions and then made the recommendations that if we could get a little change here or there from the administration, then we could get the additional concessions from Congress. And it worked."

Similarly, in Congress, Arkansas Governor Bill Clinton assiduously lobbied his fellow Democrats while Delaware Governor Michael N. Castle did the same among balky Republicans.

"Governors don't have the time to worry about strategy and how to do all that needs to be done," Martin says. "But hopefully we can arrange their schedules to fit so that we can bring them in when needed. Sometimes all they have to do is make a phone call."

Robert Fulton, now Oklahoma Governor Henry Bellmon's secretary of social services, was a top Senate Budget Committee staffer from 1977 to 1983, when Bellmon was the

Governors Scramble Signals

The nation's governors, active participants in efforts to craft a federal child-care bill, apparently got some of their wires crossed the week of Oct. 2 [, 1989].

The problems started when Rep[s]. Charles W. Stenholm, D-Texas, and E. Clay Shaw Jr., R-Fla., asked the National Governors' Association (NGA) whether their substitute for the child-care provisions contained in HR 3299, the fiscal 1990 budget-reconciliation bill, was consistent with NGA's official policy regarding federal child-care legislation.

After consulting by telephone with Arkansas Democrat Bill Clinton and New Jersey Republican Thomas H. Kean, the organization's designated "lead governors" on the issue, NGA Executive Director Raymond C. Scheppach wrote Stenholm an affirmative response. "Only your bill is consistent with the governors' child-care policy, because it provides for a grant program that allows states the flexibility to tailor programs to meet their individual needs," said the Oct. 3 letter.

That upset backers of the provisions already in the bill, because they had purposely included language close to that of the Senate-passed child-care measure, S 5, which the NGA had officially endorsed.

It apparently upset Clinton as well. He disavowed the language in an Oct. 4 letter to Education and Labor Committee Chairman Augustus F. Hawkins, D-Calif. "Neither I nor to my knowledge any other Democratic governor authorized the version of the National Governors' Association letter to Reps. Stenholm and Shaw stating their bill is the 'only' bill before the House consistent with the NGA policy," Clinton wrote.

Scheppach said Oct. 5 that the wording in the Oct. 3 letter to Stenholm was a mistake. "We had a screw-up in staff where the 'only' got in inadvertently," he said, noting that another Oct. 3 letter to all members of the House said only that the Stenholm-Shaw substitute "is consistent with the governors' child-care policy."

But that did not end the fight. Nine Democratic governors, led by Maryland's William Donald Schaefer and Ohio's Richard F. Celeste, wrote an Oct. 4 letter to House Speaker Thomas S. Foley, D-Wash., stating that even the correct version of Scheppach's letter "does not represent the views of many governors."

They added: "Please note that the letter does not carry the signature of any governor." Noting that the Stenholm-Shaw plan would delete "over a billion dollars in critically needed federal child-care authorization from the reconciliation bill," the nine governors continued, "We are urging our congressional delegations to support the child-care provisions included in reconciliation and to oppose the Stenholm-Shaw and Edwards substitutes."

Source: Julie Rovner, "Governors Scramble Signals," *Congressional Quarterly Weekly Report* (October 7, 1989), 2640.

committee's senior Republican. Fulton recalls that Martin "was not tremendously visible on the Hill. Jim was around, but he's never a witness, for example, at hearings. He's always prepping governors—a real behind-the-scenes man."

Stewart Gamage, former head of Virginia's Washington office under Democratic Governors Charles S. Robb and Gerald L. Baliles and now an aide to House Majority Leader

Richard A. Gephardt, a Missouri Democrat, says of Martin, "For 20 some years, he's been out there taking the governors through the 101, 102 and post-graduate courses, but you would never know that to talk to him. He is never there to take the credit. The credit always goes to the governors."

While Martin banks heavily on the governors' influence, perhaps as important as that medium is the message each governor carries.

The NGA adopts its policy positions at its annual winter and summer meetings, after at least two-thirds of all governors approve. Martin is guided by those general positions in mapping his stance on more specific legislation and proposed administration regulations.

Understanding as well as anyone in Washington that information is power, he marshals all the data and intelligence he can, both to keep abreast of proposals critical to the states and to make sure that federal policy makers are aware of the proposals' possible impact on the states and their governments.

"Jim is a good lobbyist of the kind I call the informational lobbyist, the kind I liked," says Richard N. Brandon, former staff director of the Senate Budget Committee. "It's not the pressure thing with him."

In the 1980s, with the White House and Congress consumed by budget cutting and states on the defensive, Martin has focused on the executive branch offices and the congressional committees responsible for budget and tax laws. Their proposals in hand, he gathers the information about the costs to states.

Much of that is within Martin's grasp in the Hall of the States, an office complex a few blocks from the Capitol that is home not only to NGA's staff, which has grown in Martin's time from four to more than 100, but also to the Washington liaison offices of 27 states, the National Association of State Budget Officers and the Federal Funds Information for the States, which provides computerized break-downs and projections for the flow of federal money.

Armed with timely printouts of some proposal's adverse impact, Martin mobilizes opposition among the states' lobbyists and, in turn, among their senators and representatives; in conversation, he seems always to be reaching for some sheet crammed with numbers to make a point. "He's found a niche that's data-oriented," says Fulton.

Such ammunition was a factor in 1981, when the NGA helped defeat Reagan's proposed cap on federal Medicaid spending, one of the president's few setbacks in his honeymoon budget outing. Martin and NGA have been less successful since then in dissuading Congress from mandating expanded state Medicaid spending. At best, they have been able, working with the Senate and the administration, to limit the proposals that seem to perennially come out of the House.

The fiscal minutiae that Martin relies on to make his arguments is actually the work of others. He is best known for taking a broad-brush approach to federal-state relations, so much so that some associates have said privately that he's not a detail man. "I see Jim as someone with broader vision, and given his responsibility to the governors, that's appropriate," says Frank Shafroth, who is the director of federal relations for the National League of Cities. "I think he complements Ray [Scheppach, the NGA executive director] in that capacity, and there's good staff behind him. . . . Jim gets really excited about a program or an idea and loves to talk about it, and presumes that the idea on its merits is what's going to move the thing."

Shafroth said both he and Martin puzzled colleagues by the tenacity of their work in the past year to soften the economic impact of an agreement between the White House and Congress to close a number of military bases. "How it will spell out in the end is not fully clear," Shafroth says, "but the law now provides the flexibility to state and local governments to have access to those base facilities. They aren't going to be sold automatically to the highest bidder in the private sector.

"I think a lot of people thought we were both a little crazy to devote as much time to it as we did, but these are important things because in the end they're going to make a difference to a lot of states and communities. But for Jim, I think the law would have been very different in the end."

Martin's work with Shafroth on that issue was just one of many examples over the years of the alliances among public-sector lobbyists. But just as well known are their fights, especially the prolonged tug-of-war between state and local governments over the division of revenue-sharing funds and the Reagan-era debate over New Federalism. Perhaps nothing, however, so threatened Martin's standing among his public-sector contemporaries as the *Bellas Hess* issue.

[In 1989], some representatives of local governments complained that NGA, in cahoots with House Judiciary Committee Chairman Jack Brooks, a Texas Democrat, had reneged on a deal to back legislation that would overturn the Supreme Court's 1967 decision in *National Bellas Hess v. Illinois Department of Revenue* and force mail order houses to collect both state and local sales taxes from their out-of-state customers. Under the since-abandoned compromise, the taxes would have been paid to the states, which in turn would have remitted appropriate shares to localities. Brooks instead introduced simpler legislation that would not require states to collect revenues for the localities.

A round of name-calling and finger-pointing ensued, some of it directed at Martin.

"We had an agreement, and then I see him up there [at the Capitol] lobbying for something that was not the agreement," says

Lance Simmens of the U.S. Conference of Mayors. "It leaves a sour taste in your mouth."

Martin vigorously denies that he and NGA bargained covertly with Brooks. And one of the most embittered parties, Cochran of the mayors' conference, says, "Believe me, I have no bad feeling about Jim Martin. I'm just very disappointed in the process."

Likewise, Shafroth says he does not blame Martin, but—like Cochran—he notes that some others do if only because Martin is so identified with the states, the beneficiaries under Brooks' bill. "I certainly have one staff person in mind who felt that Jim was not always honest and forthright," Shafroth says. "I don't agree with that. I've never known Jim to be in any way dishonest."

Martin is known among both his friends and some professional colleagues for his commitment to his religion: He is a fundamentalist Christian. That's not because he is known to proselytize or preach. Rather, it is the evidence they see that Martin's religious beliefs, not political ideology, guide his approach to his job.

"He's committed in many ways to what the Conference of Mayors is committed to on a daily basis: the disadvantaged and the people who are hurting in this country," says Cochran, citing such problems as AIDS, poverty and drugs. "It's a moral thing with him. You can sense that he feels it personally."

Bernard F. Hillenbrand, for many years the executive director of the National Association of Counties [NACo], hired Martin as his assistant in 1963. Now a Methodist minister, Hillenbrand says that Martin views his job the same way that Hillenbrand saw his at NACo: as "a holy mission."

For his part, Martin simply says, "I'm working where I'm supposed to work. There is an element of seeking justice and rightness for poor people that enters into everything you do in public service." . . .

Outside NGA, some of Martin's colleagues wonder why, after all the years, Martin isn't tapped to run the association, to be its executive director. "That's not to say anything against Ray Scheppach, but it's just that Jim is like the Gromyko of the governors' association," Cochran says, referring to the late Soviet official who held top posts for decades, surviving a succession of Communist Party leaders. "Executive directors come and they go, and Jim is always there."

Martin says simply of his longtime post, "It's a good job." And Farber suggests that the executive directorship is not in Martin's sights. "Jim's love is not administration. It is not the oversight of a large organization. His love is lobbying for the governors' interests."

In recognition of that, in 1987 the governors gave Martin a standing ovation and a warm proclamation in honor of his 20th anniversary with NGA. One line is Martin's obvious favorite. It's the one that says he's "the only person who's lived in Washington, D.C., for 20 years who still thinks governors are the best public officials in America." And the best lobbyists, Martin might have added.

VII. STATE BUREAUCRACIES AND ADMINISTRATION

Departments and agencies within each state carry out the laws passed by the legislature and approved by the governor. These departments vary in size and in responsiveness to executive control. Transportation, human services, corrections, education, and health usually are large departments with sizable budgets and staffs. These "big ticket" agencies perform services quite visible to the public, and governors and legislators alike pay close attention to them. Governors appoint the heads of these agencies with great care, and the legislature often must confirm the appointments.

Many parts of the state bureaucracy, however, appear to be remarkably immune to the vagaries of legislative and gubernatorial politics. The key to successful bureaucratic politics is to keep a low profile. Governors come and go, legislators come and go, but some agencies keep on doing what they have always done with minimum intrusion from outside. State government encompasses so many agencies and activities that it is virtually impossible for the governor and the legislature to keep track of them all.

Between a Rock and a Hard Place?

State bureaucrats—this is not a derogatory term—often are torn by competing values: economy and efficiency on the one hand and political expediency on the other. In the results-oriented world of politics, points often are scored for achieving an electorally advantageous goal rather than for saving money or doing a job efficiently.

Another problem is accountability. To whom are state employees accountable? To the governor, the legislature or particular legislators, the interest served by the agency, the public at large, themselves? The numerous lines of accountability give those in the state bureaucracy the opportunity to play one group against another and thereby do what they want.

In recent years important changes have been made that have improved the caliber of the states' work forces. The standards for hiring, promotion, and retention have been raised. Educational requirements are more exacting. In-service training has been upgraded. State employees who report wrongdoing in state government—"whistleblowers"—are better protected against retaliation. And more employees are covered by civil service and merit systems, which has reduced the number of patronage positions. Moreover, now minorities have better opportunities for employment and advancement within state government.

Another related development has been the growing political influence of state employee organizations. State employee groups and state employee labor unions have become stronger in almost all of the states. Like other interests, they lobby their own concerns and proposals before the governor and the state legislature and with increasing effectiveness. What do they want for their efforts? Higher wages, better health and retirement benefits, and more recognition of their professional status. When it comes to preparing the budget, the most influential parties often are those who carry out the intent of the budget—namely, state employees.

Organizational Problems

How are state agencies organized? Some would argue they aren't. Governors trying to "run" state government or citizens trying to find out where to get help often are baffled by the apparent organizational chaos of the many departments and agencies. Periodically, the states reorganize their executive branch departments. This usually is done either to improve economy and efficiency, to clear up the lines of accountability so that the governor is the chief executive in fact rather than in theory, or to gain control over some agencies that are perceived as out of control—usually the control of the governor or of the legislature.

Not surprisingly, reorganization often is resisted by the agencies themselves and by groups with vested interests in the way things are. Those who know how the system works prefer the status quo and are extremely reluctant to learn new ways. And when the goal is to give the governor more power and influence, the agencies fight hard: they are far from willing to lose or share their power. Organizational battles are so difficult to mount and win that many governors and legislatures avoid them, believing victory is not worth the political costs.

Republican governors have been particularly attracted to setting up economy and efficiency commissions to survey state government programs, organizations, and policies in an effort to find ways to save the taxpayers money. These commissions, which usually are made up of members of the business community and supported by an out-of-state consulting firm specializing in such studies, review a state's budget, governmental organization, and programs. The commission issues a well-publicized final report pointing out waste in state government and indicates 300-400 suggested changes as to how the state could save millions of dollars.

Some of the suggested changes make sense; others do not. They usually include some reorganization and consolidation of agencies, turning over some of what the agencies do to the private sector (privatization), eliminating some programs, charging or increasing user fees for some services, or transferring a program to another level of government.[1] One observer concludes that such studies have "been largely discredited" and may be more "a political than an administrative tool."[2] Even reorganizations have been criticized as doing more to spawn confusion "about program goals and work responsibilities" and sparking "political brushfires" that keep "managers from getting back to those basic issues of responsibility and accountability."[3]

Major executive branch reorganization efforts have occurred in twenty-three states since the 1960s. The goals usually articulated in these efforts were "modernization and streamlining of the executive branch machinery, efficiency, economy, responsiveness, and gubernatorial control."[4] These reorganizations are not apolitical events; they involve a battle for power among the branches of government. Aside from the built-in resistance that state bureaucrats have to such changes, governors and legislatures often are at odds over some of these proposals because they usually increase the power of the governor over the executive branch at the expense of the legislature. For example, the number of independent boards, commissions, and agencies usually declines precipitously, such as in Georgia, where the number of such units dropped from 300 to 22, or in Louisiana, where the drop was from 300 to 19.[5] Going from the many to the few, with the few being directed by gubernatorial appointees rather than by a multiperson board, means more control for the governor and less access for the legislature. The most recent example of success in this occurred in 1989, when West Virginia Governor Gaston Caperton gained legislative approval for consolidating 150 executive boards and agencies into seven departments.[6]

Rather than seek major reorganization of the bureaucratic structure, state leaders may attempt partial reform when there is a pressing need to consolidate overlapping and confusing jurisdictions, or when they wish to tackle a particular problem facing the state and eliminate organizational barriers. This has been especially important in economic development, in the environmental area, and in the actual administration of state government.

Since the mid-1970s, thirty-six states have followed Colorado's lead and adopted some form of sunset legislation—legislation that calls for the automatic termination of an agency, board, or commission unless the legislature reauthorizes or reestablishes it. Licensing and regulatory agencies are the agencies most often governed by sunset laws. However, six states have since repealed their sunset laws, and six other states have allowed their laws to lapse into inactivity.[7] Many states also have passed "open government" laws to give the media and interested citizens better access to the activities and records of state government.

Management and Personnel Changes

Where the states have made the most headway is in adopting new management techniques. Budgets no longer are worked out in the back rooms of statehouses by employees wearing green eye shades; they are part of a larger policy-management process headed by the governor. In many states, policy, planning, and budgeting are treated as a whole process, not to be separated by competing political fiefdoms. However, according to two recent surveys, more than half the states still have poor central management of state government.[8]

Changes in state government administration and personnel have been made but not without considerable furor. Controversies over affirmative action (Should minorities have a leg up in hiring and promotions?) and comparable worth (Should men and women be paid equally for dissimilar jobs of similar skill levels?) are bedeviling state legislators and administrators. A March 1987 U.S. Supreme Court decision, *Johnson v. Transportation Agency, Santa Clara County, Calif.,* support-

ing the promotion of a woman over a slightly more qualified man in a local government personnel situation, indicates judicial branch support for affirmative action principles. Another Supreme Court decision, *City of Richmond v. Croson* (1989), declared unconstitutional another state and local government affirmative action effort called set-asides, in which a fixed portion of public works funds are reserved for minority-owned companies. Using the legal concept of strict scrutiny, the Court argued any such programs must meet a compelling state interest to be used. The concept of strict scrutiny historically has been difficult to specify legally, especially in the area of racial discrimination.[9]

Politically, it makes sense to open up jobs for women and other minorities; they are becoming more active in politics and their support often is needed to win elections. Hence, it is no surprise that the number of women in state-level cabinet positions increased by 114 percent between 1981 and 1989. In a 1989 survey of the forty states with a cabinet structure of government, women held 150 of the 703 cabinet-level positions, or 21 percent. The number of women in these cabinet positions varies from zero in Missouri to eight in Illinois and ten in Vermont.[10] The director of administration in Louisiana said she still sees evidence of male chauvinism in state government but felt "the good ol' boy network is aging and it is likely I will live to see their replacements." [11]

There have been considerable changes in the type of personnel working at the administrative level in state governments. According to Deil Wright, who has studied state administrators since 1964, the 1988 cadre of administrators differed from their 1964 counterparts in the following ways: there were fewer males (83 percent in 1988 vs. 98 percent in 1964); fewer whites (91 percent vs. 98 percent); they were younger (median age of 46 vs. 52); and better educated (only 1 percent had a high school education or less vs. 18 percent, and those with graduate or professional degrees rose from 40 percent to 55 percent over the period).[12]

Ethics

How government officials, elected or appointed, behave while in office is increasingly a topic of concern at the state level. We generally recognize a corrupt act—or do we? Handing cash to a public official to influence a decision would seem to be a corrupt act. But what about a public utility political action committee that contributes funds to incumbent legislators' campaigns so that legislators might look more favorably on revising the utility rate structure? Is that a corrupt act? Or is that politics?

Like beauty, corruption and ethical misbehavior often are in the eye of the beholder. Some states are trying to clarify this definition by establishing ethics codes, standards, and commissions. Recently, several states have established inspectors general offices to probe into allegations of wrongdoing in state government. In some instances, the inspectors general have the authority to "identify programs or departments that *might be vulnerable* to corruption. . . ."[13] Some observers suggest that these steps, along with measures to open up electoral and governmental processes and to develop accountability measures, "have . . . been at least as significant as the other reforms" occurring in the states over the past few decades.[14]

While there are several state governments with a history of ethical and corruption problems, few can match the current situation in West Virginia. Over the past year the following events have occurred: the popular, recently reelected state treasurer, A. James Manchin, was impeached and resigned in July 1989 after auditors found losses of

nearly $300 million in the state's Consolidated Investment Fund; state attorney general Charlie Brown resigned one month later after being accused of perjury during a custody hearing involving his ex-wife and daughter, and a grand jury that was investigating the perjury charges also subpoenaed Brown's campaign finance records from 1984 through 1988; three state senators were forced to resign, two over charges of taking money in return for votes, the other over a felony income tax charge; up to fifty other state and local officials were under investigation for alleged wrongdoing; and in April 1990, former governor Arch Moore (R, 1969-77, 1985-89) pleaded guilty to federal charges of extortion, mail fraud, tax fraud, and obstruction of justice.[15]

But that wasn't all. Shortly after the newly elected governor, Gaston Caperton (D), settled his messy divorce suit, his former wife announced her intention to seek the office of state treasurer. She won the Democratic Party nomination in May 1990. And the governor announced in May that he planned to marry the conductor of the Wheeling (West Virginia) Symphony.

Part VII explores some of these and other controversies concerning state bureaucracies. In *North Carolina Insight*, Tim Funk takes a critical look at the role and future of governors' efficiency study commissions. From *State Legislatures* comes two articles, one by Lon Mackelprang and Fred Becker, who review the practice of "contracting out" for government services, and the other by William T. Waren, who assesses the condition of minority set-aside programs after the U.S. Supreme Court's 1989 decision, *Richmond v. Croson*. Elder Witt from *Governing* looks at the question of corruption in state and local governments, and Fran Burke and George C. S. Benson examine how some states are addressing ethical problems.

Notes

1. Tim Funk, "Efficiency Study Commissions: Is an Old Idea a Bad Idea?" *North Carolina Insight* 11:4 (August 1989): 42-43, 46-50.

2. James K. Conant, "Reorganization and the Bottom Line," *Public Administration Review* 46:1 (January/February 1986): 48.

3. Les Garner, "Managing Change Through Organization Structure," *The Journal of State Government* 60:4 (July/August 1987): 194.

4. James K. Conant, "In the Shadow of Wilson and Brownlow: Executive Branch Reorganization in the States, 1965 to 1987," *Public Administration Review* 48:5 (September/October 1988): 895.

5. Ibid., 902.

6. Elder Witt, "A Governor Seeks Less Government," *Governing* 2:9 (June 1989): 66.

7. Richard C. Kearney, "Sunset: A Survey and Analysis of the State Experience," *Public Administration Review* 50:1 (January/February 1990): 66.

8. Coalition to Improve Management in State and Local Government, *The Governor's Management Improvement Program: How to Do It* (Washington, D.C.: National Academy of Public Administration, 1985); and Office of State Services, *Reorganization and Management Improvement Initiatives: An Essay on State Experience* (Washington, D.C.: National Governors' Association, 1986).

9. Linda Greenhouse, "Ruling Ends Part of Affirmative Action Debate," *New York Times News Service,* reprinted in [Raleigh] *News and Observer,* January 25, 1989, 2A.

10. National Women's Political Caucus, "More Women Hold Top State Positions," *USA Today,* February 27, 1989, 6A.

11. Mireille Grangenois Gates, "More Women Join State Cabinets," *USA Today,* October 24, 1986, 3A.

12. Data for 1988 provided by Deil S. Wright. For the comparison between the 1964 and 1984 results, see Peter J. Haas and Deil S. Wright, "Research Update: The Changing Profile of State Administrators," *The Journal of State Government* 60:6 (November/December 1987): 270-278.

13. Cheri Collis, "State Inspectors General: The Watchdog over State Agencies," *State Government News* 33:4 (April 1990): 13.

14. Fran Burke and George C. S. Benson, "Written Rules: State Ethics Codes, Commissions, and Conflicts," *The Journal of State Government* 62:5 (September/October 1989): 198.

15. No one has put together the whole story yet, but some of the pieces can be found in: "In Briefs: West Virginia," *Comparative State Politics Newsletter* 10:2 (April 1989); "West Virginia Woes," *State Policy Reports* 7:17 (September 1989): 30; "West Virginia Problems," *State Policy Reports* 7:24 (December 1989): 9; LaDonna Sloan, "In Briefs: West Virginia," *Comparative State Politics* 10:6 (December 1989): 37; and "West Virginia Problems," *State Policy Reports* 8:8 (April 1990): 24.

Efficiency Study Commissions:
Is an Old Idea a Bad Idea?

by Tim Funk

When prim, scholarly Woodrow Wilson stepped before Cornell University's Historical and Political Science Association in late 1886, he threw out what was then a young idea. Government should be studied, the college professor and future president told the group, to determine how it can do its job "with the utmost possible efficiency and the least possible cost either of money or of energy."

Edwin Siegelman, one of the editors of the then-new *Political Science Quarterly*, thought so much of Wilson's address that he asked to publish it in his magazine. The resulting article, "The Study of Administration," is noted today for establishing the confines of American public administration. Wilson eventually left academia for Democratic politics, taking his ideas about government to New Jersey's executive mansion and later to the White House.

Today, Wilson's "efficiency" banner is still being hoisted in the political arena—but mostly, it seems, by Republicans. President [Ronald] Reagan's Grace Commission recommended cost-cutting measures on the federal level. And, in North Carolina, GOP Govs. James E. Holshouser and James G. Martin launched "efficiency study commissions" shortly after taking office in 1973 and 1985.

Both Governors charged groups of North Carolina business executives with ferreting out waste and proposing ways to run government more like a business.

Do such efforts work? Academics have become skeptical of politicians' highly publicized attempts to make government more efficient by eliminating waste. But politicians still trumpet startling results: millions upon millions of tax dollars saved by the volunteer efforts of a part-time panel of sharp eyed businessmen, guided by a team of consultants.

In April 1988, Martin—like Wilson, an academic-turned-politician—summoned reporters to the state Administration Building to deliver a status report on implementation of his commission's recommendations. "It should be remembered that the commission's study had two goals," said Martin, whose high-minded words sometimes echoed Wilson's.

Tim Funk is a reporter for *The Charlotte Observer*. This article is published with permission of the N.C. Center for Public Policy Research, an independent research and educational institution formed to study state government policies and practices. It originally appeared in *North Carolina Insight* 11:4 (August 1989): 42-50, the quarterly journal of the North Carolina Center for Public Policy Research.

"The first was to pinpoint changes that could be made to save time and money. But the second goal was to infuse an overall attitude of efficiency into state government operations. It has done that, and this is one of the many reasons behind its great success."

Of the 414 recommendations, state agencies agreed to implement 301, Martin said, although some of these would need legislative approval. Four others were to be given "further study." Some of the ideas implemented were small and amounted to little more than common sense; the Lieutenant Governor's office agreed to buy a $900 "envelope imprinter" so a clerk didn't have to spend her time addressing the envelopes manually. Others were structural and ambitious, although in at least one case the Martin administration claimed credit for a major structural change that did not take place. The 1988 status report claims a savings of $20.6 million for "reorganizing the office of chief engineer." Jim Sughrue, the department's assistant secretary for external affairs, says the chief engineer's office has not been reorganized. Sughrue says efficiency-related changes such as using private contractors to mow grass along highways and paying entry-level workers an hourly wage with limited benefits account for the $20.6 million in savings. "We've instituted some of the spirit of the recommendations," says Sughrue. "I don't think it was the direct result of their recommendations."

And some of the recommendations were more like hidden tax increases than efficiency measures. The Revenue Department, which had been charging merchants a one-time registration fee of $5, boosted the fee to $20 to "cover related processing costs." The change was to bring in $465,000.

In his news conference, the Governor said implementing the 301 recommendations would save the taxpayers more than $127 million a year. He also said there would be an additional one-time savings of $22 million—most of it from the sale of surplus property. This bonanza of savings came at minimal cost to the state, Martin administration officials said. Businesses donated the time of 73 loaned executives, and cash contributions covered the roughly $500,000 in consultant fees and publication expenses. The only direct cost to the state was the time of State Budget Office employees who provided administrative support and other state employees who were interviewed during the course of the study.

Nobody has come forward to challenge Martin's figures. But according to prevailing opinion among political scientists and public administration professors, claims of saving significant sums of money through efficiency studies are questionable. "In sharp contrast to this optimistic political rhetoric, reorganization for economy and efficiency has been largely discredited in the contemporary academic literature," writes James Conant, an assistant professor in public administration at New York University, in a 1986 article, "Reorganization and the Bottom Line." Indeed, Conant adds, "modern political scientists tend to think of reorganization as a political rather than an administrative tool."

Efficiency commissions often advise reorganizing and consolidating government operations to save money. Martin's commission, like the Holshouser commission before it, was no different in this regard. But Les Garner, president of North Carolina Wesleyan College and a former business professor at the University of North Carolina at Chapel Hill, concludes in a 1987 article that reorganization also can make government *less* efficient. He cites Florida's efforts in the mid-1970s to streamline its human services delivery system as an example. "Reorganization spawned confusion about program goals and work responsibilities," writes Garner, who served on a 1986 review team assembled by the Florida

Governor's Constituency for Children. "It also sparked political brushfires, the resolution of which kept managers from getting back to those basic issues of responsibility and accountability."

Conant argues that while efficiency studies may identify areas of potential savings, these dollars are generally applied toward other purposes rather than returned to the taxpayers.

So whom is one to believe about the latest North Carolina efficiency effort? Martin, who says his commission's ideas saved the state millions? Or the academics, whose articles suggest that such efforts are largely political?

Conant attempted an evaluation of an effort similar to Martin's in his article. Conant sought to calculate the real impact of New Jersey Gov. Thomas Kean's 1982 efficiency study—dubbed the Governor's Management Improvement Program. Kean, [a Republican] like Martin . . ., claimed that implementation of his recommendations—produced by a corps of business executives—saved New Jersey $102 million.

Conant sorted through conflicting claims of the Republican administration and the Democratic legislature and found both lacking. The Kean administration based its $102 million figure on what it labeled "cost avoidance." The administration took a four-year average of department-by-department increases in the state budget to arrive at a projected need for fiscal year 1984. The actual 1984 appropriations then were subtracted from the projected need figures and the total difference was touted as the "cost" avoided by Kean's efficiency panel. Democratic lawmakers used a bottom-line argument; the overall actual budget increased by 5.9 percent in fiscal year 1984; therefore, Kean's commission produced no savings. Conant undertook what he considered to be a more objective review than either the

Republican Kean administration or the Democratic legislature. He conducted exhaustive interviews to compile a series of "departmental inventories"—lists of actual savings in five of 20 departments, savings that could be documented.

Assuming the savings in the five departments were representative of savings throughout state government, Conant postulated that the New Jersey plan did produce some real savings—about half the amount claimed by the Governor. But he also found that these savings did not produce a net reduction in the bottom line because the money saved was used elsewhere in government. "The most important finding of this analysis is that no matter what the size of the savings increment . . . the bottom line will probably go up, not down," he writes. "New programs will be added, costs will increase, and the savings achieved through reorganization will be used to meet unfunded costs or be reinvested in higher priority areas. If government officials want to reverse this trend, if they really want to reduce the bottom line, they must resort to curtailment of public services and programs. Administrative reorganization will not provide the means to get a net reduction in the bottom line."

What Conant said about New Jersey may hold for North Carolina. Martin's commission produced just over $127 million in recurring, annual savings, or a little more than 1 percent of the overall state budget. This amount, cited by Martin at his 1988 news conference, represents money the Governor says otherwise would have been spent. But an inspection of Martin's own proposed budget for 1989-1990 shows that, if approved by the legislature, appropriations and the number of state employees would go up, not down. The Governor even proposed a 1-cent increase in the state sales tax to raise more money to spend. . . .

Hiring Outside Help

by Lon Mackelprang and Fred Becker

Hiring private businesses to provide government services re-emerged in the late 1970s as an important political idea and is likely to remain a controversial issue to the end of this century.

At issue is how far state and local governments should go with private contracting. And according to a recent survey conducted by Sangamon State University, lawmakers have very definite viewpoints.

Using private companies as an alternative means for providing public services is as old as the Republic itself. In 1792, Pennsylvania delegated to private organizations broad franchise powers to finance, construct, operate and maintain some of its roadways and bridges. Other states pretty much followed Pennsylvania's lead at that time, but as states grew stronger fiscally, the need for private highways diminished.

These early private transportation systems set a precedent, however, and the idea of private contracting spread into other areas. Over the years, outside contractors have been used in public works, refuse collection, maintenance and support services and for various social administrative services.

What is new in the 1980s is the accelerated growth in private contracting by government and its extension into new areas. Caught between the public's demand for more services and dwindling resources, states and local governments have turned to private providers in an attempt to "do more with less."

Today private contractors are:

- Administrators of a public school district in Massachusetts;
- Operating a state mental hospital in Florida and a state mental retardation facility in Kentucky;
- Financing, constructing and operating public tollways in Virginia, California and Colorado (in the planning stage);
- Managing and operating at least five state or local prisons for adults and several for juveniles;
- Delivering fire protection services in at least 36 jurisdictions;
- Providing local police protection in several suburban jurisdictions in California;

Lon Mackelprang is professor of public administration at Sangamon State University in Springfield, Illinois. Fred Becker is associate professor of health services administration at Florida International University. This article is reprinted with permission from *State Legislatures* 16:1 (January 1990): 19-20. © 1990 by the National Conference of State Legislatures.

● Assessing property for taxation in at least six Michigan communities.

While these examples may not be representative of current private contractual practices among state and local governments, they raise important philosophical questions about where we are going. In a democratic society, how far should governments go in allowing public functions to be performed by private providers? More particularly, to what extent is it feasible and proper to delegate the coercive powers of government (represented most prominently in such areas as taxation, public safety and regulation—functions that significantly intersect with issues of life, liberty and property)? Where should the line be drawn between activities that require public agencies to be solely responsible and those that allow for appropriate roles for private organizations?

These are political questions. State legislators, because of their key role in determining public policy, will play an important role in providing the answers. Until recently not much was known about state legislators' attitudes on these issues.

To find out how state legislators feel about these issues we mailed questionnaires to all lawmakers in the 50 states asking them to indicate the extent to which they feel it is proper for state governments to contract with private organizations to provide public services in 12 specific program areas. They were also asked to indicate why they favor or oppose private contracting. The survey had roughly a 10 percent response—about 740 legislators.

According to the survey, the degree of tolerance legislators have for private contracting varies greatly depending on what is to be contracted out. For example, legislators generally feel that governments' use of private contracting is proper in the areas where it has traditionally occurred, such as:

● Support services like employee cafeterias and guarding of public premises;

● Maintenance services for equipment and grounds, and janitorial work;

● Consultant services for management studies, computer programming and other professional needs;

● Services that are not critical to the safety and security of society, like mental health services to those not a danger to themselves or others, and public mass transportation.

Nearly three-quarters of the legislators responding (73 percent) believe it is proper for state governments to contract with private organizations for these services. About 12 percent of those responding said they oppose contracting for such services.

The areas where legislative support and opposition are most evenly divided are:

● Support services performed by receptionists, secretaries, clerks and data entry operators;

● The involuntary care and treatment of the mentally ill who are a danger to themselves or others;

● Operating—not just managing—state prisons;

● Serving as intermediaries for payments to recipients of AFDC [Aid to Families with Dependent Children], Medicaid and other entitlement programs;

● Collecting delinquent state taxes.

While there is strong support for contracting in these areas, there is also significant legislative opposition. Forty-two percent of those responding were in favor and 37 percent were opposed to private contracting for these services. The remaining 21 percent of the legislators answering expressed neutrality.

Legislators were most opposed to hiring outside contractors to perform these kinds of government jobs:

● Delivering public services that are critical to the safety and security of society, such as fire and police protection;

• Drafting regulatory rules for state agencies such as those designed to protect the environment and health of the public;

• Auditing tax returns and serving as intermediary mechanisms to receive, deposit and account for state taxes.

Slightly more than half of the respondents (56 percent) believe that contracting for these services is improper. About a quarter (24 percent) were in favor of private contracting in these areas.

State legislators clearly reflect the quandary facing governments at all levels as they try to define the areas where government should use outside help. Influencing the positions of the survey respondents were such things as accountability, effectiveness, efficiency and public liability. For a majority of state legislators (eight out of 10), accountability is the key issue in determining propriety of relying on private organizations to provide services for government. When the potential lack of accountability is not a primary concern, legislators are most likely to cite issues of effectiveness and efficiency as key factors influencing their attitudes.

In those areas involving the coercive powers of government, where reservations about contracting are greatest, lawmakers are most concerned about issues of public liability. Sixty-four percent of the respondents indicated this is a significant concern for them. More than half (60 percent) feel there are no circumstances in which state governments can properly delegate to private organizations the authority to use coercive force. And two-thirds say that state government should not allow private contractors to use force in performing law enforcement services for government.

Minority Set-Aside Programs: How Can States Respond to *Croson*?

by William T. Waren

Many states and localities now face the possibility of lawsuits by contractors who can allege that race-conscious preferences for minority businesses are unconstitutional. This is the result of the U.S. Supreme Court's decision on Jan. 23, 1989, in the case of *Richmond vs. Croson,* that Richmond, Va.'s minority business enterprise program discriminated against whites in violation of the equal protection clause of the 14th Amendment.

The holding in *Richmond vs. Croson,* in essence, is that race-conscious measures in minority business programs will be subject to strict scrutiny. Such measures must be justified with a detailed, evidentiary record identifying past discrimination, and plans must be narrowly tailored for purposes of remedying such discrimination.

Benna Solomon, chief counsel for the State and Local Legal Center, cautions that too much emphasis should not be placed on Justice Sandra Day O'Connor's strict-scrutiny analysis in this context because she also "recognized that remedying past discrimination is a compelling state interest" that may justify a race-conscious remedy. Professor David Strauss, of the University of Chicago Law School, agrees that minority business set-aside programs will be upheld by the courts where

they are narrowly tailored and carefully documented remedies for past discrimination. According to Strauss, "The Court shows a little skepticism about affirmative action, but it has by no means closed the door."

How far the door remains open for minority set-aside programs remains in question and is a likely subject for additional litigation. Charles J. "Chuck" Cooper, who served as assistant attorney general in the Reagan administration, says states and cities must realize that "the decision attempts to prohibit racial set-asides in all but the most extreme circumstances." States and cities must justify race-conscious programs on the basis of a detailed record. "Establishing that evidentiary basis may well be difficult," Cooper says. "It is not easy to prove past discrimination, but it is possible."

The door for affirmative action in government contracting is open wider than Cooper suggests, in the view of Barry Goldstein, a California civil rights lawyer and former

William T. Waren covers commerce, labor, and regulation issues for the National Conference of State Legislatures. This article is reprinted with permission from *State Legislatures* 15:6 (July 1989): 32-36. © 1989 by the National Conference of State Legislatures.

Washington director for the NAACP Legal Defense and Education Fund. He says that if a state or locality has "the political will to establish a set-aside program, the decision provides ways to increase the share of contract dollars going to minority businesses." Cities and states, Goldstein says, will have to devote the necessary resources to documenting past discrimination in order to meet the Court's requirements.

While it may be read narrowly or broadly, O'Connor's opinion in *Croson* sets the limits of debate on set-aside programs. Even Chuck Cooper agrees that "the Court did not go as far as Justice [Antonin] Scalia would have gone—to say that the Constitution in no circumstances permits class-based, racial quota relief." And even Barry Goldstein concedes that the *Croson* decision "has brought into question hundreds of set-aside programs."

The case that has resulted in such controversy had its origins in 1983 when the city of Richmond adopted its minority business set-aside program. At a public hearing, the Richmond City Council heard testimony that only 0.67 percent of prime construction contracts awarded by the city in the previous five years had gone to minority-owned businesses, despite the fact that Richmond's population is 50 percent black. The city manager testified that there was widespread discrimination against minorities in the Richmond construction industry. No direct evidence, however, was presented that Richmond had in the past discriminated on the basis of race in awarding contracts or that city contractors had in the past discriminated against minority subcontractors.

On the basis of the testimony, the Richmond City Council adopted a minority contract set-aside program, modeled in most respects on the federal program upheld in 1980 by the Supreme Court in *Fullilove vs. Klutznick*. Prime contractors on city construc-

tion jobs were required to subcontract at least 30 percent of the value of the prime contract to businesses at least 51 percent owned and controlled by members of minority groups. The Richmond ordinance reflected the language of the Federal Public Works Employment Act by defining minority group members as "Blacks, Spanish-speaking, Orientals, Indians, Eskimos, or Aleuts." Waivers of the set-aside quota were allowed where the prime contractors could show that minority businesses were unwilling or unqualified to accept the subcontracted job.

Shortly thereafter, the city of Richmond sought bids for the installation of stainless steel urinals and water closets in the city jail. The only bidder was the J. A. Croson Company. After attempting to line up minority subcontractors, Croson applied for a waiver of the minority set-aside requirement, which the city denied. Croson filed suit in federal district court, alleging that the Richmond set-aside program discriminated against whites in violation of the 14th Amendment's equal protection clause.

When the case finally reached the U.S. Supreme Court, the attention of civil rights groups, contractors, states and local governments focused on the case. It was headline news when the Court decided in January [1989] that Richmond's "treatment of its citizens on a racial basis violates the dictates of the Equal Protection Clause."

Justice O'Connor, who wrote the majority opinion, differentiates between the Richmond case and *Fullilove vs. Klutznick*, where the Court upheld a federal law providing set-asides of construction contracts to minority firms. The 14th Amendment, she says, gives Congress wide-ranging authority to remedy "society-wide discrimination," but serves as "an explicit *constraint* on state power." To allow states and localities to adopt race-conscious measures in response to societal discrimination, according to O'Connor, "would be to cede control over the content of the Equal Protection Clause to the 50 state legislatures and their myriad political subdivisions. . . ."

What are states and localities to do in response to the *Croson* decision?

One approach is to shift program emphasis from minority businesses to disadvantaged businesses. Contracting preferences for small businesses, disadvantaged entrepreneurs, or businesses operating in distressed communities may address many of the same purposes as minority business set-aside programs, without the race-conscious categories that will trigger strict scrutiny by the federal courts. Several jurisdictions, including Texas, Tennessee and New York City, currently use the disadvantaged business approach.

States and localities that want to retain programs that are explicitly directed at minority businesses, on the other hand, will have to ensure that they comply with the Court's very specific and demanding requirements for building a record of past discrimination and narrowly tailoring their program to remedy that discrimination.

The first stage is to build the record. Representative Daniel T. Blue Jr., chairman of a North Carolina House judiciary committee and chair of NCSL's [National Conference of State Legislatures] Committee on Law and Justice, comments that in North Carolina they are moving to "establish the factual record." Blue says: "It's going to be a little more work to document a history of discrimination that everyone knows is there." The administrative burden of identifying and documenting past discrimination should not prove unreasonable in Blue's view. "We have become accustomed," he says, "to doing that kind of fact-finding for a wide range of issues."

Developing statistical evidence may prove especially demanding. The Court in *Rich-*

mond vs. Croson required that the data show a disparity not between minority populations in a locality and the percentage of contracts awarded to minorities, but rather between the number of minority contractors in a specific market and contracts awarded to them.

Census data on minority businesses are dated and incomplete. Census employment data are more complete but may only suggest the potential talent pool for minority entrepreneurs. Unconventional data sources like trade association records and local business registrations may be helpful. Some jurisdictions may want to increase their own reporting requirements or commission their own surveys. Given the limits of the data base, building an economic model that can estimate accurately what the level of minority firm participation would have been, absent discrimination, will be challenging.

More promising are the opportunities for developing historical information of value in establishing a record. The past proceedings of state and local human rights commissions and the record of past lawsuits against the jurisdiction, for example, may prove to be documentary treasure troves. New studies and investigations can also be commissioned.

A new record may also be developed in legislative hearings. Witnesses might testify to specific instances of discrimination (as opposed to conclusory statements about the well-known tradition of discrimination in the community and industry). For example, immediately following the *Croson* decision, over 60 minority businesses in Seattle completed affidavits detailing specific instances of past discrimination and submitted them to the city's Human Rights Department.

The second stage, of course, is for the state or locality to "narrowly tailor" its new minority business statute or ordinance.

One important step in drawing narrow legislation is to consider race-neutral alternative policies and to proceed with race-conscious measures only where neutral policies have shown to be inadequate. Indeed, race-neutral policies may reinforce affirmative action. Creating a market through a preference policy may not be helpful to a potential minority contractor unless he or she also has access to capital, receives help with bonding requirements, and receives training and technical assistance in how to negotiate through the contracting process and how to meet the terms of the contract successfully.

The second and most important step is to craft legislation and administer the minority business program in a way that benefits only those minority groups which have been identified in the record as victims of discrimination. The remedy should be limited to the appropriate geographic market, which may be quite different depending upon what goods or services are involved. The remedy should also be tailored to the appropriate economic market, i.e., construction contractors. Finally the remedy should benefit only those minorities that were discriminated against locally, i.e., not Eskimos in Richmond.

A third step is to ensure the remedial character of the program. Justice Sandra Day O'Connor suggests that the remedy should be limited in time and should be regularly evaluated. The record may suggest a logical point for the program to stop. Another means of

ensuring the remedial character of the program is to require firms that prosper in the protected market to graduate to the unprotected market.

A fourth step is to ensure that the remedy is flexible. Goals or targets are probably preferable to set-asides that can be disparaged as rigid quotas. Where minority firms are unavailable or their bids are economically unreasonable, waiver provisions should be available.

States, cities and countries with minority business plans have their work cut out for them as they seek to meet the Supreme Court's requirements. Some jurisdictions may take the opportunity to drop programs or move to race-neutral disadvantaged business plans. Minority business plans have been criticized as likely targets for front operations run by whites, or other scams. And, in contrast to affirmative action in hiring or college admissions, which benefits those seeking an initial boost onto the ladder of success, it is alleged that affirmative action in contracting benefits those who are already successful or influential.

Representative Blue, on the other hand, disagrees with critics and urges states and localities to "take the extra effort to ensure we continue to make progress" and "to root out the vestiges of a system of discrimination." He says that "if you take into account 350 years of history in the United States then you have to take some action to level the playing field."

Is Government Full of Crooks, or Are We Just Better at Finding Them?

by Elder Witt

The figures are startling. Ten times as many state, city, county and other local officials are convicted on federal corruption charges today as were 20 years ago. For all the reforms over those two decades, the government that is supposed to be closest to the people seems more corrupt than ever.

"Our democratic system is in crisis," declares New York's Commission on Government Integrity, ranking New York City's recent scandals the worst since the ones that shattered the empire of Tammany Hall more than half a century ago.

In 1970, 10 state and 26 local officials faced federal indictment. By 1987, that annual number had climbed to 102 state and 246 local officials. That does not even include prosecutions under state and local law; no reliable figures exist for them. But no one who has studied the issue disputes the trend: more public officials facing trial and jail than anyone in politics would have dreamed possible two decades ago.

Every locality has its own story. Pennsylvania state Treasurer R. Budd Dwyer shot himself to death in front of rolling television cameras after being convicted of bribery. Former Syracuse, New York, Mayor Lee Alexander, one-time head of the U.S. Conference of Mayors, faces 10 years in prison for extorting over $1.2 million from city contractors. More than 150 county commissioners in Oklahoma have gone to jail for defrauding taxpayers of millions of dollars through an intricate kickback scheme. Sixty of Mississippi's county supervisors have been convicted of similar crimes. An elaborate FBI sting operation probing illegal campaign contributions has ensnared several key members of the California legislature.

One lawyer in Chicago, asked how many traffic court judges he had bribed over a 10-year period, had this to say: "I didn't count them. I just bribed them. It was kind of like brushing your teeth. I did it every day."

It sounds like an epidemic. But is it? Some of those who have studied the issue longest don't think so. "Almost certainly, we are less corrupt than we were," says Suzanne Garment, a resident scholar at the American Enterprise Institute. She is at work on a book about corruption. "Read any of the histories of states and cities of 75 years ago," she says, "and you see a system that is very different. Less gets stolen from the public now."

Elder Witt is a staff writer for *Governing*. This article appeared in *Governing* 2:12 (September 1989): 33-38.

Are we electing rascals to office in record numbers, or are we simply finding and punishing actions that used to be routinely ignored? Is it massive corruption, or just massive exposure? The question is simple enough, but the answers are many and complex.

For one thing, there are a lot more laws for public officials to break than there used to be. New laws are the standard legislative response to scandal. . . . "Revolving door" statutes are an example. They scarcely existed 20 years ago. The law showed little interest in what a public official did when he left office. Today, there are all sorts of restrictions. In Connecticut, to cite one example, any former executive-branch official is forbidden for life to represent anyone but the state on any matter he previously handled and in which the state has an interest. A state regulatory official risks going to jail if, during his first year out of office, he goes to work in the industry he once regulated.

In Massachusetts in the 1960s, the average state legislator would have thought nothing of hiring members of his immediate family to work in his legislative office. Today, he could be slapped with a $2,000 fine if he did that. Nepotism is a clear violation of the state conflict-of-interest law enforced by the state ethics commission.

The catalyst for much of this was Watergate. That national political scandal involved federal officials, but it set off an explosion of new laws in the states. In 1973, only a handful of states had ethics agencies. By 1978, half had set them up. Today, all states have designated some office to fulfill this function, and 38 of them have independent agencies. Cities and counties are also busy setting up such boards; Maryland's Ethics Commission reports that there are nearly 100 local ethics agencies in that state alone.

What has emerged from the past 20 years, however, is not a clear system of rules, but an inconsistent and confusing patchwork. It is not always easy for either public officials or those doing business with them to be sure of what they can and cannot do. In some states, says Page Bigelow of the Institute of Public Administration, "there's one county where you can take someone in government to lunch, and in the one next door you can't and you're breaking the law by even asking."

A fair number of state and local officials indicted in the 1980s have thus run afoul of laws that did not exist in the 1960s. But a larger number have fallen victim to increasingly sophisticated federal prosecution. The federal presence in state and local corruption cases has grown steadily in the past two decades, and it has involved the use of weapons that local law enforcement generally does not possess.

Some of this is a simple matter of technology. Twenty years ago, for example, it was very hard to tape the conversation of a public official under suspicion unless he conducted it in a room already wired for sound or over a tapped telephone line. Today, the use of "body wires"—difficult-to-detect recording equipment placed on the person of a government informer—allows a prosecutor to tape the suspect anywhere: in a parking lot, on a sidewalk, even in the middle of an open field.

"Audio tapes are crucial," says John R. Hailman, the assistant U.S. attorney who has overseen the Mississippi corruption cases for the northern half of the state. Once a public official on trial sees or hears himself in the actual process of making a questionable transaction on tape, he can usually expect to receive the full wrath of a jury. "You just can't answer a tape," says Hailman.

Not all state courts accept evidence procured with body wires. But federal courts do, and federal prosecutors can use it to try state and local officials in federal court for a variety of federal offenses. Without such wires, many of the public corruption cases prosecuted in the past decade would never even have been brought, and the total number of officials convicted would be much lower.

The same is true of elaborate undercover operations in which law enforcement agents set up fictitious criminal schemes or entire business enterprises to catch corrupt public officials. Before the 1980s, this was not often done; such "stings" were used mainly to pursue drug suspects or identify and convict professional thieves. But the FBI's Abscam operation of 1980, in which agents posed as Arab sheiks and offered congressmen bribes to introduce immigration bills, changed the situation in a dramatic way.

In the years following, Abscam came under considerable attack by critics who considered it entrapment, but it stood up to U.S. Supreme Court scrutiny and has been copied, in one variation or another, all over the country. Undercover enterprises snared local judges in Chicago and, most massively, the county commissioners in Mississippi and Oklahoma.

In Operation Pretense in Mississippi, three FBI agents went to work for a construction equipment company whose owner was outraged at the dishonesty he found in dealing with county government. The undercover agents, in the words of John Hailman, one of the federal prosecutors in charge, "had the appropriate accents and 'good ole boy' demeanors to be accepted as crooked local salesmen. They wore caps saying Mid-State Pipe and chewed liberal amounts of tobacco." They used body wires to tape their conversations with the county supervisors who received kickbacks.

In both the Mississippi and Oklahoma cases, state officials actually took the first steps toward gathering evidence. The Mississippi auditor's office discovered that counties had not only paid far too much for heavy equipment, but sometimes couldn't find it when

asked about it. Oklahoma's auditor noticed that one county reported purchasing enough lumber to rebuild every bridge in the area four times—and yet none of the bridges had been repaired.

Strong political ties and weak state laws hamstrung local district and county attorneys when they tried to pursue these clues. In Mississippi, state law requires that a person be tried in his home county. The county supervisors, who were the target of the investigations, were also the employers of the sheriff and the county attorney. In Oklahoma, there was an additional problem: The kickback scheme involved suppliers and officials in almost every county in the state. The power of the county attorney stopped at the border of his county.

And in both states, as in most of the country, the attorney general had relatively limited law enforcement authority. He could not convene a grand jury with authority to subpoena witnesses. So it was the federal government that prosecuted the county supervisors, who were convicted of extortion and mail fraud.

The prosecutors who went after these supervisors say that it was not a matter of finding new forms of corruption. They are convinced that bribery has existed in county government in their states throughout the century. What happened was the arrival of modern evidence-gathering technology and a federal will to act in these particular states. . . .

But the massive increase in corruption cases is not entirely a matter of new laws or new technology. It also in part reflects the higher monetary stakes involved in state and local government decisions.

"Corruption follows money," says Diana Henriques, author of *The Machinery of Greed,* a study of abuse of public power. "The larger the budget, the greater the allure." The amount of money spent by state and local government has increased nearly eightfold over the past 20 years, to more than $900 billion a year, an enormous increase even in constant dollars.

It is one downside of the devolution of federal power to other levels of government. As state and local governments expand in size and power, they become more attractive targets of corruption.

Increasingly, governments are setting up special districts, commissions and government "authorities" to handle their expanded responsibilities in a more "business-like" fashion. This is a governmental frontier that many of the public access and disclosure requirements that affect more traditional agencies do not penetrate.

In some cases, the officials who run these new entities are corrupt; in others, they are simply corruptible. "When you give people the authority to make 'red light, green light' decisions that are very valuable to people, you've created a situation that's vulnerable to abuse," says Henriques. "Unless you vaccinate that situation somehow, you are placing enormous temptation on the frailties of human nature."

Corruption in a special government authority usually has a modest and relatively innocent beginning, Henriques found. "No one worries that a few contracts out of so many are being steered in a certain direction. But no one knows when to stop, and so it proceeds until the authority is so riddled with abuse that the program can't be saved."

In the end, a much-needed and very well-intentioned program may be scrapped, and the people it was supposed to serve are the ultimate victims. "The political fixers and influence peddlers move on to some other program, wherever the money is," she says.

A local government horror story in Bergen County, New Jersey, came to light this summer as a result of investigative reporting by a local newspaper, the *Record*. The paper spent months looking into the work of the Bergen County Utilities Authority and found "an agency out of control." The authority was $600 million in debt, having awarded multi-million-dollar bond underwriting contracts on a no-bid basis to investment banking firms that had made large campaign contributions to county officials.

The *Record* portrayed Wall Street as the instigator of "pay for play," the strategic use of campaign contributions by bond underwriters to ensure that they would win bond business. When Bergen County had its first election for county executive in 1986, the Wall Street investment firm of Bear, Stearns, through individual and corporate donations, was the biggest campaign contributor. In the two years preceding the election, Bear, Stearns had earned millions for underwriting bond issues for the Bergen County Utilities Authority.

The New Jersey Senate has asked the State Commission on Investigation to determine whether any laws were broken in the relationship between the securities industry and the public authority.

"You can't fault the bond dealers for playing by rules, written and unwritten, which confront them," says Henriques. "They'll play the game any way the public officials demand. If the officials want competitive bidding, they'll give competitive bids. If they want tickets to the Giants game, they'll get tickets to the Giants game."

The corruption of the Bergen County Utilities Authority could not have taken place on anything resembling the same scale 20 years ago. The authority existed in those days, but it did not build sophisticated facilities and therefore did not need to raise huge sums of money. It was a small-scale sewer commission. Wall Street had no reason to be interested in it.

In this case, corruption was more than anything else a function of growth and development. The fast-growing county's need for waste treatment facilities, and government institutions that could provide them, far outpaced its ability to keep those institutions under control. And the utilities authority, as a modern special-purpose unit of government rather than an old-fashioned unit, lay outside the traditional mechanisms of accountability.

Special units of government are not inevitable centers of corruption. The numerous state lotteries created in recent years illustrate how government can protect itself against corruption by acknowledging its vulnerability, selecting leaders who will guard against even the appearance of impropriety (the first lottery directors in many states were former FBI agents) and providing adequate oversight for the operation. The key to avoiding trouble in most of the lotteries was the recognition in virtually every state that a gambling operation was inherently corruptible and required special controls. Where the threat is less obvious, the safeguards tend to be less thorough. These are the kind of situations, Henriques warns, in which "the temptation is enormous and the perception of risk minuscule."

The same warning applies to another common state and local innovation of recent years—the creation of partnerships between government and private institutions. Those moves are made to save money and improve services, and sometimes they do. But they represent one more step away from accountability, and from clarity as well. As the line between public and private blurs, the night-and-day world of extortion and bribery fades into a twilight zone of ambiguous shades and shifting standards.

Earlier this year, Milwaukee County Zoo Director Gilbert Boese experienced firsthand the difficulties of operating in this situation. He resigned as zoo director after the county ethics board began investigating charges that he had failed to disclose benefits provided him by the Zoological Society of Milwaukee County, the zoo's private "partner." The benefits included a yearly 10 percent addition to his county-paid salary as well as travel expenses, including an African safari. Boese's wife was, at the time, the executive director of the Zoological Society. After leaving his public post, Boese become the society's president and his wife moved to another organization.

There was no crime involved here, and it could be argued that no serious ethical violation even took place. Nonetheless, these events became a major news story in the Milwaukee papers and ended up tainting not only Boese but also his superior, Milwaukee County Executive Dave Schulz. The publicity that surrounds issues such as these creates a heightened ethical sensitivity in the public, a greater willingness by prosecutors to investigate corruption charges and, ultimately, more indictments and more convictions.

And when it comes to explaining the "epidemic" of corruption cases, the point about public values may be the most important point of all. They have changed for a variety of reasons in the past 20 years, but they have changed. Public values determine what level of corruption a democracy will tolerate, and what acts it will prosecute. . . .

For a blunt-spoken comment on the dramatic changes that have taken place in those rules, one can do no better than Lou Farina. The former Chicago alderman spent more than a year in prison after being convicted of extorting $7,000 from a building contractor.

"Anyone who goes into politics today is nuts," Farina says. "If a restaurant owner donates $500 to your campaign and then gets in trouble with a health inspector, he'll bring the citation to you and ask if you can help. Years ago, if you were an alderman, you'd say, 'Give it to me, I'll do the best I can.' You'd call the judge up, say, 'This is a good man, can you help him out?' Today you go to jail for that!"

Written Rules: State Ethics Codes, Commissions, and Conflicts

by Fran Burke and George C. S. Benson

... [T]he mid-20th century has spawned the demand for increased citizen participation, which has led to more open government meetings and documents. The practice of openness in government is based on the principle of visibility in which decisions and actions open to the public are less likely to be unethical. This push during the last several decades to diminish fraud, waste, abuse and corrupt practices also has led states to establish standards of conduct through written codes of ethics.

Some state laws forbidding conflicts of interest date back to common law provisions. The 19th and early 20th century laws often forbade officials from acting in cases of conflict of interest or required disclosure of potential conflicts before letting a government contract or voting on a bill. Enforcement of these laws by criminal prosecution was not the norm; enforcement was more usually by court action to void the contract. But by 1957, 27 states had conflict of interest laws. In the 1970s, publicity about Watergate coupled with "good government" campaigns by organizations (notably Common Cause) resulted in more than a score of states passing ethics legislation. This legislation focused mostly on officials disclosing their personal finances ... as a means to reduce conflicts of interest.

As states move toward the final decade of the 20th century, these efforts towards the pursuit of public integrity are more stringent, demanding and clearly sighted on improving the ethical operation of state governments.

State Codes of Ethics

State government codes most often appear in statute form, couched in legalistic language with few inspiring phrases. States have dispensed leaflets to officials and employees describing in simple language their responsibilities under the code. State codes vary greatly in length. Most include a list of forbidden actions and identify conflicts of interest such as bribes, influence peddling, leaking confidential information, forgery and other means of cheating the government or its citizens.

The main objective of a code is to strengthen integrity within public organizations by fostering high ethical standards. Additionally, codes provide guidance in making ethical decisions, especially those which fall

Fran Burke is a professor in the School of Management at Suffolk University in Boston. George C. S. Benson is president emeritus at Claremont McKenna College. This article is reprinted with permission from *The Journal of State Government* 62:5 (September/October 1989): 195-198. © 1990 by the Council of State Governments.

within the "gray areas" of ethical choice. And, finally, codes are promulgated in order to increase public confidence in the operations of government.

The American Society for Public Administration (ASPA) Code with guidelines, adopted in 1983, has been widely distributed to heads of state and local governments. Some state leaders have redistributed the ASPA code; for example, Gov. Thomas Kean of New Jersey sent it to all state agencies. Georgia reprinted its code to send to all inquirers.

The ASPA Code urges its adherents to apply the principles behind the code not merely "to prevent wrong, but to pursue right through timely and energetic execution of responsibilities."

Financial Disclosure

State ethics laws of the 1970s introduced the newer enforcement mechanism of financial disclosure. Legislation in two-thirds of the states mandates that candidates for or holders of specified official positions must disclose certain aspects of their income and property holdings. Would-be city officials must file this statement with city clerks, elected county candidates or officeholders with a county official, and state officers or candidates with the secretary of state. Such individual statements are in almost all cases available to public inquiry.

How useful is this device of disclosure? Dr. Anthony Quinn, member in 1975 of the California Ethical Commission, thought it made more officeholders aware of the dangers of conflict of interest but that it is seldom used. According to the Council on Governmental Ethics Laws *Blue Book* (COGEL), however, only seven states (Idaho, Missouri, New Hampshire, New Mexico, Utah, Vermont and Wyoming) seem not to require financial disclosure from some groups of state employees. The officials required to disclose some of their financial holdings vary greatly, according to

the 1988-89 *Blue Book*. Legislators are required to disclose personal finances in 33 states. County elected officials must file in only 18 states. Limited disclosure of interests and associations in many states also applies to family members. So, disclosure is still used, but is it useful?

Jerry Crump, deputy counsel of Los Angeles County and lawyer in that office for 25 years, has a more optimistic view of the disclosure policy. At meetings of the Board of Supervisors, he said citizens cite data from the disclosure forms. Data from the forms is often cited by political investigative reporters in stories on political campaigns and leadership.

In many states, thousands of disclosure reports are filed. The COGEL report, however, indicates that there is only a "desk review" of most of them. Few citizens, reporters, investigators or others request these disclosure statements. Yet, the *Blue Book* reports from 11 to 50 investigations in eight states: California, Florida, Illinois, Nebraska, Pennsylvania, Rhode Island, South Carolina and Wisconsin. There are more investigations in New Jersey, New York and Washington. While there are valuable effects of disclosure, the requirement needs further analysis to ascertain its usefulness.

Conflicts of Interest

The ASPA code and guidelines forbid "undue personal gain from the performance of official duties" and command officials to "avoid any interest or activity which is in conflict with the conduct of our official duties."

Laws on conflicts are involved and difficult to write. The U.S. Office of Governmental Ethics made commendable efforts to condense these complex laws into simplified form. In March 1989, President Bush's Commission on Federal Ethics Law Reform recommended standardization of ethical principle[s] and practices, which would apply equally to the

Congress, the executive and to the departments. Almost all of the knotty problems concern conflicts of interest. . . .

The Indiana Code of Ethics clearly lists potential conflict of interests. Written in language that a non-legally trained state employee can comprehend, the code covers moonlighting, outside compensation, privileged information and actions to take to avoid possible conflicts. Like the Ten Commandments, it reads as a list of negative injunctions, but its importance lies in its ability to educate and sensitize elected and appointed officials to the ethical concerns of daily operations.

The "Revolving Door"

Several states have tried to forbid employees from leaving government service to serve as well-paid lobbyists to former governmental associates. The South Carolina statute prohibits "any public official or . . . employee [from receiving] any compensation including a promise of future employment to influence his actions, votes." The New Jersey law has a similar clause, but neither law is as stringent and detailed as the federal law.

Pennsylvania and Alabama place specific limits on former government employees lobbying former employers. The Pennsylvania code is particularly thorough, setting timetables for lobbying former employers, mandating strict punitive measures and authorizing binding "advisory opinions" for ambiguous "revolving door" situations.

While many states may be criticized for ignoring the problem of "revolving doors," care should be taken not to draw too strict barriers. Too tight a "revolving door" provision may make it difficult to recruit administrators.

State Ethics Commissions

About 35 states have established a state ethics commission, agency, department, division or similar body. The unit, appointed by the governor, or by the governor and legislative leaders, or by elected staff officers, usually employs an ethics director and a small staff. The jurisdiction of the commissions varies greatly from oversight of all legislative and executive personnel to the executive or legislative alone or a limited number of executives. Each commission is responsible for interpreting provisions of the ethics law, making supplementary rules and referring violations to the attorney general or county attorney for possible prosecution. In 37 states the commission (or designated agency) may impose administrative fines for breaking the ethics code. In the less populated states, the function of the ethics director often is handled by the secretary of state or the attorney general.

With a few exceptions, state statutes apply to local political subdivisions as well as state officers and employees. However, the means of enforcement varies. In Alabama, Pennsylvania and South Carolina, for example, substate ethics infractions come under the jurisdiction of the state commission and the state statute that established the commission. Other states encourage agencies and localities to promulgate laws that more closely fit their needs. New Jersey and Indiana encourage their administrative agencies to draw up ethics codes, while Maryland suggests that localities do so. In Maryland, the power to enforce codes for local matters is usually in the hands of the county prosecutors.

The Ethical Future

There has been some agreement that the quality of state government has improved in recent decades. The U.S. Advisory Commission on Intergovernmental Relations (ACIR) in 1985 issued a report on "The Question of State Government Capability," which reported improvement over the last three decades. One can quarrel with aspects of the report, for example, it credits the U.S. Supreme Court decision on reapportionment as a major reform (which it was), but it does not mention the impetus to gerrymandering resulting from that decision. It is true, as noted by the ACIR, that legislative reform, state executive reorganization, merit recruitment procedures and constitutional modernization have contributed to the general improvement of states. However, scant attention was paid to the reforms of the 1970s and 1980s that opened the electoral process, fostered accountability measures and increased clarification of conflict of interest. Each of these measures appreciably strengthened state government capability. Finally, observers may wonder if the introduction of state ethics codes and legislation, which set standards of quality, have not been at least as significant as the other reforms.

VIII. STATE COURTS

The Furor Over One Juror

The third branch of state government, the judiciary, probably is the one part of state government with which most citizens would prefer not to have any dealings. State courts handle the crimes reported in the news—drunk driving, child abuse, robbery, murder, and rape. Personal disputes, divorce cases, and other civil matters also are tried in state courts.

Despite the importance of the judiciary in state politics, it is perhaps the least visible branch. One reason is because citizens want it that way; they want the courts to be above the hurly-burly of politics. The legislature may conduct its business in a circuslike atmosphere and the governor may crisscross the state to keep an impossible schedule of appointments, but the courts must be a model of decorum, a place where the rational presentation of facts and arguments leads to truth and justice.

The Court System

The several levels of state courts each have differing responsibilities. At the lowest level are trial courts, where cases are argued and juries may be called to weigh the facts presented. Intermediate appellate courts, the next level in the state judicial system, are where the decisions of the trial courts and other lower courts can be appealed. (Thirty-five states have intermediate courts.) Finally, each state has a court of last resort, usually called the Supreme Court, but in Maine it is called the Supreme Judicial Court; in West Virginia, the Supreme Court of Last Resort; and in New York, the Court of Appeals. Here, the final appeals to lower court decisions are made unless a federal question is involved, which then means that appeal to the federal appellate courts is possible.

State court judges rule on a variety of concerns. Part of their work load is administrative (for example, the probating of wills).

Another part involves conflict resolution (for example, deciding which party is correct in contested divorce settlements and property disputes). And still another area of responsibility includes the criminal prosecution and appeals process.

In a broader sense, state court judges are policy makers. It is often in court decisions, rather than in legislation or constitutional amendments, that state policies are modified or set aside. Courts are reactive institutions of government, and their decisions are limited by the nature and timing of the cases brought before them. Judges establish new norms of acceptable behavior and revise existing norms to match changing circumstances. Their interpretations of the law may or may not have the backing of the public or of the governor or state legislature. Nonetheless, what they say goes—that is, of course, unless it is overturned by another court decision or by another decision-making body. In some instances, court decisions simply are ignored because the judiciary has no bureaucracy of its own to enforce decisions.

The norm of separating partisan politics from the judiciary is part of our national and state political cultures. But judges must be selected in some manner; and inevitably, politics become a factor.

Judicial Selection

The methods used to select judges vary from state to state. Sometimes judges are appointed by the governor and confirmed by the state senate. In Connecticut, the legislature appoints judges from nominations submitted by the governor. In Texas, judges are elected as Democrats or Republicans. Other states—Montana, for example—elect judges on a nonpartisan basis.

Some states have adopted a variation of

the "Missouri Plan" to remove politics from the selection process as much as possible. In this process, a nonpartisan group such as the state or district bar association screens the many candidates and recommends the top contenders to the governor, who then makes the final decision. The argument is that merit will be the foremost criterion in the screening and nomination process.

The Missouri Plan also provides that when their terms expire, judges can "run again" on their record. The voters are asked: Should Judge X be retained in office? If the voters say yes, the judge serves another term. If the voters say no, the selection process starts anew. In this way, the judiciary is accountable to the citizens of the state.

In 1990, Florida voters will show how volatile even a retention election can be. Leander J. Shaw, Jr., a member of the Florida Supreme Court, will seek another term on the court that begins in 1991. However, antiabortion groups have targeted Shaw's tenure because they are angry at him for writing a unanimous 1989 state supreme court opinion striking down a state law that required teenage girls to obtain parental consent or judicial approval prior to having an abortion. This isn't partisan politics, but single-issue politics of the most direct kind.[1]

And the world of partisan elective judicial politics also is in considerable ferment. Political observers were startled in 1986 when three states—California, North Carolina, and Ohio—all had well-publicized, negative, and very expensive partisan races for their state's chief justiceship. California voters rejected liberal Democratic chief justice Rose Bird, appointed to that post by former Democratic governor Jerry Brown. The divisive campaign was centered around Bird's consistent objection to capital punishment. In North Carolina, the long standing tradition whereby the governor appoints the longest-serving Su-

preme Court justice to the post of chief justice when that office is vacated was violated by Republican governor Jim Martin. Martin refused to appoint ranking Democratic supreme court justice Jim Exum and instead elevated his own newly-appointed Republican supreme court justice Rhoda Billings. This led to a series of political maneuvers, resulting in Exum's resignation and a subsequent successful challenge of Billings in the 1986 general election. In Ohio, Chief Justice Frank Celebrezze was defeated in a heated campaign after serving in a manner that provided for "rancorous controversy and political infighting of a sort rare for state high courts."[2]

In early 1987, a U.S. district court judge in Jackson, Mississippi, ruled that Section 2 of the Voting Rights Act of 1965 applies to judges elected at the state level. At issue was the question of whether electing judges from at-large, multimember districts dilutes minority voting strength. The impact of the decision probably will mean that state judges will be elected from single-member districts, thereby offering the possibility of greater minority representation in the state judiciaries.[3]

In December 1989, a three-judge federal appeals court upheld the concept that the Voting Rights Act applies to judicial election districts.[4] So, in those states covered by the provisions of the Voting Rights Act, any changes in judicial district lines or the addition of judges must be precleared with the U.S. Department of Justice before being implemented.[5] In April 1990, the Department of Justice threw out Georgia's system of electing judges because it was discriminatory against blacks. The problem with the system was the election of judges in broad judicial circuits by a majority vote, rather than by a plurality vote. This has the same effect as at-large elections often do: diluting the strength of minority groups.[6]

In 1988, political fights swirled around

the Texas Supreme Court as nine justices came up for election. This was the first time since Reconstruction that a majority of the court faced the voters at one time. The political contest had several elements:[7]

• In 1987, two justices were criticized separately by the Texas Commission on Judicial Conduct for improper ties to lawyers;

• The state supreme court was criticized by Texaco and the national press for refusing to hear the appeal of the $10.53 billion judgment by a state court trial judge against Texaco in favor of Pennzoil;

• Some of the leading contributors of political funds to the members of the current court turned out to be Pennzoil lawyers, although Texaco lawyers also gave money to some candidates (though they were outbid $315,000 to $72,700);[8]

• The resignation of Chief Justice John Hill in January 1988 to campaign for an appointed system of judgeships was quickly followed by the resignation of senior justice Robert Campbell to campaign for continuing the electoral system for selecting judges;

• Republican governor William P. Clements, Jr., appointed Texas's first Republican supreme court chief justice of the twentieth century and two well-known Democrats, all of whom ran for election to the court as Republicans.

The 1988 Texas Supreme Court campaigns, which cost an estimated $10 million, had "the nastiest, most negative campaigning I have ever seen," one Texas legislator told North Carolina's Judicial Selection Study Commission. "If you are before a judge in Texas now, you've got to be worried if you are a Democrat and he is a Republican."[9]

Is justice for sale as some critics suggest? Giving money to political campaigns, even judicial campaigns, is legal and "that's the problem," according to a Texaco spokeswoman.[10] One Houston lawyer suggested that "it looks just as bad for a lawyer to give a lot of money to a judge as for a judge to take a lot of money from a lawyer."[11] This is all cannon fodder for those wanting to remove the judicial selection process from electoral politics.

Tides of Judicial Policy Making

A current issue in the states concerns who should take the lead in the judicial system—the federal judiciary interpreting the U.S. Constitution, or the state judiciaries interpreting the individual state constitutions. For decades, the loud cry of "states' rights" masked inaction by state courts on segregation, malapportionment, and other unconstitutional practices.

During the 1950s and 1960s, under a broad interpretation of the Constitution (especially the Fifth and Fourteenth Amendments), the U.S. Supreme Court moved to upset the states' intransigence and, in some cases, illegal activities. Led by Chief Justice Earl Warren (the governor of California from 1943 to 1953), the U.S. Supreme Court overturned state laws upholding segregation, forced state legislatures to apportion themselves on a one-man, one-vote basis following each census, expanded voting rights, legalized abortion, and broadened the rights of the accused in the state criminal justice system. The Warren Court set minimal standards for the states to follow in these areas. The Warren Court often reversed state court decisions that narrowly construed the rights of individuals.

In recent years, the U.S. Supreme Court has become more conservative in its decisions. It has even backed away from some of the minimal standards it set earlier. Several state courts have decided not only to uphold these minimal standards but to exceed them. U.S. Supreme Court justice William J. Brennan, Jr., describes this trend as "probably the most important development in constitutional jurisprudence today."[12] Ronald Collins, an expert on state constitutional law, estimated that between 1970 and the mid-1980s state high courts have issued approximately 400 decisions based on the higher standards of the state constitutions as opposed to the minimum standards established by the U.S. Supreme Court in interpreting the U.S. Constitution.[13] As New Jersey Supreme Court justice Stewart G. Pollock suggests, "Horizontal federalism, in which states look to each other for guidance, may be the hallmark of the rest of the century."[14]

California Supreme Court justice Stanley Mosk argues that liberals and conservatives alike can support this trend—liberals because it is a continuing expansion of individual rights begun under the Warren Court, and conservatives because such decisions are being made in the state capitals rather than in Washington, D.C.[15] North Carolina Supreme Court justice Harry Martin feels that this trend also gives "the people of the individual states greater protection of their individual rights because of the way people live in the different states." He argues that the state constitutions were designed to respond to the needs of each state, while the U.S. Constitution must respond to the needs of all fifty states. He cites as examples Florida's protection of citizens from unreasonable searches and seizures on boats, Alaska's similar protection of passengers on airplanes, and the right of North Carolina's citizens to a system of inexpensive higher education—all critical parts of each state's economy.[16]

Not all legal scholars and participants agree that this activism will have positive results. Oregon attorney general David Frohnmayer argues that "superimposing new and different state doctrinal rules on top of federal law is an open invitation to confusion and error on the enforcement front." He says the movement also means a greater responsibility will now be placed on the state legisla-

tors who draft state constitutional provisions and pass the statutes that can be questioned under the constitutional provisions.[17]

Why does such activism develop in a state's supreme court? One study of six state supreme courts from 1930 to 1980 found that dramatic shifts by state high courts from a relatively passive role to an active role take place in a relatively short period of time and are due mainly to a change in the composition of the court. The appointment of a "maverick" judge to a state's supreme court begins a process in which that judge dissents from the previous consensual and passive court decisions, soon gaining some supporters to the minority position. With additional appointments of more activist-oriented jurists, the court changes direction. Of import is the fact that once a transition to activism occurred, none of these courts moved back in the direction of nonactivism, at least not during the period studied.[18]

However, there still may be a question as to whether federal or state court decisions will affect states more. In recent years the U.S. Supreme Court has been making significant decisions affecting state politics. In *Davis v. Bandemer* (1986), the Court changed the ground rules of reapportionment by allowing a losing political party in a redistricting plan standing in a court suit to challenge the plan. In *Tashjian v. Republican Party of Connecticut* (1986), the Court threw out a state law mandating a closed party primary, thereby allowing independents to participate in the party nomination process. In *Johnson v. Transportation Agency, Santa Clara County, Calif.* (1987), the Court upheld local government affirmative action plans and decisions that discriminate in favor of women and minorities.

Open Courts

Courtroom dramas such as "Perry Mason," "L.A. Law," and "The People's Court" portray how Hollywood feels justice is carried out. But these shows are misleading since most "real" justice proceeds at a very slow pace and is based on the rule of law and facts rather than on emotion. In fact, one lawyer argues that "trials are as exciting as watching paint dry." After the 1981 U.S. Supreme Court decision *Chandler v. Florida* rejected the argument that a defendant's right to a fair trial was violated by allowing cameras and microphones in a state courtroom, states have moved rapidly to allow such coverage by the media.[19] As of mid-October 1987, forty-four states allowed either still-picture cameras, microphones, or television cameras into their courts.[20] Interestingly, federal courts still ban these electronic devices.[21]

What is the impact of having cameras in the courtroom during trials? Some feared they would lead to behavior changes by participants in trials, such as grandstanding by lawyers. Not so, according to one Kentucky judge who feels the cameras cause lawyers and witnesses "to be a little bit more respectful because they know the tape will show the appellate court their tone of voice and body language, not just sterile written words." Other observers worried the cameras might be intimidating to lawyers or witnesses. To date there have been no such complaints in the Kentucky courts.[22]

Can videotapes replace the written record? In one Kentucky case, the tape playback refuted an appeal to a guilty plea entered when the defendant was supposedly insane. The tape showed the defendant to be "cogent and responsible." But there are some problems: it is often more difficult to find particular points or references on a tape than in a written transcript for a jury or appellate court seeking clarification.[23] Importantly, though, cameras in the courtroom increase the public's understanding of our states' judicial systems. According to the Kentucky judge, it "brings a

whole new dimension to the idea of a public trial."[24]

Part VIII, State Courts, includes five articles that explore different aspects of the judicial branch. Peter Buchsbaum, in *New Jersey Reporter,* argues that while courts may be more active, they are the least changed branch of government. David M. Jones, in *Comparative State Politics,* describes the politics involved in a recent judicial election in Wisconsin. Elder Witt of *Governing* profiles one of the states' top jurists, Hans A. Linde of the Oregon Supreme Court. Linda Wagar of *State Government News* explores the resurgence of judicial activism and the conflicts that have resulted between the judicial and legislative branches of state government. Finally, Ed McManus, in *Illinois Issues,* shows how important one juror can be in a case.

Notes

1. Stephen Wermiel, "Florida Judge Faces a Trial by Voters as Ruling on Abortion Is Big Issue in 'Retention' Election," *Wall Street Journal,* February 26, 1990, A10.
2. Katherine A. Hinckley, "Four Years of Strife Conclude with Ohio Chief Justice's Defeat," *Comparative State Politics Newsletter* 8:2 (April 1987): 13. Reprinted in Thad L. Beyle, ed., *State Government: CQ's Guide to Current Issues and Activities, 1988-89* (Washington, D.C.: Congressional Quarterly, 1988), 174-181.
3. "Mississippi Ruling Could Aid N.C. Suit on Judgeship Elections," [Raleigh] *News and Observer,* April 5, 1987, 32A.
4. The Voting Rights Act of 1965, extended in 1970 and 1975, banned redistricting plans that diluted the voting strength of black and other minority communities. The law suspended literacy tests and provided for the appointment of federal supervisors of voter registration in all states and counties where literacy tests (or similar qualifying devices) were in effect as of November 1, 1964, and where less than 50 percent of the voting age residents had regis-

tered to vote or voted in the 1964 presidential election. State or county governments brought under the coverage of the law due to low voter registration or participation were required to obtain federal approval of any new voting laws, standards, practices, or procedures before implementing them. The act placed federal registration machinery in six Southern states (Alabama, Georgia, Louisiana, Mississippi, South Carolina, and Virginia), Alaska, twenty-eight counties in North Carolina, three counties in Arizona, and one in Idaho.

5. "Federal Court Applies VRA to State Judicial Districts," *Intergovernmental Perspective* 16:1 (Winter 1990): 20.

6. Peter Applebome, "U.S. Declares Georgia Judge Selection Illegal," New York Times News Service, in [Raleigh] *News and Observer*, April 27, 1990, 3A.

7. Peter Applebome, "Texan Fight over Judges Illustrates Politics' Growing Role in Judiciary," New York Times News Service, in [Raleigh] *News and Observer*, January 24, 1988, 14A.

8. Sheila Kaplan, "Justice for Sale," *Common Cause Magazine* (May/June 1987): 29-32.

9. Jane Ruffin, "Texan Warns N.C. Commission to End System of Electing Judges," [Raleigh] *News and Observer*, November 12, 1988, 3C.

10. Kaplan, "Justice for Sale," 29.

11. Applebome, "Texan Fight over Judges," 14A.

12. Robert Pear, "State Courts Move Beyond U.S. Bench in Rights Rulings," *New York Times,* May 4, 1986, 1.

13. Lanny Proffer, "State Courts and Civil Liberties," *State Legislatures* 13:9 (September 1987): 29.

14. Pear, "State Courts," 16.

15. Stanley Mosk, "State Constitutionalism: Both Liberal and Conservative," *Texas Law Journal* 63:6/7 (March-April 1985): 1081.

16. Katherine White, "North Carolina's Constitution Comes of Age," *North Carolina Insight* 10:2/3 (March 1988): 118-119.

17. Proffer, "State Courts and Civil Liberties," 28.

18. John Patrick Hagan, "Patterns of Activism on State Supreme Courts," *Publius* 18:1 (Winter 1988): 97-115.

19. *Chandler v. Florida,* 449 U.S. 560, 101 S. Ct. 1802 (1981). John Bacon, "Across State Lines: Mich. Joins Pack, Allows Cameras in Courtrooms," *USA Today,* October 15, 1987, 8A.

20. Radio-Television News Directors Association as cited in note 19.

21. Ibid.

22. Eileen Shanahan, "The Cameras Are Rolling in Kentucky Courts," *Governing* 2:1 (October 1988): 32-35.

23. Ibid.

24. Ibid.

The Courts:
The Least Changed Branch

by Peter Buchsbaum

Among the three branches of government, the judicial branch has undergone the least change in the course of the nation's history. The 20th-Century executive branch no longer resembles, either in size or diversity of function, its 18th-Century ancestor. The Legislature, with its committee systems, large staffs, and diffusion of power among individual legislators, no longer functions as it did 20, let alone 200, years ago.

In contrast, the courts have undergone little change. Individual judges, assisted by perhaps a single law clerk, pass on whatever range of cases happen to be assigned to them. The core of the process has remained intact for two centuries.

We may not be able to afford this judicial conservatism any longer. The disastrous fire in an illegal trash dump at the Hub Recycling and Scrap Co., which resulted in a near-meltdown of Interstate 78 in Newark, [New Jersey,] capped two years of judicial wrangling over the issue of whether the state's contention that the facility was a public-health hazard outweighed the owners' property rights.

The actions of [New Jersey] Superior Court Judge Paul B. Thompson—who ruled in May [1989] that Hub posed no immediate hazard, allowing the site to remain open by staying his own earlier order to shut it down—may demonstrate that the system simply cannot cope with the number and complexity of disputes which must be resolved today. The single generalist judge system adequately responded to society's needs during much of our history, when lawsuits were few and concentrated mainly on private issues. These few generalists had time to concentrate on the occasional complex or public issue case. A nonbureaucratic judiciary could meet [New Jersey's] needs for dispute resolution.

Compare that model with the situation in which Judge Thompson found himself when the state of New Jersey requested . . . that the Hub Recycling and Scrap Co. be shut down. Essex County, the busiest judicial vicinage in [New Jersey], has an overwhelming number of cases. The time and attention that can be given to any one case must be carefully rationed by the judges, or the system will simply break down. In addition, the Supreme Court and the

Peter Buchsbaum is a partner in the Trenton, New Jersey, law firm of Hannoch Weisman. Reprinted by permission of the Center for Analysis of Public Issues, © 1989, from the September 1989 issue of *New Jersey Reporter* magazine, 32-33.

Administrative Office of the Courts require that judges dispose of cases promptly, to avoid a logjam in the system. Accordingly, Judge Thompson and his brethren do not have the time that a judge in the 1850s or even the 1950s would have had to mull over a complex case like the Hub dispute.

Moreover, the case was apparently not an easy one. The environmental risks probably had to be explained by technical testimony, which a lay judge, with little specific scientific or technical background, would not resolve through a simple analytic process.

In fact, the environmental problems which come before the courts today are typical of a whole species of cases, such as product-liability, land-use, and housing disputes, whose resolution requires real expertise. Yet these issues must be resolved by judges who have less time than ever to acquire the knowledge necessary to make informed judgments.

To some extent, the status of the judge within the judicial system has declined. There are hundreds of judges now. As a rule, they earn less money than many of the lawyers who appear before them. Psychologically, this may work to the detriment of judicial performance. The person who perceives himself or herself to be one of hundreds of average paid officials may feel more like someone on an assembly line than the person who was once regarded by the bar and by society as "The Judge."

Finally, the pace of the judiciary's deliberations simply does not jibe with that of real-world events. Judge Thompson may have had good reason for staying his initial decision to shut down Hub. After all, the state had taken a long time before even requesting the injunction. And it is difficult to say, at this stage, whether the evidence submitted by the state about imminent danger was really all that persuasive. In fact, the state's failure to appeal the stay in May suggests that the state attorney general's office may have had some doubts about the quality of the state's evidence. Further, totally shutting down a business before an appeal is heard, as the state requested, is a drastic remedy which would give any normal, thoughtful judge grounds for hesitation.

The real problem may not have been Judge Thompson's decision to issue the stay, but the fact that the courts take so long to render rulings. The fire broke out in August [1989], more than three months after Judge Thompson granted his stay pending Hub's appeal of his earlier order to close the dump down. In the normal course of judicial events, the appeal would not have been decided for a year, in this case, the spring of 1990. This leisurely pace to reach a resolution makes no sense in light of the environmental concerns involved. . . .

During these delays, nothing happens. In another context, Judge Thompson's stay might have been tolerable—even sensible—giving a private business a chance to appeal before shutting it down—if the appeal could have been heard in months, rather than years. In this case, the outcome of the delay was a disaster.

What can be done? Only *ad hoc* remedies have been offered so far. [New Jersey] Chief Justice Robert Wilentz's mandate for creation of a special environmental appeals panel should help in this one specific area. The panel will be made up of judges who have the necessary expertise in environmental issues, who have prestige by virtue of their special selection, and who, in theory, will have sufficient time to concentrate on each case.

But the broader problems will remain. Land-use and housing disputes, and issues concerning other state regulations, will still be remitted to the normal process, which is inadequate to the demands of the subject matter and the volume of cases.

A genuine solution to the judiciary's problems requires more than a targeted response to a particularly acute emergency, such as the Hub fire. Nor will the problem be solved simply by enlarging the existing system through the addition of more generalist judges.

Rather, the question is whether a judiciary reliant upon the unassisted generalist judge can really serve the public today. Judge Thompson's stay in the Hub case provides a lesson in the consequences of the perpetuation of an obsolescent system. The Supreme Court must address this problem before obsolescence gives way to a near system-wide breakdown in its ability to deal quickly but thoroughly with complex public issues.

Ideology and Judicial Elections in Wisconsin

by David M. Jones

This spring [1989], for the first time in more than two decades, an incumbent Justice of the Wisconsin Supreme Court faced a serious challenge in a reelection bid. The incumbent, Justice Shirley Abrahamson (the only woman on the Court), has been considered a judicial liberal by most commentators. Her home base is Madison, the state capital. Her challenger in this nonpartisan race was Judge Ralph Adam Fine of Milwaukee, an outspoken conservative. Judge Fine, who had recently defeated an incumbent in a State Court of Appeals race, had gained some fame (some would say notoriety) for his stand on plea bargaining, which he opposed as being too lenient on criminals. Indeed, his book *Escape of the Guilty,* an attack on that practice, had earned him a spot on the television program "60 Minutes."

Abrahamson, who had been appointed to a vacancy on the bench in 1976, and who had subsequently been elected to a full seven year term, had also been a subject of some controversy. In 1987, the *Milwaukee Journal* published a series of articles, "Discord on the Court," alleging that personality conflicts on the Wisconsin Supreme Court were undermining its productivity. Much of the blame for these conflicts was placed at the feet of Justice

Abrahamson, who was characterized as being arrogant and abrasive (a charge she denied). Political observers had been predicting for some time that this race between the two ideological opponents would take place.

Fine announced his candidacy in late November, stating that he would focus his campaign on "crime and judicial fairness." The judge, who had written an opinion piece in the *Wall Street Journal* supporting Robert Bork's nomination, campaigned for harsher sentencing, against plea bargaining and for the closing of legal "loopholes" which (he alleged) allowed guilty persons to go free. Abrahamson, he charged, was one of those justices who seemed to find such unnecessary loopholes. He also attacked her as being a judicial liberal who was far out of the mainstream.

Abrahamson, for her part, said she was in favor of judicial accountability, fairness and a greater concern for victims' rights. She denied being a liberal (implying such labels were inapplicable to judges) and suggested that if

David M. Jones is associate professor of public affairs at the University of Wisconsin-Oshkosh. This article is reprinted from *Comparative State Politics* 10:4 (August 1989): 6-8.

Fine wanted to achieve his stated objectives, he should run for a "political" office rather than a position on the Wisconsin Supreme Court.

The campaign was marred by charges and countercharges in which each side accused the other of making misleading and/or false statements about the opposition. The candidates also, after some hesitation on Abrahamson's part, engaged in a number of debates, many of which were quite rancorous.

In spite of her "liberal" label, Justice Abrahamson received endorsements from approximately three-quarters of the state's sheriffs, the Milwaukee County District Attorney and several prominent Republicans, as well as victims' rights groups and a number of Democrats. Many of the state's newspapers also endorsed her candidacy. Fine, for his part, argued that it was inappropriate for judicial candidates to seek endorsements in their campaigns.

The campaign was, by Wisconsin standards, an expensive one. Both candidates reached the spending limits of $215,000 imposed by the state's public financing law. Most of their funds appeared to have gone for television "spots" that appeared in the state's major media markets.

In spite of the expenditures, the heat of the campaign and its ideological overtones, voters seemed to be largely unaffected. A poll taken by the *Milwaukee Journal* a week prior to the election showed that Abrahamson led Fine by the same three percent margin with liberals, as she did with conservatives. She had, however, a much higher margin among moderates.

These preelection polls were vindicated on April 11 [, 1989] when Abrahamson beat Fine rather decisively. Unofficial tallies showed Abrahamson receiving 482,388 votes to Fine's 395,227. Preliminary analysis indicates that "friends and neighbors" voting may explain voting patterns at least as much as ideology. Fine did very well in the Milwaukee area (including heavily Democratic Milwaukee County) while Abrahamson's strongest base of support came from around Madison. She also did well in traditionally conservative out-state areas.

Because the position of Chief Justice of the Wisconsin Supreme Court is based on seniority and because Justice Abrahamson's tenure on that body is third in length, it is possible that, within a few years, she will become Wisconsin's first woman Chief Justice.

Hans A. Linde: The Unassuming Architect of an Emerging Role for State Constitutions

by Elder Witt

Hans A. Linde has made a career out of not following the crowd. Now there's a crowd following him.

To a country fascinated with the federal courts and the federal Constitution, Linde has been repeating the same message: State constitutions should get more respect. That was the theme of a lecture a decade ago. "State bills of rights are first in two senses; first in time and first in logic," and state judges should look to them before turning to the U.S. Bill of Rights.

It is a message at odds with conventional wisdom. "It is common knowledge that the rights all Americans prize . . . come from the first 10 Amendments of the United States Constitution. It is common knowledge, but it is false," he continued in that 1979 address, his sentences sprinkled with the broad As and W-shaped Rs of his native Germany. "Far from being the model for the states, the federal Bill of Rights was added to the Constitution to meet demands for the same guarantees against the new central government that people had secured against their own local officials."

Linde began his campaign on behalf of state constitutions as a young law professor at the University of Oregon in the 1960s. The influence of his ideas has grown steadily since he became a member of the Oregon Supreme Court in 1977.

Since 1980, dozens of state courts, in more than 350 cases, have declared their constitutions more protective of individual rights than the federal Constitution. That's triple the number of such decisions in the 1970s. No individual is more responsible for that trend than Hans Linde.

A small, scholarly man of 65, bald and bespectacled, Linde is commanding in neither appearance nor tone. He answers his own telephone, eats at the sandwich shop across the street from the justice building and buzzes around Salem in a blue Honda. He operates with a single clerk and a judicial assistant.

Yet he is acknowledged as the intellectual architect of this newly emerging judicial federalism. Without drama or rhetoric, without flourish or flamboyance, in speeches, articles, seminars and decisions, he has promulgated the state courts' declaration of independence.

That independence is in part a reaction to an increasingly conservative U.S. Supreme Court. When that court, after the departure of

Elder Witt is a staff writer for *Governing*. This article is reprinted from *Governing* 2:10 (July 1989): 56-60.

Chief Justice Earl Warren in 1969, began to pull back from its activist posture on questions of individual rights, some state courts began to look for a reason not to follow suit. They found that reason in Linde's writings.

His "first-things-first" approach to constitutional law was the vehicle they needed to stay where they wanted to stay—or go where they wanted to go. "State judges are looking around for creative tools to solve problems in new ways," says Utah Supreme Court Justice Christine Durham. State constitutional law is just such a tool. In the past decade, it has developed into a school of judicial thought that stands on its own as a philosophical approach, not merely a reaction to the decisions handed down by the federal courts. "That's due to Linde; he's both its generative force and its instructive force," says Jacob Tanzer, a former member of the Oregon Supreme Court who is now in private practice.

This might not have happened if then-Governor Robert Straub, a Democrat, had not decided to appoint a scholar named Linde to Oregon's high court 12 years ago. "There are lots of professors with lots of theories. But only when theories have the official force of the state's highest court are they regarded as more than interesting theories but also valid options for other courts to follow," Tanzer explains.

Like state constitutions themselves, Linde's ideas are rarely stunning in their novelty. Their power is in his timing, his juxtaposition of problem and solution. He has a talent for rubbing the old brass lamp to cast new light on difficult questions. "There is about him a feeling that you're seeing a much deeper reality being penetrated," says Hardy Myers, former speaker of the Oregon House. "Things are turned over and looked at from a standpoint that most people simply don't think of. Suddenly a light just goes on, and you wonder, 'Why didn't I think of that?'"

That was the case when male inmates at the state prison complained that their privacy was violated when they were body-searched by female guards. The Oregon Supreme Court agreed and halted the practice.

But Linde didn't base its ruling on the federal right to privacy cited by the inmates. Instead, he cited a long-ignored provision of Oregon's constitution that protected inmates from being treated with "unnecessary rigor." A number of other states have similar guarantees, and within three years, Linde's opinion had been cited at least eight times by courts outside Oregon.

Other Linde opinions and articles are often cited, less to justify a particular result than to validate a court's shift to state laws and state constitutional rulings rather than federal ones as grounds for its decisions.

There's one very important side effect to that shift. State judges don't like being second-guessed by the federal courts, and the U.S. Supreme Court has said it won't review rulings that are based plainly on state constitutional law. Even though the federal justices sometimes breach their rule, it remains a strong incentive for state judges to follow Linde's lead.

Linde's emphasis on state constitutions is just the most visible aspect of revolutionary legal philosophy.

The Warren Court ignored state constitutions, explains Ron Collins, a visiting professor of law at Temple University, and thereby "left in the minds of a whole generation the idea that as long as government conduct comported with the commands of the federal Constitution as interpreted by the U.S. Supreme Court, it was legal."

To Linde, this federal-first emphasis is upside down. He's doing his best to turn things right side up. "You can often get to the same result without dealing with a constitutional claim," he explains. "That used to be conventional wisdom until Earl Warren."

The first question he asks when a state action is challenged in his court—whether it's a police request for a driver's license or a regulatory board's revocation of a dentist's license—is whether the action is authorized by law. If it is not, the government loses. If it is, he asks whether it is in line with the state constitution. If it is not, the government loses. If it is, only then does Linde look to a challenge based on the federal Constitution.

That's sequence, that's process, and that's Linde, a man with a passion for the law governing government. It is a passion born of experience.

Linde doesn't dwell on the early part of his journey from the family apartment on Berlin's bustling Kurfurstendamm to the sunny, flower-encircled old farmhouse in Salem where he lives today with Helen, his wife of 44 years.

But it is not surprising that the nine-year-old Jewish child who left Germany in 1933 as Hitler came to power, and then left a happy life in Copenhagen six years later as Germany was plunging Europe into war, already saw a need for laws to confine the exercise of government's power. Reflecting on his childhood experiences, Linde recalls that the news unfolding around him—the Spanish Civil War, the rise of Nazi power in Germany, the Italian invasion of Ethiopia—made obvious the necessity of protecting the rights of the individual.

Law provides that protection in a democratic system, and law to Linde is far more than what judges decide. He believes it is the job of the courts to clear the channels by which people can alter their laws as values and situations change. That, in his view, is why sequence is so significant: Judges should base their decisions on state law, which can be changed with relative ease, or, if necessary, on the state constitution, which is not nearly as difficult to amend as the U.S. Constitution.

Linde's own court took this inherently conservative tack when it faced a dispute over the public funding of abortions. Under pressure from the state Emergency Board, which acts as an appropriations committee between sessions of the legislature, the state agency responsible for medical assistance to the poor moved to limit who could get abortions. When that action was challenged, it was struck down by the Oregon Supreme Court, not because it was unconstitutional, not because it violated any individual's right, but because it was not authorized by law.

The Emergency Board had authority only to appropriate money, not to change state policy, Linde explains. "The operating agency was responsible for the program as the statute had set it up, and should not change it to please the Emergency Board, which is not a small legislature.

"I'm a great believer in legislatures," Linde continues, leaving his desk to join a visitor in a more comfortable corner of his spacious office in Salem's marble Supreme Court building, older by two decades than the U.S. Supreme Court building.

That belief is based on close acquaintance. Linde spent four years in Washington, D.C., as legislative assistant to Oregon's U.S. Senator Richard M. Neuberger, a Democrat. After returning to Oregon, Linde worked closely on a variety of issues with friends in the Oregon legislature, taught legislative process to law students and literally wrote the book, the law school casebook, on the subject.

Nevertheless, Linde is chagrined to be praised as a lawmaker, as New York University Law School did in dedicating its annual survey of American law to him in 1984. Judges aren't supposed to be lawmakers, he contends; their role is to keep the process working correctly so that others can make law.

Questions of process are the focus of the field of administrative law, an area in which

Table 1 Preemption of State Law Cases Heard by the U.S. Supreme Court

	Number of preemption cases	Number of cases finding preemption (losses by states)	Typical cases
Recent decisions (1985, 1986, 1987 terms)	39 (9% of docket)	22 (56% of all preemption cases)	Business interests seeking relief from state or local regulations: 31 cases, 17 wins (55% success rate)
Earlier decisions (1962, 1963, 1964 terms)	10 (2% of docket)	6 (60% of all preemption cases)	Union seeking National Labor Relations Board protection: 5 cases, 4 wins (80% success rate)

Source: Data from Stewart A. Baker, chairman of the State and Local Legal Center Advisory Board, which appeared in "Court to Decide Cases Important to States," *Governors' Weekly Bulletin* 23:40 (October 13, 1989): 1. Reprinted with permission from the National Governors' Association.

Linde was well known as an authority long before the current wave of attention to his ideas about state constitutions. "He has this very systematic, rather global approach, that authorizes government to act based on statutes and limits government action in ways that are clear and can be figured out and don't boil down to platitudes about discretion," says Tanzer.

A prime example was the Oregon court's reversal of a decision of the State Board of Dental Examiners to revoke a dentist's license for "unprofessional conduct." Nothing in the board's rules gave the dentist fair notice that he could lose his license for giving an insurance company misinformation about his employees, declared Linde. He then went on to point out an avenue by which administrative agencies could develop consistent standards to guide their work.

Analyzing the legislators' decision to authorize the dental board to make rules for the conduct of those it supervises as well as to resolve individual cases, Linde said that the legislature had intended the board to use its rule-making power to define such key terms as "unprofessional conduct," rather than merely permitting that definition to evolve through the patchwork of case-by-case decisions.

"I preach about this decision, about what

Hans started by presenting a rationale for requiring state agencies . . . to make their law by rule rather than by ad hoc orders, case by case," says Arthur Earl Bonfield, who teaches administrative law at the University of Iowa law school. . . .

In 1958, Linde [accepted] a teaching position at the University of Oregon law school. He accepted the job, he says, because it offered him a chance to return to Oregon and stay in the area of public law, the law governing government. "At the time, you couldn't practice that body of law in Oregon," he explains. "You could either be in government or you could teach."

So teach he did, but that wasn't all. Summers were spent consulting—on the international issues in which he had become expert during his State Department years—in Washington, D.C., at the Arms Control and Disarmament Agency or in California at the Rand Corp., the Santa Monica-based think tank.

Oregon considered revising its constitution in the early 1960s, and Linde was in charge of drafting the changes. Friends and former students like Dave Frohnmayer, now Oregon's attorney general, became executive branch officials or legislators; Linde advised them on policy. His reputation grew. Other law schools wooed him, but all were rejected.

He and Helen had a son and a daughter, and life in Eugene was pleasant. He traveled to lecture, to teach as a visiting professor in the United States and in Germany.

Frohnmayer was a first-year law student at Berkeley when he met Linde, a visiting professor there, in the mid-1960s. Frohnmayer took Linde's course, and their friendship grew. When Frohnmayer's path led to a position on the law faculty in Eugene, Linde taught the young newlywed professor's first classes so that the Frohnmayers could complete their honeymoon.

Few scholars sit on state supreme courts, but when a vacancy occurred on Oregon's court in 1976, Frohnmayer, then a state legislator, wrote Governor Straub to suggest that he appoint Linde to fill out the unexpired term, and Straub took the suggestion. "Judging," says Linde, "would not have been my first choice" of a government job, all things being equal. By the time Straub offered the appointment to Linde, however, the professor had concluded that if he wanted a senior public position, "it had to be judging or nothing."

Frohnmayer remains a friend and admirer of his former professor, though as attorney general, he's lost his share of arguments to the Linde logic. And friendship doesn't stifle some reservations about Linde's views.

Independent state constitutional interpretation is fine up to a point, Frohnmayer says, but "there's a fine line to be walked between this declaration of independence and a declaration of unreality." That's particularly true in criminal law, where double standards cause severe everyday problems. "You can say, 'Well, that's okay for the feds, the state can do its own thing.' But as a matter of fact, we have a lot of joint federal-state law enforcement task forces, and to have two sets of rules presents a serious practical problem.

"Hans has his eye on the long ball," Frohnmayer adds. "Some of us would like to know a little bit more clearly where the ball is going to land."

While Linde's work as a justice has stimulated a resurgence of intellectual activity and interest in state courts across the country, not all of his decisions have been precedent-setters.

"When we had a really knotty problem without precedent, the chief justice would assign it to Hans," says Tanzer, his former colleague. "One way or another, Hans could unravel the problem in a logical way." Whether the lawyers who had to live with that decision could understand it, however, was another matter. Several of Linde's most innovative decisions have gone uncited by lawyers and judges who simply agree to ignore them because they can't figure them out.

"His strength is in his intellect, but that's also his greatest weakness," says another close observer. "Linde's so smart he can't believe he's ever made a mistake."

If Linde finds it hard to acknowledge his mistakes, he is frank about his flaws as a candidate. "I'm not the kind of person to be elected to office," he says. Yet judges in Oregon are elected, so when Governor Straub talked with Linde about his appointment, he made sure that the new judge had the stomach for the political campaign that would be necessary to win a six-year term of his own.

Despite his long fascination with politics, Linde had never considered running for office himself. "I'm not a backslapper," says Linde. "I don't have a lot of patience with repeating the same cliches over and over again for one audience and then another audience. I'm strictly a substance person."

His first election in 1978 was a breeze: He had no opposition in the non-partisan race for the job, which now pays $70,000 a year. But to win re-election in 1984 required a hard-fought effort against two opponents. One opposing candidate was a judge, the other a prosecutor backed by law enforcement groups and Mothers Against Drunk Driving. Both were critical of Linde rulings limiting police power to search suspects and government's power to impose the death penalty.

Traditionally, the senior member of the Oregon Supreme Court is elected by his colleagues as chief justice. Linde is the senior justice, but he had no interest in the administrative responsibilities that go with the chief justice's job. It went instead to Linde's good friend and chess partner, Ed Peterson.

The seven justices hear cases the first week of each month, usually in their spacious, amber-toned courtroom under a stained-glass ceiling, but sometimes in the more informal, and better-attended, setting of a law school classroom.

Like [Supreme Court] Justice [William O.] Douglas, [for whom Linde clerked,] and unlike many judges, Linde writes his own opinions, and Linde's clerks are well advised not to presume to question their boss's style. "One learns quickly to be humble in his presence," says Temple University's Ron Collins, who is one of Linde's former clerks. "His intellectual power is just overwhelming. As far as I know, no Linde law clerk has ever written a Linde opinion or even a portion of one."

Unlike Douglas, however, Linde forms a close working relationship with his clerks, who usually emerge from their year with him as disciples. David Schuman, who clerked the year that Linde battled for re-election, recalls the experience as "a one-year intensive seminar in legal thinking conducted by an articulate, brilliant and considerate tutor."

Linde's clerks learn their lessons well. Collins has taught state constitutional law at a variety of law schools from coast to coast. And he and another former Linde clerk, Jennifer Friesen, who now teaches at Loyola Law School in California, are both writing books on state constitutional law.

Linde's second term ends next year. He will be 66. Will he run again? The intellectual man has a practical moment. "I like the work and don't mind staying on, but I don't want to do it for nothing." His brown eyes twinkle with impish humor: "If the difference between working and retirement is only $300 a month," he says, "you look at yourself and say, 'Am I smart enough to be a judge?'"

Judicial Activism Raises Ire of the Legislature

by Linda Wagar

There rests a thorn in the side of some lawmakers and it's called the judicial system.

State courts have reared their independent heads in a variety of ways in recent years, provoking the baser emotions of lawmakers who think the line between legislative and judicial powers has grown decidedly narrow.

Court rulings that have overturned abortion statutes, limited punitive damages and ordered more equality in education funding have prompted some legislators to decry judicial activism—accusing courts of setting public policy rather than interpreting the constitution.

West Virginia lawmakers did not hesitate to object when they felt the state judiciary had overstepped constitutional boundaries with a 1982 ruling on the funding of education. A West Virginia judge not only ruled the state funding system unconstitutional but outlined exactly how the Legislature should rectify the problem.

"The court produced a very detailed finding without a lot of public input," said West Virginia House Speaker Robert Chambers, who noted that many of the changes have never been implemented because of lack of public support.

Georgia Supreme Court Chief Justice Thomas O. Marshall said he disagreed with courts that try to "road map the legislature" by detailing how a ruling should be implemented.

"Courts should stick to interpreting the laws," Marshall said.

Kentucky Chief Justice Robert Stephens agreed, adding that courts should be reluctant to change longstanding interpretations of their state constitution even in response to political or social circumstances.

But Oregon Attorney General Dave Frohnmayer, a former legislator, said it is often the vague laws of legislators that prompt activism in the courts.

"Many laws give executive branch entities almost unbridled discretion to regulate important aspects of human life," Frohnmayer wrote in an article for *The Journal of State Government*. "They virtually compel our court system ultimately to impose extensive procedural safeguards and substantive policy definitions, which are largely if not wholly of judicial creation."

Wisconsin Supreme Court Chief Justice

Linda Wagar is a staff writer for *State Government News*. This article is reprinted with permission from *State Government News* 32:12 (December 1989): 34. © 1990 the Council of State Governments.

Nathan Heffernan said he grows irritated with lawmakers who accuse activist courts of robbing the public of its voice as expressed by the legislature. Heffernan said courts often are forced into action to meet constitutional mandates the legislature has ignored.

"The voice of the constitution *is* the voice of the people and that supersedes the voice of a lethargic legislature," said Heffernan.

Some lawmakers accept Heffernan's view and say they are not bothered by what others might perceive as judicial activism.

Georgia Sen. Thomas Algood said he had little problem with a court spelling out for a governing body what it can or cannot do. Algood described his own state Supreme Court as "more conservative than it should be," noting that at times he wished the court had made rulings on areas that were too politically sensitive for the Legislature to handle.

Wisconsin's Heffernan said he believed most lawmakers welcome court intervention when it saves them from making politically unpopular decisions. Such, he said, was the case in 1964 when the Wisconsin Supreme Court gave the Legislature several months to reapportion itself.

"They didn't act and the court reapportioned the state for them," Heffernan said. "I think the court saved the Legislature from a lot of heat and they were delighted that someone else was willing to take the rap."

Heffernan said judges have the ability to accomplish measures that lawmakers cannot because judges, in most states, do not face frequent re-election or run in partisan races.

"We don't have the political constraints that legislators have," Heffernan said.

Texas Chief Justice Thomas Phillips said that despite lawmaker complaints about judicial activism, courts have a legitimate and large lawmaking role. "Most of the law that governs our conduct is judge-made law," Phillips said. "Part of the reason such a system works well is because of its flexibility. You can apply precedent day by day."

Kentucky's Stephens acknowledged that no matter what a court does, some lawmakers will never be pleased.

"When a court declares a statute as unconstitutional they [lawmakers] are very resentful of that," Stephens said. "Personally, I think judicial activism lies in the eyes of the beholder. It depends on whether your ox is the one being gored."

The Furor Over One Juror

by Ed McManus

It was an especially brutal case of child abuse. Two-year-old Jasmine Ferguson had been severely beaten and placed in scalding hot water. When paramedics were called to the home of her grandmother, they found the child nearly comatose. She died two days later, and the grandmother, 38-year-old Miriam Watt of south suburban Harvey, [Illinois,] was charged with murder.

The state sought the death penalty and, as is customary, questioned prospective jurors about their feelings on capital punishment. Eventually, 12 jurors who said they weren't opposed to it were selected, and . . . they found Watt guilty. .

But then the state's plan went awry. When the jury began considering whether to declare Watt eligible for a death sentence—a procedure which precedes the deliberation on whether to actually sentence a defendant to death—one juror resisted. The jury foreman told the judge that the man refused to declare Watt eligible "because of his disbelief in the death penalty."

What happened? We don't really know. Perhaps the man deliberately lied during jury selection. But what would someone's motivation be to do that? Maybe he just changed his mind.

And what can (or should) be done about it? As in many aspects of our criminal justice system, it depends on your point of view.

The prosecutors were outraged, and Robert Clifford, head of the sixth district of the Cook County state's attorney's office, said his office might prosecute the man for perjury. This statement provoked even more outrage from defense lawyers, who denounced Clifford. But no one ultimately did anything to the juror. He was never interviewed by the judge or the attorneys, so we don't know what he said in the jury room other than what the other jurors said he said.

(The judge subsequently sentenced Watt to life in prison without parole.)

The prosecutors felt double-crossed.

"He sabotaged the system," said Assistant State's Atty. Henry Simmons.

"It's so frustrating," said another assistant state's attorney, Celeste Stewart. "The guy lied to us."

"It's not fair that a member of a jury can

Ed McManus is an assistant editor of the *Chicago Tribune*. This article is reprinted with permission from *Illinois Issues* 15:6 (June 1989): 40-41, published by Sangamon State University, Springfield, Illinois 62794-9243. © *Illinois Issues*.

misrepresent himself and go unpunished," said Clifford. He said it would be possible to hold a hearing on whether the man was in contempt of court or to prosecute him for perjury. Clifford turned the matter over to his superiors, who took no action.

But the defense lawyers were still mad at Clifford. A group of 10 lawyers, led by Cook County Public Defender Randolph N. Stone, issued a statement, which said in part:

"Clifford should be reminded that in a democracy, the voice of dissent is not sabotage, but a necessary and valuable part of the 'system.' Clifford's statements constitute not only a blatant threat to punish a juror for depriving the state's attorney's office of a death verdict, but an insidious attempt to intimidate future jurors with the specter of prosecution for disagreement with the government. Such threats and intimidation have no place in our criminal justice system.

"Jury deliberations are sacrosanct. No juror ever need justify his or her vote in a criminal case. The dissenting juror in the Watt case, for whatever reason, concluded that the defendant should not be sentenced to death. Perhaps the juror felt lingering doubt about Watt's guilt, since the evidence against her was completely circumstantial. Perhaps the juror felt the evidence did not warrant the death penalty. Perhaps the juror chose to extend mercy to Watt. Any of these reasons is completely legitimate and above questioning or criticism.

"Moreover, even if the juror in the Watt case simply refused to consider the death penalty, there was no 'perjury' involved. The decision to sentence a fellow human being to death is unlike any other. A potential juror being questioned before a trial may sincerely believe that he could, under the proper circumstances, sentence someone to death. Yet that same juror, after hearing the evidence and considering the sentence in deliberations, may find himself unable to do so. Such a good faith realization by a juror is not crime.

"Our jury system will cease to work if jurors are forced to worry that they may be punished for their decisions."

Clifford and Stewart stressed that their anger over the juror's action was magnified by the fact that it occurred' while the jury was deciding whether Watt was eligible for a death sentence—not whether she should be sentenced to death. Under Illinois law, people can be sentenced to death only if they fit within certain categories—in this case, according to prosecutors, because it was a "brutal and heinous" murder of a child.

As a matter of fact, one member of the jury, interviewed by the *Chicago Tribune*, said the other jurors, although they wanted to declare Watt eligible, "were not going to vote for death."

The courts have held that a juror is guilty of misconduct if he falsely misrepresents his interest or situation during jury selection. But, as the defense lawyers pointed out, we don't know if that was the case here. Clifford had a point when he said during an interview, "What if the shoe was on the other foot? What if those lawyers had been assured that a juror wasn't hostile to them, and then he turned out to be?"

So it seems to come down to who's side you're on.

IX.   STATE ISSUES

One might think that the goal of state government is to provide the services that citizens need and then raise the money to do so. Actually, the process is just the reverse: the governor and state legislature raise the money they can and then decide the extent of services the state can provide. It comes as no surprise, therefore, that financial issues are at the top of state policy agendas. How should revenues be raised—taxes, user fees, bonds, lotteries? What kinds of taxes should be imposed—sales, income, inheritance, property? Who will bear the burden of these taxes—the rich, the poor, the consumer, the property holder? These are the most important questions state governors and legislatures address.

During the nationwide recession in the early 1980s, state revenues dropped precipitously. In 1982, twenty-two states imposed major tax increases. The following year, thirty-eight states raised at least one kind of tax. The fiscal crisis necessitated layoffs, hiring limits, travel restrictions, and delays in expenditures. The budget crunch of the early 1980s greatly lowered expectations of what state government could and would do.[1]

In 1984 and 1985, the states continued a wait-and-see attitude, with nineteen states raising taxes and thirty-two states decreasing them. States were waiting to see how the national government would handle the federal deficit, and how that decision would affect state and local finances. Then, in 1986, a major fear of state leaders' came true: the president and Congress decided to solve part of the national deficit crisis by letting the states pay for a considerable part of it. Saving a program that formerly was funded in whole or part with federal funds means increasing state and local taxes. And to many lawmakers, increased taxes can mean defeat at the polls.

In recent years another problem has occurred in many states: the deterioration of their fiscal health resulting from reduced tax revenues to support state government programs and services. But state leaders are learning how to cope with these problems. In 1987, twenty-four states had to cut their budgets at midyear due to fewer revenues than forecast, thirty-four states had to raise tax levels to fund their proposed 1988 budgets, and twenty-four states adopted moderate-to-major tax reforms. In 1988, eighteen states had to cut back their enacted budgets, and by April 1989, ten had to do so for fiscal 1989.[2]

Now the states face new budget problems: keeping their budgets balanced. In October 1988, the National Association of State Budget Officers (NASBO) reported "states are in a precarious position" and cannot afford to have any bad economic news. "They have very little reserves to deal with shocks."[3] Note the irony here: the bad news for the states is their low budget surpluses; for the federal government it is the large budget deficit! But that is just the problem, according to a later NASBO report: the "federal government continues to try and solve its own problems by passing costs on to the states."[4]

What can the states do? As already noted, one option is to raise taxes. States also can seek new sources of tax revenue. For example, more and more states are considering instituting a state lottery, which seems to be a painless way to raise money. But recent research on state lotteries indicates that they amount to a "heavy tax"—one that is sharply regressive—because it is levied in part on those who cannot afford it. The economics of the state lotteries in 1988 indicate that of each dollar spent on a lottery ticket ($16 billion), 48 cents went for prizes, 15 cents for administration, including promotion and sales, and only 37 cents ($5.7 billion) for government purposes.[5]

In 1989 and 1990, finances have domi-nated the agendas of most state governors and legislatures. While many economists argue the country is not in a recession, many state leaders do not agree. State leaders feel an economic slowdown has occurred, which has translated into decreasing state tax revenues or in a decline of the revenue growth they had experienced in recent years. This often means tax increases must be considered if programs are to be maintained at their current levels, let alone starting new initiatives.

But increasing taxes can lead to citizen and voter dissatisfaction. Three of six gover-nors in economically troubled New England who are up for reelection in 1990 have decided not to seek another term. This is partially due to the problems in their states' budgetary situation, which has necessitated tax increases and caused voter resentment. Some blame President George Bush's famous 1988 cam-paign promise of "Read My Lips, No New Taxes" as setting a tone that affects all levels of government. However, Maine governor John R. McKernan (R, 1989-   ) believes that reasoning amounts to "whining . . . President Bush didn't say the governors shouldn't raise taxes. . . ."[6]

By March 1990, more than half of the states were in the throes of budgetary prob-lems in their current budget year (which ends on June 30 for all states except New York, which ends March 30). One observer indicated the imbalances in the state budgets were the worst since the 1982 recession.[7] Worst hit were the New England states and the mid-Atlantic states down through North Carolina. The energy and farm states of the Southwest and Midwest were in better shape since they already had experienced these economic and fiscal problems and had adopted an "austerity budget" approach, in addition to finding their economies improving. Many western states were still enjoying robust, growing economies

with the attendant growing tax revenues that often lead to healthy budget surpluses.[8]

After taxes, what are the issues of greatest concern to the states? Or, to put it another way, what do states spend the most money on? Funding levels are a good indication of com-mitment.

Large sums are spent each year on educa-tion, health programs, state highways, eco-nomic development, and environmental protec-tion. In 1986, state government expenditures topped $424 billion with education ($140 bil-lion or 33 percent) and welfare ($73 billion or 17.2 percent) taking over half of these funds.[9] There was a projected jump of 6.3 percent in state expenditures between fiscal 1988 and fiscal 1989 with Medicaid as the fastest grow-ing major program, and support for primary and secondary education growing faster than overall growth at 8.2 percent.[10]

Of course, different regions of the country have different priorities. In the Southwest, water policy is a dominant issue. In the Midwest, farm problems, the declining indus-trial base, and lack of economic development are major concerns. And under the prodding of the U.S. Department of Energy, the states have been grouped into a series of regional interstate compacts (legal agreements) to seek processes and sites for the disposal of radioac-tive waste within each region.

Issues also vary from one state to another. Policy makers in Florida must address the many social and environmental problems cre-ated by the state's population boom and break-neck development. Connecticut and New York have different troubles, such as the deteriora-tion of public highways and bridges, which was made evident by the collapse of the New York state thruway bridge into the Scoharie Creek in 1987. These states have been suffer-ing from a declining tax base as industry and people move out. And in Nevada and New Jersey the infiltration of organized crime in state gambling casinos has officials on the watch. More recently, these casinos have been losing money.

Setting the Agenda

How do particular concerns become priorities on the states' agendas? Although state constitutions provide for the education, health, and safety of citizens, events can trigger new interest in these issues. For example, the Soviets' nuclear disaster at Chernobyl revitalized the antinuclear power movement in some state capitals. Campaign promises and court decisions also influence policy making. A gubernatorial candidate who promises to lower utility rates will try to keep this promise once elected. And if a state court finds that some citizens, such as the mentally handicapped, are not receiving the state services to which they are entitled, chances are the governor and state legislators will pay closer attention to this issue.

A public health issue state leaders are frantically groping with now is Acquired Immune Deficiency Syndrome (AIDS), a disease without a cure. Between 1981 and 1987, AIDS was considerably more likely to be found in the larger urban states, such as California (8,348 cases) and New York (10,870 cases), while smaller rural states virtually escaped the disease, such as in North and South Dakota where only five cases each were reported in this period. But AIDS is on the rise and an estimated 1.5 million people carried the virus in 1987.[11] This public health crisis is being addressed by the medical profession, but AIDS also intrudes into other public concerns that state leaders must consider. [12]

Provisions of the U.S. Constitution also can force issues onto a state's policy agenda. Since the 1950s, there has been a series of U.S. Supreme Court decisions on "separate but equal" education, reapportionment, and criminal justice based on lawsuits challenging state and local government policies and actions as violations of the plaintiffs' constitutional rights. These decisions have caused state and local government lawmakers considerable anguish as they address and adopt often controversial and expensive new policies, which usually translate into tax increases.

Forty-two states currently are under a federal court order to ease prison crowding; only Alabama, Alaska, Minnesota, Montana, Nebraska, New Jersey, New York, and North Dakota are not. The states were expected to spend more than $4 billion in 1989 to expand existing prisons and build new ones.[13] With all the calls to get tougher on those involved in drug transactions, state prisons will only become more crowded, exacerbating already difficult problems.

The only alternative to prompt action by the states to relieve prison overcrowding is to have the federal courts take over this major state government function and mandate that the states take even more controversial and expensive steps.

However, the U.S. Supreme Court also can be supportive of state policy initiatives. For example, in an important 1989 decision, the Court upheld state antitrust laws that in 1977 the U.S. Circuit Court of Appeals had declared preempted by federal law. The winning argument indicated federal antitrust laws were supplemental and not preemptive of state laws, an important constitutional distinction in our federal system of government.[14]

In 1989, the U.S. Supreme Court decided to return to the states some of the questions over abortion rights in a celebrated case, *Webster v. Reproductive Health Services*.[15] This partially reversed the Court's 1973 decision in *Roe v. Wade*, which had taken the power to restrict abortions in the first two trimesters of pregnancy from the states. The ferment in the states began quickly when prolife and prochoice groups organized to press their positions on state legislators and governors.

Florida governor Bob Martinez (R, 1987-   ) called a special fall 1989 session of his legislature to consider legislation restricting abortion. The legislators, who were not happy with the position this placed them in, "bottled up all four of Martinez's abortion bills in committee and adjourned the session early." [16] In Pennsylvania, the governor and the state legislature were of the same mind on abortion and readily passed prolife legislation. In 1990, the Idaho legislature passed very restrictive prolife legislation, only to have their prolife Democratic governor, Cecil Andrus, veto it as being too restrictive. The abortion issue played a large role in the 1989 gubernatorial races in New Jersey and Virginia, as discussed in the introduction to Part I.

In addition to the basic philosophical and religious arguments in the abortion debate, some of the key issues being deliberated in the state legislatures are: public funding of abortions for those who cannot afford them; use of public facilities for abortions; requiring parental consent for minors; abortion as a method of birth control or sex selection; specifying time limits for an abortion and determining the viability of a fetus; and birth control and abortion counseling.

Federal program requirements also can play a role in state policy making and administration. For example, in the early and mid-1980s, the states had to raise the legal drinking age to twenty-one and limit interstate highway speeds to 55 miles per hour or face the loss of federal highway funds. However, federal encroachment on setting speed limits came to a head in a highly publicized and controversial vote to override President Ronald Reagan's veto of a multibillion dollar transportation bill in March 1987. The override allowed those states that wished to raise the limit to 65 miles per hour on rural interstates.

Innovations and programs in other states can influence a state's agenda, as a new form of activity in one state may lead to similar action elsewhere. Some of the specific steps taken by the states that had to deal with the AIDS crisis in the early 1980s are now being copied by other states. Some states are copying other states' attempts to develop technology centers to attract industry. This "copycat" method of decision making has proved to be very popular: How did State X handle this?

Events not only in another state but in another part of the world occasionally determine the issues that state governments must address. The 1973-1974 Arab oil embargo rapidly escalated world oil and gas prices. As a result, the tax revenues of states with oil and gas reserves (such as Alaska, Louisiana, Oklahoma, and Texas) greatly increased. These states impose severance taxes on the sale of oil and gas—taxes that motorists in other states pay at the gas pump.

In the mid-1970s, the oil-rich states confronted the happy problem of deciding how to spend all their money: should they expand services, create new facilities, reduce taxes, or share the wealth with their citizens by issuing dividends? All of these options and others were tried. Alaska was so flush that it provided citizens with a cash dividend and even considered moving the state capital to another location.

The energy windfall raised the expectations of politicians and the public concerning what state government could accomplish. But after the average well-head barrel price of oil peaked at almost $32 in 1982 and state severance taxes peaked at $7.8 billion, the price of oil has dropped steadily. The states collected only an estimated $4.1 billion in severance taxes in 1987. Texas saw its budget revenues savaged as severance taxes dropped from 25 percent of all state revenues in 1982 to 10.6 percent in 1987. North Dakota felt a similar drop from 35 percent to 15.9 percent.[17] Obviously, oil states must sharply reduce government spending or raise other taxes: neither option is a pleasant choice. But what will they do? In April 1989, true to their fierce antitax tradition, Louisiana voters rejected by a 55-45 percent vote a major tax reform package actively pushed by the governor, forcing the governor and legislature to begin taking drastic steps to slash the budget with its $700 million deficit.[18]

Now there are signs of more trouble brewing for the states from outside the nation. Although the recent decrease in tension between the United States and the Soviet Union has spawned the "peace dividend"—a budget windfall from cuts in the defense budget—the states will bear the cost of the dividend. Cuts in the defense budget mean the closing of military bases in some states, reducing military personnel, and cutting back or canceling contracts for military hardware and weapons systems and funding for military research. Like the high rolling energy states of the 1970s, many states and localities have greatly benefited from the defense budget in years past. Now, as times and concerns change, so will their economies and fiscal health.

Implementation

Once policy goals and priorities are set by governors and legislators, important decisions must be made concerning who will implement them. This not only means which agency in state government will have the responsibility, but which level of government—state, local, or both.

Implementation decisions are often made with the considerable interest and involvement of the federal government. State and local governments administer some federal programs: food stamps, child nutrition, social services, community action, and senior citizen centers. In other areas federal and state governments *share* administrative and fiscal responsibility: public welfare, Medicaid, interstate and federal highways, hazardous waste, and water supply and sanitation.

But in many program areas the federal presence is minimal or nonexistent—especially since the passage of the 1985 Balanced Budget and Emergency Deficit Control Act, commonly known as the Gramm-Rudman-Hollings bill after its sponsors. This intensely controversial legislation mandates extensive across-the-board federal budget cuts if deficit targets are not met. Even before Gramm-Rudman-Hollings, federal aid to state and local governments had declined 23.5 percent in real money terms between 1980 and 1985.[19]

Even leaner times are ahead. The federal government is picking up a smaller and smaller share of the state tab for primary and secondary schools, state and community colleges, public hospitals, police and fire protection, state prisons and local jails, local streets and roads, public utilities, state and local parks, public libraries, and facilities for the disabled. During the 1988 presidential election campaign we heard candidates address the problems created by the declining federal presence. The first eighteen months of the Bush administration show no indication of reversing these trends; in fact, the trend may become worse as Congress and the president try to reduce the national budget deficit.

Current Issues

To put today's issues into perspective, the top seven discipline problems in California public schools in 1940 were "talking, chewing gum, making noise, running in the halls, getting out of turn in line, wearing improper clothing and not putting paper in the waste baskets." In the 1980s, the top seventeen problems were "drug abuse, pregnancy, rape, assault, arson, murder, vandalism, gang warfare, venereal disease, alcohol abuse, suicide, robbery, burglary, bombings, absenteeism, extortion and abortion." [20]

For the future, four powerful trends are taking shape: the growth of *environmental concerns* in the wake of a deteriorating environment; the rapid *racial diversification* of our population with the attendant tensions of racism; the *changes in the age structure* as the population grows older and society shifts programmatic needs and costs between generations; and the increasing amount of *physical and sexual violence* occurring within the family and society at large.[21]

The articles in Part IX focus on five issues that are currently at the top of the states' agendas. At the most personal level, Wendy Kaminer in *State Government News* looks at the abortion issue in the states, while Myra C. Lewyn reviews how states are coping with the problems caused by AIDS. Malcolm E. Jewell in *Comparative State Politics* details how Kentucky's supreme court has caused that state to rethink its educational system since the current system was declared unconstitutional. Paul Furiga in *Governing* discusses the dilemmas the states face in handling low-level radioactive waste. Finally, John Herbers of *Governing* raises some interesting questions about foreign investment in the states.

Notes

1. National Governors' Association, *The State of the States, 1985,* 6.
2. National Association of State Budget Officers and National Governors' Association, *Fiscal Survey of the States, 1989* (Washington, D.C.: April 1989).
3. *Fiscal Survey of the States, 1988* (October 1988).
4. Marcia Howard, author of *Fiscal Survey of the States, 1989,* quoted in John Bacon, "Strapped U.S. Passes the Buck," *USA Today,* May 10, 1989, 5A.
5. Peter Passell, "Duke Economists Critical of State Lotteries," *New York Times News Service,* reported in the *Durham Morning Herald,* May 21, 1989, 11A.
6. New York Times News Service, "Budget Woes Put Pinch on Many States," in [Raleigh] *News and Observer,* March 4, 1990, 1A.
7. Ibid.
8. Ibid., 8A.
9. "Education, Welfare," *Governors' Weekly Bulletin* 21:46 (November 20, 1987): 4.
10. "State Spending," *Governors' Weekly Bulletin* 23:11 (March 17, 1989): 4.
11. Kate Farrell, "Cutting the Cost of AIDS," *State Legislatures* 13:9 (September 1987): 24.
12. Ibid. and "Effective Policies to Combat AIDS," *Governors' Weekly Bulletin* 21:38 (September 25, 1987): 1-2.
13. "Population Explosion Fuels Prison Spending," *USA Today,* March 27, 1989, 6A.
14. "Supreme Court Upholds State Antitrust Laws," *Governors' Weekly Bulletin* 23:16 (April 21, 1989): 4. The cases involved were *Illinois Brick v. Illinois* (1977) and *California v. ARC America Corp.* (1989).
15. *Webster v. Reproductive Health Services* (1989).
16. John Koenig, "Bob Martinez: The Governor of the Polls," *Governing* 3:8 (May 1990): 44.
17. Karen Benker, "Severance Tax Revenues Parallel Energy Prices," *Governors' Weekly Bulletin* 22:4 (January 29, 1988): 3.
18. Bill Nichols, "Mission: More Taxes: Governor Battles Tradition," *USA Today,* April 14, 1989, 3A; and Thomas B. Edsall, "All the King's Men Can't Put Louisiana Back Together Again," *Washington Post National Weekly Edition,* May 22-28, 1989, 34.
19. Congressional Research Service, "The Effect of Federal Tax and Budget Policies in the 1980s on the State-Local Sector," *Governors' Weekly Bulletin* 20:9 (March 7, 1986): 2.
20. Remarks of William Bondurant, executive director, the Mary Reynolds Babcock Foundation, to the National Development Conference in Dallas, Texas, June 12, 1987.
21. Ibid.

From *Roe* to *Webster:*
Court Hands Abortion to States

by Wendy Kaminer

In 1973, the U.S. Supreme Court ruling in *Roe vs. Wade* took from states the power to prohibit abortions in the first six months of pregnancy. [In 1989], *Webster vs. Reproductive Health Services* gave a little of that power back. [In 1990], state power to limit the availability of abortions will probably be expanded further by three pending Supreme Court cases, involving minor's rights and restrictions on abortion clinics. "Who decides," the rallying cry of the pro-choice movement, is a question coming squarely before the states.

When *Roe vs. Wade* gave women the right to choose abortion before fetal viability in the first two trimesters of pregnancy, it gave state legislators the opportunity not to choose sides in a wrenching political debate. Now, a newly constituted, newly conservative Supreme Court is shifting the abortion battle from the federal courts back to the states. Abortion is a "political issue," Justice Antonin Scalia suggested in *Webster;* it should be decided by "popular will." While the *Webster* court narrowly declined to overrule *Roe,* to Justice Scalia's dismay, it did weaken the constitutional protection *Roe* provided women and the limits it imposed on the states.

The *Roe* decision always has been highly controversial, not just because it extended the constitutional right for an abortion but because of the way those rights were defined. The court balanced women's right to choose (which it located in the 14th Amendment right of privacy) with the state's interest in potential life by charting the course of fetal development. Drawing a line at viability, the point at which a fetus can live outside the womb, the court held that states had a compelling interest in preserving fetal life only after viability, which generally occurs in the 24th to 28th week of pregnancy (or the third trimester). The court recognized another compelling interest in protecting maternal health during the second trimester when abortion becomes more risky for women. Thus, under *Roe,* abortions must essentially be available on demand during the first trimester of pregnancy, they may be regulated in the interests of the mother's health during the second trimester and they may be prohibited to preserve potential life after viability in the third trimester.

Wendy Kaminer is a lawyer and a visiting scholar at Radcliffe College in Cambridge, Massachusetts. This article is reprinted with permission from *State Government News* 32:11 (November 1989): 12-14. © 1990 the Council of State Governments.

Table 1 Status of State Abortion Laws Enacted Since the 1973 *Roe vs. Wade* Decision

Type of laws	Number of states
Parental consent or notice	35
Provide Medicaid funding for abortion. only in cases where it is necessary to save the life of the pregnant woman	30
Viability assumed (weeks)	13
Provide funds for medically necessary abortions	12
Preamble protection of fetus	9
Provide public funding in certain circumstances, i.e., rape, incest or deformed fetus	8
Would make abortion illegal if *Roe vs. Wade* is overturned	5
Prohibit abortion counseling	4
Prohibit use of public facilities	4
Prohibit involvement of public employees	2
Require viability tests	2

Source: State Government News 32:11 (November 1989): 16-17. Reprinted with permission from the Council of State Governments © 1990.

In cases following *Roe vs. Wade,* the court held firmly to this trimester framework, invalidating efforts to limit women's abortion rights before viability. In *Planned Parenthood of Missouri vs. Danforth,* the court in 1976 struck down a spousal consent requirement and a prohibition of a common and accepted method of abortion (saline amniocentesis) during the second trimester. In *Akron vs. Akron Center for Reproductive Health,* the court in 1981 struck down a requirement that second trimester abortions be performed in hospitals and an informed consent law that required physicians to tell women about fetal development and the "physical and emotional complications" of abortion. In *Thornburgh vs. American College of Obstetricians,* the court in 1986 struck down a Pennsylvania informed

consent law and a reporting requirement that was held to infringe upon women's privacy rights.

Before *Webster,* the court allowed significant abortion restrictions only in two important classes of cases—those involving minors and those involving women dependent on public funds. In *Bellotti vs. Baird,* the court in 1979 held that minors may be required to obtain either parental or judicial consent to abortions. In *Harris vs. McRae,* it upheld in 1980 a federal cutoff of Medicaid abortion funding.

Supreme Court opposition to abortion rights grew in the 15 years between *Roe* and *Webster* as the composition of the court gradually changed. Now, four justices appear ready to overrule *Roe vs. Wade*—Chief Justice William H. Rehnquist, Justices Byron White, Anthony Kennedy and Scalia. Justice Sandra Day O'Connor has expressed serious reservations about *Roe*'s trimester formulation but declined the opportunity to overrule it providing the swing vote in *Webster*. Justices Harry Blackmun, William Brennan, Thurgood Marshall and John Paul Stevens comprise what has become a pro-choice minority, no longer able to hold the line on state regulation drawn by *Roe*.

In *Webster vs. Reproductive Health Services*, the court upheld a Missouri law imposing two significant new restrictions on abortion rights. The court upheld 1) a requirement that women seeking abortions past the 20th week of pregnancy undergo tests to determine if the fetus is viable, and 2) a prohibition on the use of public facilities and public employees in performing or assisting abortions not necessary to save the mother's life.

Pro-choice activists point to *Webster* as the beginning of the end of a woman's right to choose to have an abortion. Opponents of abortion rights and some moderates tend to minimize *Webster*. They say the court allowed a cutoff of public funding some 10 years ago, in *Harris vs. McRae*, and that viability testing is not tantamount to an abortion prohibition or a reversal of *Roe vs. Wade*.

But, as a matter of constitutional law, *Webster* does suggest a break with the court's prior rulings on abortion rights. As a practical matter, it sanctions substantial obstacles to abortions in Missouri.

The Missouri law upheld in *Webster* goes well beyond a cutoff of direct abortion aid to Medicaid recipients: Its prohibition of public assistance is broad enough to prohibit abortions in private hospitals merely located on public land. The viability testing provision raises the cost of abortions and represents a partial dismantling of *Roe*'s trimester scheme. By allowing the state to presume viability and

State Regulation of Private Conduct

The U.S. Constitution and particularly . . . the Bill of Rights . . . limit the powers of state governments. Those rights and state police powers often conflict, as in cases of state power to prosecute criminals and federal rights of criminal defendants and in the state police power to regulate weapons and the Constitutional right to bear arms. But these rights are not so absolute that state regulation of their exercise is prohibited. . . . Constitutional law generally reflects the balancing in the phrase, "There is no right to yell fire in a crowded theater."

Many cases match the right of an individual to deal with his or her own body and the right of the states to exercise their powers. [Examples:] Can states make it a crime for a person to commit the ultimate body-damaging act—suicide—when the lives of others aren't threatened? If so, can states prohibit body-damaging actions such as deliberately cutting off a finger, piercing an ear, getting tattooed? Can a person be permitted to die by inaction such as denying medical treatment for himself or can courts order treatment against the informed determination of the individual not to receive it? Does the right of the state extend to a Christian Science parent who refuses to consent to medical treatment of a child, [or extend] to defining as criminal the conduct of a pregnant woman who refuses to give up cocaine, alcohol, tobacco, overeating?

Source: State Policy Reports 7:13 (July 1989): 19-20.

require viability testing in the 20th week of pregnancy, *Webster* allows state intervention in the abortion decision on behalf of the fetus during the second trimester. It also imposes a new limitation on physician autonomy. States may "superimpose" regulation on the "medical determination of whether a particular fetus is viable," Chief Justice Rehnquist suggested. Under *Webster,* the process of determining viability becomes a political as well as a medical question.

Whether *Webster* is only a qualification of women's abortion rights or a first step toward practical elimination of those rights may become clearer this term. In *Turnock vs. Ragsdale,* the court will decide whether Illinois officials may require clinics performing first trimester abortions to comply with onerous licensing requirements found in federal court to be medically unnecessary. If the court upholds the Illinois law, it will significantly limit the availability of first trimester abortions, making abortion rights moot for many women without formally withdrawing them. In *Ohio vs. Akron Center for Reproductive Health* and *Hodgson vs. Minnesota,* the court will decide the constitutionality of parental notification requirements for minors seeking abortion. The court has generally treated minors as a separate class of pregnant females, so a decision upholding parental notification laws, with or without a judicial bypass, would not necessarily signal a new approach to abortion rights. It would, however, impose new hardships on pregnant minors, particularly those without harmonious family relations: The Minnesota law requires notification of both biological parents of a pregnant minor, regardless of whether the parents ever married or divorced.

Of course, states need not exercise all the power the Supreme Court may give them. Unless the court declares that fetuses are people, endowed with equal constitutional rights, states will be allowed but not required

to promulgate whatever abortion restrictions the court upholds. The *Webster* case, for example, is a grant of permission, not a mandate, for states to regulate the determination of viability; it doesn't decide that viable fetuses are people. The court does not seem intent on making a decision about fetal personhood: Its currently prevailing distaste for *Roe v. Wade* appears grounded in concern for states' rights not fetal ones.

But questions of fetal life not addressed by the Supreme Court may be answered by the states, consistent with the court's pronouncements on women's rights. Following Missouri's lead, state legislators may decide when life begins: *Webster* upheld a declaration by the state of Missouri that life begins at conception and that "unborn children" enjoy the same rights as people who've been born.

But this declaration of rights, while facilitating abortion prohibitions, may have troublesome consequences for states. Soon after *Webster* was decided, a lawsuit was filed on behalf of the fetus of a woman incarcerated in Missouri, claiming its due process rights had been violated. Pro-choice lawyers in Missouri have devised a series of similar actions: As dependent persons, fetuses are said to be tax deductible; and, if life begins at conception, lawyers argue, age should be measured from date of conception, not date of birth, making Missouri's citizens eligible for driver's licenses or Social Security benefits nine months earlier than they were before Missouri's abortion law took effect. As these claims point out, myriad laws and social policies are based on the notion that fetuses are not quite equal human beings, with equal legal status and rights. The states' newfound power to regulate abortions in the interests of fetal life will have to be handled with care.

AIDS: Lifesaving Lessons

by Myra C. Lewyn

Since the 1925 uproar over teaching evolution in Tennessee public schools, state and local governments have analyzed the merits of public instruction of such sensitive topics as evolution, sex, and, most recently, AIDS.

The Human Immunodeficiency Virus (HIV) that causes the Acquired Immune Deficiency Syndrome (AIDS) is indeed a sensitive topic, for its vocabulary includes words like "homosexuality," "intravenous drug use" and "condom." But unlike other sexually transmitted diseases, AIDS is an incurable, lethal condition, the spread of which has all the making of a modern-day plague.

Since the virus is transmitted almost exclusively by behavior that individuals can modify, education programs that influence behavior can be effective in curtailing its spread.

"Adolescents and pre-adolescents are those whose behavior we wish to especially influence because of their vulnerability when they are exploring their own sexuality and perhaps experimenting with drugs," said C. Everett Koop, former Surgeon General of the U.S. Public Health Service under President Ronald Reagan, in his 1986 report on AIDS. "Teen-agers often consider themselves immortal, and these young people may be putting themselves at risk."

According to the Centers for Disease Control, of the 88,096 people with AIDS (as of Feb. 28 [, 1989]), over one-fifth of those are in their twenties. And because the latency period between HIV infection and the onset of symptoms is about 10 years, most of these people probably contracted the virus as teenagers. In addition, a report issued in early June [1989] by the American College Health Association found that one in every 500 college students tested was infected with the virus.

Those statistics would appear to support AIDS education in schools, but such instruction is not universally favored.

Support for AIDS Education

At the end of May [1989], 28 states and the District of Columbia required HIV/AIDS education in public schools, according to a ... report by the National Association of State Boards of Education [NASBE]. These states are Alabama, Connecticut, Delaware, District of Columbia, Florida, Georgia, Illinois, Indi-

Myra C. Lewyn is a contributing editor to *State Government News*. This article is reprinted with permission from *State Government News* 32:8 (August 1989): 15-17. © 1990 the Council of State Governments.

ana, Iowa, Kansas, Kentucky, Maryland, Michigan, Minnesota, Nevada, New Mexico, New York, North Carolina, Oklahoma, Oregon, Pennsylvania, Rhode Island, South Dakota, Tennessee, Utah, Vermont, Virginia, Washington and West Virginia.

"Strong state policies and adequate funds are essential steps for assuring that all students receive effective HIV/AIDS education statewide, education necessary for them to protect themselves from a fatal disease," recommended NASBE in its report.

Although the number of AIDS cases increased by more than 50 percent among 13- to 19-year-olds between February 1988 and February 1989, AIDS education is not required in all states. Of the states requiring instruction, Michigan and Minnesota students can be excused from AIDS discussions. And Nevada requires written permission from parents for student participation.

Voters in North Dakota may decide in a referendum whether public schools will discuss AIDS and other health topics if more than 13,000 signatures can be obtained by July 27 [,1990] in opposition to a 1989 law mandating health education in public schools.

After much debate in the Senate, the health education bill, which called for instruction on such subjects as drug and alcohol abuse, AIDS and other sexually transmitted diseases, was signed by Gov. George Sinner.

Sen. Donna Nalewaja, R-Fargo, led opposition to the health education bill in the Senate, calling it "a knee-jerk reaction to the AIDS epidemic." Other critics of the bill claimed health classes would promote immorality and lead to birth-control clinics in schools.

Sex Education vs. AIDS

Because AIDS is a deadly condition, AIDS education is required by more states than the broader subject of sex education.

Furthermore, while states are developing detailed AIDS curricula, a study by the Alan Guttmacher Institute involving educators' views revealed that general sex education programs often are not updated. Classes remain focused on the clinical aspects of human sexuality such as reproductive systems, puberty and pregnancy. The social aspects of dating, marriage and the responsibilities of parenthood are explored rather than the touchy, more relevant issues of sexually transmitted diseases, AIDS and pregnancy prevention.

Only 17 states and the District of Columbia mandate sex education, which is an increase over the three that did in 1980 (Kentucky, Maryland and New Jersey), according to the study. And, only seven states require instruction about pregnancy prevention. These are Arkansas, Delaware, Iowa, New Mexico, South Carolina, Vermont and Virginia. But while Alabama frowns on such instruction, Utah forbids it.

Additionally the study revealed that although no states prohibit sex education in public schools, nine states take no position on the subject. These states are Arizona, California, Illinois, Louisiana, Massachusetts, Mississippi, North Carolina, Texas and Wyoming.

Where to Teach

Discussions of AIDS and sex should take place at school and home, some believe.

"The PTA believes that teens and children must be educated about AIDS. The spread of the AIDS virus can and must be stopped. The only way to prevent AIDS is through education," said the National Congress of Parents and Teachers (PTA) in the brochure, *How to Talk to Your Teens and Children About AIDS.*

"But discussions about sex and AIDS shouldn't happen just in school and shouldn't happen just at home," said Laura Abraham, a spokeswoman for the National PTA.

As surgeon general, Koop advised in his initial report that AIDS education should start early in elementary school and at home "so that children can grow up knowing the behavior to avoid to protect themselves from exposure to the AIDS virus."

Only 16 states and D.C., however, require HIV/AIDS education in early education (some beginning as early as kindergarten), seven require it in grades six through eight, one requires it be taught in high school and four states require no specific grade level.

Funding for AIDS Education

AIDS education not only gets more attention than sex education, it also receives more funding. The NASBE report stated that the Centers for Disease Control funds every state at an average of $250,000 for HIV/AIDS education. This is not enough, however, to cover the costs involved in establishing HIV/AIDS education programs.

The NASBE report also disclosed that for the 1988-89 school year, seven state education agencies received state funding that was appropriated specifically for HIV/AIDS education: Florida, $500,000; Hawaii, $150,000; Kansas, $1.5-million; Maine, $80,000; Minnesota, $900,000; New York, $1,165,000; and Washington, $314,000.

In New Hampshire, funding was appropriated to the state education agency for HIV/AIDS education staff positions but was not granted due to a hiring freeze.

Several state education agencies reported that they utilized funds from their general health education budgets for HIV/AIDS education: Massachusetts, New Mexico, North Carolina, Oregon, Rhode Island, Tennessee and Vermont.

What to Teach

Certainly, sex education has been complicated by the advent of AIDS and all that

word implies. As a matter of fact, educators do not always agree that HIV/AIDS and discussions of other sexually transmitted diseases be included in general sex education. "There is now no doubt that we need sex education in schools and that it must include information on heterosexual and homosexual relationships," said Koop in *You Can Do Something About AIDS,* a public service publication. But "the threat of AIDS can provide an opportunity for parents to instill in their children their own moral and ethical standards," Koop said in his 1986 report on AIDS.

The Centers for Disease Control agrees. "The specific scope and content of AIDS education in schools should be consistent with parental and community values," said the Centers in *Morbidity and Mortality Weekly Report.*

Two states address homosexuality in the content of HIV/AIDS education: Alabama and Oklahoma, according to the NASBE report.

Although states are saying what teachers can and cannot teach regarding sex and AIDS education, they have not set policies as to how to present materials and information, and teachers consider this among the problem areas.

In the study "What Public School Teachers Teach About Preventing Pregnancy, AIDS and Sexually Transmitted Diseases" reported in the March/April [1989] issue of *Family Planning Perspectives,* researchers Jacqueline Forrest and Jane Silverman of the Alan Guttmacher Institute said, "Sex education teachers regard pressure from parents, the community or the school administration as the major problem they face in providing sex education. Other important problems are the lack of appropriate materials on the subject, and students' reactions or lack or interest."

AIDS Affects Other Important Issues Confronting Governors

Discrimination Issues
- Ensuring access to health care
- Ensuring the rights of the handicapped and the disabled to a variety of needed services
- Ensuring access to employment, housing, and public facilities

Health Care and Prevention Issues
- Controlling and preventing IV drug use
- Preventing teenage pregnancy
- Providing services for the terminally and chronically ill
- Containing the costs of highly specialized or expensive health services
- Protecting the supply and ensuring the availability of blood, tissue, and organs
- Preventing the increasing spread of other sexually transmitted diseases
- Ensuring safe work environments

Confidentiality Issues
- Protecting personal medical information and individuals' rights to privacy
- Creating separate standards for special conditions
- Imposing a duty to warn
- Imposing professional and provider liability for providing information

Testing Issues
- Ensuring informed consent and counseling before invasive procedures
- Providing testing after workplace exposure

Finance Issues
- Choosing among competing social needs
- Covering the uninsured and uninsurable
- Covering catastrophic illness
- Financing/providing long term care
- Mandating benefits in the public and private sectors
- Financing care for behavior-related illness

Research/Economic Development Issues
- Determining the federal, state, and private role in supporting basic medical research
- Supporting research and development for new medical technologies or less costly drugs

Surveillance and Public Health Control Issues
- Reporting HIV and other sexually transmitted diseases
- Notifying sexual partners
- Controlling behavior that threatens public safety
- Maintaining the safety of clients, inmates, and staff in public institutions

Other Issues
- Assessing service provider liability
- Regulating the storage, treatment, and disposal of infectious wastes

Source: "NGA Guide Urges Balanced Approach to AIDS Policy," *Governors' Weekly Bulletin* 23:34 (September 1, 1989): 1. Reprinted with permission, National Governors' Association.

High-Risk Groups

Some state education agencies in cooperation with the Centers for Disease Control have addressed the problem of educating children whose behaviors put them at high risk of HIV/AIDS infection. Those include:

● Dropouts, runaway and homeless youth, migrants and incarcerated youth

● Racial and ethnic minorities, including those for whom English is a second language

● Pregnant school-age women, school-age parents, IV drug users, homosexual youth

● Those living in certain urban areas where the incidence of HIV/AIDS is high

● Those with special needs, such as emotional or physical disabilities

State education agencies are working with state departments of corrections and youth services, with migrant and special education programs, and with community-based agencies that serve youth.

The New Jersey Department of Health, for example, developed an outreach program targeting hard-to-reach children such as dropouts. One program is training ex-drug addicts to return to the streets to share information about AIDS and the IV drug use connection.

Challenge of AIDS

Teen-agers and children live in a world where HIV/AIDS is a constant threat. Information and education about the virus and its related diseases are critical to rearing children if they are to grow up healthy or indeed grow up at all.

The warnings of such experts as Koop pose a challenge for policymakers who have not dealt with HIV/AIDS education in the public schools to address the needs of children, who were once assumed to be safely out of reach of the deadly virus.

"Our kids, in a modern society, are facing more and more problems," said North Dakota Lt. Gov. Lloyd Omdahl on the subject of his state's health and AIDS education bill. "These kids can't afford to have us standing around arguing about a solution."

The Supreme Court, Kentucky's Schools

by Malcolm E. Jewell

The June 8 [, 1989] decision of the Kentucky Supreme Court, declaring the Kentucky education system to be unconstitutional, has raised a host of questions about the financing, structure, management and quality of education in the state. It is too early to predict how these questions are going to be answered, but some of the choices facing Kentuckians in the months ahead are becoming clearer.

Financing the Cost

The Supreme Court has mandated a fundamental revision in the system of financing public schools, and specified two basic principles that must be followed by the General Assembly:

1. It shall "provide funding which is sufficient to provide each child in Kentucky with an adequate education."

2. Schools throughout the state must be "substantially uniform." "Equality is the key word here. . . . The children who live in the poor districts and the children who live in the rich districts must be given the same opportunity and access to an adequate education. This obligation cannot be shifted to local counties and local school districts."

Despite this emphasis on equality, the Court has said that local school districts are not "precluded from enacting these local taxes to supplement the uniform, equal educational effort that the General Assembly must provide."

The Court appears to be saying that the basic tax structure to support education must be established by the legislature, that it must provide enough funding to insure an adequate education, and that—if the tax structure includes local property taxes—the legislature cannot give local school districts authority to lower the rates below the standard that it sets. But local districts may raise tax revenue above the level established by the legislature under certain conditions.

The Court further specifies that if part of this revenue comes from a local property tax, that tax must be based on 100% assessment and must be uniform in all districts. This requirement of uniformity has caused some confusion because it appears to contradict the statement that local districts can raise taxes above the level set by the legislature. It may

Malcolm E. Jewell is professor of political science at the University of Kentucky at Lexington and editor of *The Kentucky Journal*. This article was reprinted from *The Kentucky Journal* (July 1989) in *Comparative State Politics* 10:4 (August 1989): 1-6.

imply that this additional local revenue should come from other forms of taxation. But it seems unlikely that the Court would order any school district to cut its total revenue from local taxes.

The legislative leadership is seeking clarification from the Court about its statements on local tax rates. This is an important point because the large disparities in local spending for education result not only from differences in wealth but from differences in tax effort.

It would appear that the legislature can choose among several strategies in responding to the financial aspects of the Court's decision:

1. The state might abandon the local property tax altogether, and rely entirely on state income, sales, business and other taxes (including perhaps state property taxes) to support education.

2. The state might require that all school districts adopt a local property tax rate that was considerably higher than that now used by many districts, in addition to increasing state support for education.

Several arguments can be made for retaining local property taxes, or other local taxes, as part of the financing package. Taxpayers are accustomed to supporting schools in part by property taxes; to eliminate these in school districts would require even higher increases in the other taxes. Moreover, some persons argue that retaining a local tax for education will maintain local support for schools.

On the other hand, there are several problems with relying on local taxes—particularly those on property—as a major source of funding. In many rural counties apparently the actual assessment of property falls far below 100%, and it will be a difficult task to overcome this gap.

It is difficult to determine what a standard tax rate for all districts should be. If it is set too high, close to the rate in Fayette or Jefferson counties, it will be necessary for many of the poorer districts to raise tax rates dramatically, at least doubling them in most cases. There would obviously be strong opposition to mandating such a large change.

But if the mandated increase is more modest, perhaps up to the state average of 46 cents, large disparities will remain in the tax rates, and thus the funds available for education, among the districts. In short, the legislature must decide how much of the cost of improving education in the poorest districts must be borne by residents in those districts and how much by residents of the state as a whole.

If both state and local revenues are increased and reallocated to provide substantially equal funding for both rich and poor districts, the consequence should be that in every school district teachers with the same qualifications would get the same pay. There would be the same programs available in every district, in terms of the range of course[s], the availability of kindergartens, preschool programs, programs for handicapped children, lab equipment, computers and other supplies.

The quality of education might still vary because of the quality of teaching, the availability of skilled teachers, the skill with which resources are utilized, the willingness of local schools and teachers to use experimental techniques and (unfortunately) the level of parental support for students. But it would not vary because of the tax resources of the district.

Using Resources Efficiently

If the state is going to invest a great deal of additional money in order to provide an "efficient" system of education, it must make sure that the funds are not wasted, and are not used inefficiently. Kentucky is not a wealthy state; it cannot afford to waste education resources.

Moreover, increased spending and taxing

Lawsuits Feed on Success

... James Goetz, the attorney who represented Montana's poor school districts, said that since the Montana Supreme Court ruled in his favor [in February 1989,] he has heard from attorneys in Minnesota and South Dakota interested in filing similar suits.

Debra Dawahare, one of the attorneys who represented Kentucky's poor school districts, said she also has talked to attorneys in Minnesota as well as Tennessee and Oregon who have either filed a lawsuit or are beginning to lay the ground work for one.

Goetz and Dawahare said the success of educational equity lawsuits in states such as California, West Virginia and Michigan was instrumental in helping them win their cases.

"Courts are cautious, and when they are breaking new (constitutional) ground they get doubly cautious," Goetz said. "When there is precedent from another state it can be quite valuable."

Not every lawsuit has been successful. To date, state funding systems have been found unconstitutional by supreme courts in Arkansas, California, Connecticut, Kentucky, Michigan, Montana, New Jersey, Washington, West Virginia and Wyoming. Eleven state supreme courts, however, have dismissed equity lawsuits. But even in states where equity lawsuits were dismissed benefits have occurred.

"The conclusion of many experts who have studied these lawsuits is simply 'when in doubt sue because it helps education in the long run,'" said Kern Alexander, a distinguished scholar at Virginia Tech. Alexander, a Kentucky native and former president of Western Kentucky University helped advise the plaintiffs in the Kentucky lawsuit.

David Franklin, a professor of educational administration at Illinois State University, who has conducted a national study of the equity lawsuits filed by schools, agreed with Alexander. A case in point ... is Colorado. Despite a 1982 ruling that upheld the state's school financing system, state officials developed a more equitable system for compensating teachers and increased school funding.

Franklin, however, said it was difficult to determine how many of the Colorado changes resulted from the increased awareness of educational problems caused by the lawsuit and how many of the changes were encouraged by national efforts to improve education during that same period, such as the release of *A Nation at Risk*.

The paradox is that while failed lawsuits such as Colorado's appeared to have a positive effect on education—some successful lawsuits have not had nearly the impact that many had hoped.

In West Virginia, many of the mandates laid down in a 1982 court decision have yet to be enacted. Jerry Cook, the judge who was assigned to the case for four years, estimated that less than 5 percent of the original decision has been put into practice.

A West Virginia lawmaker blames the failure to enact the reforms on two factors: West Virginia's poor economy and the manner in which the reforms were ordered by the court. West Virginia House Speaker Robert Chambers said the Legislature is frustrated with its inability to correct the educational funding problems, but many of the stalling factors have been beyond lawmakers' control.

"We get a court decision telling us what we already know and at the same time we are hit with an economic depression and a reduction in federal aid," Chambers said.

"The court produced a very detailed finding without a lot of public input," said Chambers. "And because of that there was not a lot of public support...."

Source: Linda Wagar, "When Education Isn't Equal," *State Government News* 32:8 (August 1989): 7-8. Reprinted with permission from the Council of State Governments © 1990.

for education will be possible, in the long run, only if these steps have popular support. That support will be stronger if the public believes the money is not being wasted.

If the state is providing the resources, it has the obligation and the opportunity to oversee more carefully how it is spent. And the Court has emphasized that, even if the General Assembly delegates responsibilities to local school boards, it "must provide the mechanism to assure that ultimate control remains with the General Assembly," and must be sure that local school boards act "in an efficient manner."

The Court is even more explicit: The General Assembly "must monitor [the system] on a continuing basis. The state must carefully supervise it so that there is no waste, no duplication, no mismanagement, at any level."

Structure of Districts

The Supreme Court included the existing school districts in its sweeping judgment that the existing school system is unconstitutional. This has led to speculation about the possibility and the consequences of legislative action to reorganize and reduce school districts. The state has 177 school districts. Each of the 120 counties has a county school district and 41 of the counties also have one or more independent school districts. Some of these are urban areas, but a number of them encompass relatively small towns.

There are two distinctly different arguments that can be made for merging school districts. In some cases the independent school districts are wealthier, with higher per pupil property values; whether or not this is the case, some independent school districts have been willing to establish higher tax rates than the counties. For one or both of these reasons, approximately 80 percent of the independent districts spend more per pupil than the corresponding county districts. If no other

changes were made, a merger of these districts would dilute the resources available for the independent school districts.

If, however, the General Assembly passes legislation that provides substantial equality in the per pupil revenue available for every district, inequalities in the tax base would no longer be a problem but it would still be necessary to equalize the tax rates throughout the merged district.

The other argument for [the] merger of districts is one of efficiency and equality. In the less populated counties, there should be economies of scale that would result from merger[s]. Consolidating a county and a city high school, for example, might improve the facilities and the range of courses available to students. The arguments that are likely to develop about merging school districts would be comparable to those heard in the past about consolidating schools. The legislature will have to decide whether the gains in equality and quality of education are great enough in some of these counties to make it worth fighting the battle that is likely to develop at the local level in many counties.

There are many issues at stake in the merger of school systems: resources, the size of schools, the quality of education, local support for school[s] and questions of politics and patronage.

School Management

The Supreme Court has made it absolutely clear that the General Assembly must take the necessary legislative steps to bring about better management of the schools, and must monitor the schools to make sure that this is occurring. The legislation authorizing the Department of Education to oversee or even take over "bankrupt" school districts is a good example of such action.

Although the Court did not explicitly discuss the problems of nepotism and political machines in school districts, these are obviously subsumed by phrases such as "waste" and "mismanagement." The Court makes it clear that the only powers the school boards have are those delegated by the legislature, and the legislature obviously has wide latitude to outlaw those local practices that virtually guarantee mismanagement.

School districts that are charged with poor performance and mismanagement often argue that they lack the financial resources to make improvements and the local voters will not support higher taxes. But, if the legislature has adopted a program that substantially equalizes funding, this excuse will disappear. Moreover, if citizens in the more prosperous districts are to support large increases by the state in educational funding in the poorer districts, they must be convinced that the money is not being wasted or used to line the pockets of relatives or political supporters of the school board or the superintendent.

One problem facing the legislature is how to monitor school districts closely enough to prevent waste and mismanagement and yet give the schools enough flexibility to permit experimentation and innovation.

Improving Quality

In the wake of the Supreme Court's decision, much of the debate will inevitably center on funding formulas and sources of tax revenue. But the purpose of the Court is to improve the quality of education; higher, more equitable funding is a necessary but not a sufficient means to that end.

Once the mechanism has been established to raise educational funding and distribute it equally, the legislature will have to consider how to improve its quality.

Emphasizing quality is important not only for educational reasons but for political reasons. The taxpayers must be convinced that much higher spending is buying better educa-

Funding Equality in California

. . . Equality in funding California schools began to become a reality with a 1971 state Supreme Court ruling, *Serrano vs. Priest*, that found the funding system unconstitutional. The majority of changes, however, occurred after the 1978 voter passage of Proposition 13, which slashed property taxes 60 percent and made them uniform throughout the state. What resulted was that the state had to pick up a bigger share of the support of local schools and many systems were forced to cut costs to compensate for the loss in local property taxes.

California's current educational system is funded 60 to 70 percent by the state—prior to Proposition 13, districts received 70 percent of their funding from local taxes. Today it is illegal for school districts to have more than a $200 difference in the amount they spend on students per year. If a district was to pass a property tax increase that brought it over that amount, the extra money would be distributed to poorer districts.

Before the passage of Proposition 13, California ranked at or above the national average for money spent per student. . . . By 1982, California fell to 33rd in the country.

In addition, with greater equity came a loss of control over school operations by local districts. . . .

Source: Linda Wagar, "When Education Isn't Equal," *State Government News* 32:8 (August 1989): 8. Reprinted with permission from the Council of State Governments © 1990.

tion. In the long run, public support is essential to implement the Supreme Court's mandate; and the public expects to see results.

It is also important to emphasize programs designed to improve quality in order to convince taxpayers and parents in the wealthier, more urban school districts that they have something to gain from this reform. It is obviously the poorer school districts that will be getting a larger share of the new resources. But the programs to make good use of those resources will be available in all districts. If teachers are better trained and have more opportunities for professional development, if more innovating teaching techniques are being developed, this will benefit children in all districts.

The legislature will have to consider a number of approaches to improving quality. Better education requires better qualified teachers. This suggests the necessity of recruiting better students into teaching, improving the training of teachers and providing better opportunities for the professional development of teachers. It may require changes in certification methods to broaden the range of skills and experience that can qualify a person to teach. Another approach to higher quality is support for more innovative and flexible teaching techniques, along with greater autonomy for individual teachers and schools in developing both techniques and curriculum. . . .

One aspect of quality that was emphasized in the court testimony . . . is the need for a more varied and advanced curriculum for students, particularly in the senior high schools.

Better quality education requires more modern tools—better laboratories, more adequate libraries, more and better instructional materials and a large influx of computers into the schools—along with training so that teachers can make good use of them.

Choosing Priorities

Because the Supreme Court has emphasized that the General Assembly has respon-

sibility for the education system, it must decide spending priorities.

It can mandate the priorities that local school districts must follow in choosing among programs—or it may give these districts some flexibility in making choices.

Assuming that there is substantial uniformity in the per pupil revenue available to each district and that the total state budget for education is significantly higher, the legislature must make choices in allocating these resources.

How large a proportion of the new funds will be allocated to increase teachers' pay, and how much of that should go to longevity or "merit?"

How much of the additional funding should go to raising the pay of teachers in the poorer districts to approximate the standards in the richest district?

How much money should be allocated to reducing the size of classes, one of the goals of the 1985 educational reforms?

How much should be appropriated for particular programs aimed at improving the quality of education: more professional development of teachers, an expanded curriculum, more innovation and benchmark schools, more and better teaching materials and equipment, etc.?

How much should be allocated to preschool programs such as Head Start, PACE and kindergarten—programs that virtually all experts say have proven to be of tremendous value. These are programs that assume particular importance in the relatively poor districts where there are a larger proportion of "at risk" children.

How much funding should go to programs for particular subsets of children, including both special education programs for those who are disadvantaged and programs for the gifted and talented?

Hot Stuff

by Paul Furiga

On a Saturday morning last spring, Mario M. Cuomo, the Democratic governor of New York, donned his running clothes and jogged out of the governor's mansion in Albany, only to be met [by] a group of angry citizens carrying protest signs and pulling coffins along the street. The protesters had ridden buses from 10 different areas across New York that Saturday. They brought along a coffin for each of their communities, all of which were on the preliminary list of potential dump sites for the state's low-level nuclear waste.

Cuomo met for an hour with the crowd, outlasting a few emotional hecklers, and even climbed onto one of the coffins to be better heard. Although the governor was sympathetic, and even met a second time with the group, he told them there was little he could do; federal law requires the state to provide a dump, and the state legislature had approved a plan for it. That plan left citizens as uncertain as they were angry. "The majority of people are totally confused about what we're doing," says Angelo Orazio, a former New York Assembly member and chairman of the state's Low-Level Radioactive Waste Siting Commission.

The citizens' display of emotion points up what may be the most critical nuclear-waste issue facing state officials today: the siting of more than a dozen dumps for low-level radioactive waste. Almost everywhere, they face the necessity of healing regional differences, coming up with millions of dollars for the dumps and at the same time allaying the fears of citizens. If they fail, they could become outlaws—nuclear outlaws.

To stay within the law, states must choose between two uncomfortable alternatives: They can construct legal compacts with neighboring states, or they can go it alone in the unfamiliar role of custodian of nuclear trash. There are pitfalls along both paths. New York is an example of a state taking the solo approach. Michigan, host to a Midwestern states regional dump, illustrates some of the problems with the compact approach.

Under federal law, the states have until January 1, 1993, to form interstate compacts to build dumps for nuclear wastes from member states or else to open dumps of their own for wastes generated within their borders.

Paul Furiga is a Washington, D.C., correspondent for Thomson Newspapers who specializes in nuclear power issues. This article is reprinted from *Governing* 3:2 (November 1989): 50-54.

Congress set a second, more pressing deadline, though: Every state must have applied for a license for a specific dump site by January 1, 1990, or else certify to the federal government that it has adequate plans for temporary storage of its low-level waste. If a state fails to meet either requirement, the federal government has the authority to halt shipments of radioactive waste at state borders. That could force the facilities that produce the nuclear waste to store it themselves, probably in areas that weren't designed for the purpose.

The government's "enforcers" for these deadlines are Nevada, South Carolina and Washington, where the three existing U.S. nuclear dumps are. They have the power under the low-level waste law to refuse the nuclear trash of any "noncompliance" state, and they have demonstrated their willingness to exercise that power.

Low-level radioactive waste comes primarily from the nation's 112 commercial nuclear power plants, but it is also produced by companies that use radioactive materials in testing; universities that do research or teach nuclear engineering and medicine; and hospitals and medical centers that use radioactive materials in testing and cancer treatment. Low-level wastes include uranium, thorium, cesium and other radioactive metals from industrial and medical processes; protective clothing used by workers; and charts, glassware and contaminated equipment from power plants, hospitals and manufacturers.

Low-level waste is just about any radioactive substance or contaminated item that isn't radioactive enough to be considered high-level waste. Low-level wastes are not as "hot" as the byproducts of nuclear-weapons making, spent fuel rods from power plants and other materials that make up high-level waste, but they still can, with sufficient long-term exposure, cause cancer and other illnesses.

The nation generates more than 1.4 million cubic feet of low-level waste a year. Some states, such as New York, generate more than 100,000 cubic feet a year. Others generate hardly any. North Dakota and South Dakota each produce less than five cubic feet a year and, in several recent years, did not even bother to ship wastes to the three currently operating dumps at Beatty, Nevada, and Richland, Washington, (both run by U.S. Ecology) and Barnwell, South Carolina (operated by Chem-Nuclear Systems Inc.).

In 1979, as the nation's production of low-level nuclear waste continued to grow, leaders in those three states petitioned Congress, hoping to end their role as the nation's nuclear waste repositories. They sought to have states that generate the nation's nuclear waste share the responsibility for its disposal. There was logic to the proposal: Ten states account for about 63 percent of all of the low-level nuclear waste disposed of in this country. In order of the average volume, they are Pennsylvania, Tennessee, Illinois, South Carolina, Oregon, California, New York, Virginia, North Carolina and Alabama.

Threats by the three governors to close the dumps, plus heavy nuclear industry lobbying, resulted in the 1980 low-level waste law, written by U.S. Representative Butler Derrick, a South Carolina Democrat whose district includes the Barnwell dump. The measure envisioned a small group of regional compacts among the states—many fewer than have been created. The legislation made hosting a compact attractive by guaranteeing that no waste from outside the compact could be dumped in a host state. A host state also has a guarantee that other states will share dump costs, through the fees collected by the dump operator.

In 1993, as other states open new facilities, the states of Nevada and South Carolina plan to close their dumps; Washington, whose dump is on leased federal land, will keep its site open, greatly lowering dump costs for states in its compact.

Forty-three states have now signed as participants in nine compacts. Massachusetts, New York and Texas are planning to build their own dumps. Maine, New Hampshire, Rhode Island and Vermont have yet to make a decision on whether to join a compact or to go it alone.

The low-level waste law was seen as a way to free the federal government and the three dump states from a national burden. Yet it has often failed to work as designed. States have fought, bickered and backed out of compacts, been ostracized from them, and been forced to compromise in siting dumps that hardly anybody wants. The feuding has resulted in problems for both compact states and go-it-alone states.

For years after the passage of the 1980 low-level waste act, New York attempted to negotiate a compact with 10 other Northeastern states. The negotiations broke down over disagreements about liability: who would bear what share of damage claims that might result from accidents at the site, leaks and other problems. New York's go-it-alone decision was set in a 1986 law that also established the siting commission.

In December 1988, the commission released its list of 10 candidate areas for the dump, which included 1,154 square miles of potential sites. Not surprisingly, it provoked protests in the affected communities. More than 18,000 people have opposed sites in public hearings, arguing that they would be too close to drinking water supplies, communities and even the habitat of winged insects that favor trash sites. (Critics contend the insects might carry radioactive waste away from a site on their bodies.) "I couldn't even begin to tell you how many pages, how many volumes there are," commission spokeswoman Susan Baranski says of the challenges.

The opposition has forced the commission to postpone twice its paring of the site list to four finalists. Despite the delays, Baranski says the commission intends to meet the federal deadline of January 1, 1993.

If it were possible to do again, Baranski says, many at the New York commission believe the list of potential sites should have been narrowed considerably before the communities were publicly identified, to reduce the number of furious opponents of the plan. On the other hand, she points out, public involvement was specified in the law creating the commission, and commissioners have held to that, even when it meant six-hour meetings with angry residents. "It's not the easiest way to do it," she says. "There's a fear about the word 'radioactive,' and you tie that in with 'waste' and people get upset."

It didn't help that the state's criteria for the original sites included only preliminary determinations about site geology. Angry local citizens ridiculed the use of "windshield surveys," in which commission employees would drive by sites and merely eyeball them through the windows of their state cars. One modification that's helped somewhat: The legislature voted $500,000, as much as $50,000 per area, for local officials to investigate the state plan for the waste site and probe concerns about such a choice in their community.

The process of naming sites that so angered New York citizens has had the same effect in many of the host states in compacts, most of which are expected to miss the 1993 deadline.

The Central States compact, for which Nebraska will be the host, drew thousands to meetings, says Ron Gaynor, senior vice president of U.S. Ecology, the company selected to build and operate the dump. But he says the proposed dump also drew interest from 70 communities that wanted the jobs and tax dollars it would generate, something that didn't happen in New York. The company has selected three finalist sites from among those 70.

In general, compact states seem either to have weathered public resistance, as in Nebraska and California, home to the Southwest compact dump site, or they have yet to face it because the public has yet to see a list of proposed dump sites.

The list of compact states that must still pick sites includes almost all of the host states: Michigan, for the Midwest compact; Pennsylvania, the Appalachian compact; Connecticut and New Jersey, which somehow plan to share host status in their two-state compact; Illinois, host to the Central Midwest compact; Colorado, the Rocky Mountain compact; and North Carolina, the Southeast compact.

The Midwest compact of seven states nearly disintegrated early this year when Michigan's Democratic governor, James J. Blanchard, threatened to revoke his state's agreement to be host for a dump that would take waste from Indiana, Iowa, Minnesota, Missouri, Ohio and Wisconsin. The agreement signed by Blanchard's predecessor, Republican William G. Milliken, left too many unanswered questions about who would pay for unforeseen problems, including accidents and maintenance of waste from a state that might later pull out of the compact, says Elaine Brown, associate commissioner of Michigan's Low-Level Radioactive Waste Authority.

Michigan is the second host state in the compact and the second to suggest it might resign its host status. Illinois did so several years earlier, then signed an agreement it considered more favorable with Kentucky.

Blanchard put his threat to resign from the Midwest compact in letters to the governors of the other member states. In the letters, he expressed his hopes that they would agree to share the liability costs, which they since

have, and that the federal government would rethink the idea of having so many regional dumps. That second goal backfired. Instead of attracting the attention of federal leaders, Blanchard awakened the "enforcer" states of Nevada, South Carolina and Washington. Within days, the three agreed to ban Michigan waste from their dumps until Blanchard backed off his threat.

At a meeting of the National Governors' Association in February [1989], Blanchard produced a letter signed by the Midwestern governors agreeing to his liability demands and proclaimed victory. But the text of the letter was hardly a ringing endorsement. "We would be better served in our efforts to responsibly handle low-level waste if the access to waste disposal by our generators is not in jeopardy," the governors' letter said. "We agree to review your plan to improve the federal act. However, continued progress toward the implementation of the agreement should not be dependent on possible federal action."

As for that possibility, Brown says the governor was pleased when the federal Department of Energy announced a $5 million study of proposals to reduce the number of nuclear waste sites. That effort was bolstered in September when U.S. Representative Carl D. Pursell, a Michigan Republican, inserted language in a 1990 spending bill directing the department to "lead discussions" aimed at reducing the number of sites. "I'm sure the government never intended this," Brown says of the potential for as many as 18 sites.

While the experiences of New York and the Midwest compact may be examples of what can go wrong as states try to sort out their new roles as nuclear trash collectors, the experiences of the Southwest and Northwest compacts illustrate how states can succeed.

To begin with, those states have the benefit of geography and geology: many rainless or nearly rainless sites, far from large concentrations of people, that make them more suitable for containment of decaying nuclear waste.

In Ward Valley, California, the site of the Southwest compact's dump for Arizona, California, North Dakota and South Dakota, there is little rainfall and a distance of 700 feet below the surface to any water. And only one person lives within seven miles. Additionally, the site is federal land about to be transferred to the state—eliminating the need to buy the site from potentially recalcitrant residents.

At first, some Western states shunned California, refusing to include it in compacts for fear that its considerable waste volume, more than 100,000 cubic feet a year, would wind up in their states later on. But California has agreed to keep the dump for at least 30 years.

U.S. Ecology believes the Southwest site may be the only new low-level dump in the country to meet the 1993 deadline for operation. A similar blessing could be in store for the Northwest compact: Alaska, Hawaii, Idaho, Montana, Oregon, Utah and Washington.

The Washington dump, two decades old, is on leased federal land, and most of its capital costs have been paid. That will make it "the cheapest disposal in the country," says Gaynor, the U.S. Ecology senior vice president. Building a large dump and a small one costs about the same, and the larger the dump, the greater the base of customers over which that cost can be spread.

States that fought to keep big waste generators out of their compacts or chose to go it alone may find the costs staggering for the amount of waste they have, Gaynor says. He cites the Rocky Mountain compact of Colorado, Nevada, New Mexico and Wyoming. Those states generate just 10,000 cubic feet of waste a year, but Gaynor believes 70,000 cubic feet a year is needed to make a dump economical. Indeed, Gaynor, a senior manager familiar with most of the compacts and go-it-alone arrangements, says he doesn't think having more than a few dump sites is economical, and he questions the consequences of the 1980 law. He argues, "It really only makes sense to have three or four sites nationwide."

Such a change may be out of the question, however, Michigan's Brown says. Even with the new Energy Department study and the congressional directive requiring the department to look into limiting the number of sites, the nuclear waste issue is so unpopular that hardly anyone wants to bring it up again on Capitol Hill. "We need some kind of political mechanism to move from 17 sites to three," she says, "and it doesn't exist." Besides, New York's Orazio says, states, such as his, that have chosen a course would rather complete it than begin the debate all over again.

The Rush for Foreign Investment Ignores Serious Questions

by John Herbers

Is Kentucky, among other states, in danger of becoming a colony of Japan?

Democratic Governor Wallace G. Wilkinson doesn't think so. Japan is simply providing needed jobs, he says, for a state that has seen much of its economy decline in recent years. Wilkinson recently returned triumphantly from a trip to Japan, not only with promises of adding more Japanese plants to the 52 the state already has but also with news that Japanese banks had bought $77 million in 10-year Kentucky bonds at an interest rate of 5.4 percent, far below American market rates.

Revenue from the bonds will be used to provide low-interest loans to industries and businesses as an incentive for locating in Kentucky, a common device used by many states in the bidding wars for new industries. The loans will be available to entrepreneurs around the world, including the Japanese, who are said to be delighted with the bond sale, in part because they can draw their loan money in yen and not have to go through the money exchanges. News that Kentucky found a way to export its debt, apparently the first state to do so, piqued the interest of other states, which have besieged Kentucky officials for information and advice.

This is only the latest wrinkle in one of the most phenomenal developments in state and local government: the wholesale involvement of elected officials in foreign markets around the globe, seeking both investments in their jurisdictions and export markets for their products. Their overseas treks have become so common that they often stumble over one another as they travel the globe seeking foreign business.

According to the National Governors' Association, 41 states maintain offices in 24 countries around the world; 39 have offices in Japan, more than have offices in Washington, D.C.; 25 states assist joint ventures between firms in their states and those abroad; and 21 states have programs to help finance exports of their products. The states are not alone. Cities and counties are now major players in the foreign field.

This development has many positive aspects other than boosting state and local economies. Elected officials in obscure places have come to understand, often more than federal officials, the need for improving education and other services in order to be world-class competitors.

John Herbers is a contributing editor to *Governing*. This article is reprinted from *Governing* 2:9 (June 1989): 11.

But there are troubling aspects about the possible long-range effects of foreign involvement that have never been fully debated. The Reagan administration never made any effort to establish guidelines requiring that the national interest be served by these practices, and the Bush administration seems wedded to the same laissez-faire approach, except for barring foreign plants found to endanger national security. Each state and local government pursues its own foreign policy, whether or not it is good for the nation.

Kentucky adopted one such policy when it sold its bonds to Japan. Some states explicitly prohibit sale of their bonds abroad, and Kentucky's legislature had to change state law to make clear that there was no prohibition against such a foreign sale.

Although Kentucky got a bargain in the interest it must pay, that money nevertheless goes to Japan. Add to that the money Kentucky taxpayers put up for the many incentives, or giveaways, that the state and its localities provide to attract industry, much of it going to Japan and other countries.

The large national debt adds more to the outflow. A good portion of the money state and local governments formerly got in grants from the federal government now goes to service the debt, with foreign interests collecting a large share of that interest.

Maybe the jobs gained are worth it, but elected officials, who are intent on the quick fix, seldom mention that they come at a price. Already, elected officials with large foreign investments to protect in their jurisdictions find themselves lobbying against domestic industrialists on trade policy.

One reason they bought Kentucky's bonds, Japanese bankers told state officials, was that since so much Japanese money had already gone into American real estate, they wanted to find investments closer to the people and their productivity.

This can be a little scary. Mississippi made a big pitch a few years ago for Japanese industry, but saw it all go to Tennessee and Kentucky. Without imputing any prejudice to the Japanese, the state officials concluded that their state had too many blacks—that the Japanese prefer small towns with an easily trained white work force. Perhaps domestic industrialists would have been equally insensitive to American social needs, but their interests are here, not in Japan, and in the long run they can more easily be held accountable.

These are the kinds of questions that are in need of airing, but that are being snuffed out in the euphoria of the governors' press releases.

Reference Guide

SOURCES FOR ALL STATES

Advisory Commission on Intergovernmental Relations
 Changing Public Attitudes on Governments and Taxes (1990)
 Intergovernmental Perspective (published quarterly since 1975)
 Measuring State Fiscal Capacity: Alternative Methods and Their Uses (1986)
 1986 State Fiscal Capacity and Effort (1989)
 The Question of State Government Capability (1985)
 Regulatory Federalism: Policy, Process, Impact, and Reform (1984)
 State and Local Initiatives on Productivity, Technology, and Innovation (1990)
 State Constitutional Law: Cases and Commentaries (1988)
 State Constitutional Law: Cases and Materials (1990)
 State Constitutions in the Federal System (1989)
 Significant Features of Fiscal Federalism (1990)
 The Transformation in American Politics: Implications for Federalism (1986)

Committee for Economic Development
 Leadership for Dynamic State Economics (1986)

Congressional Quarterly
 Governing (published monthly beginning October 1987)

Council of State Governments
 The Book of the States (published biennially since 1933)
 The Journal of State Government (published quarterly since 1990,
  bimonthly from 1986 to 1989)
 State Government News (published monthly since 1956)
 State Government Research Checklist (published bimonthly since 1968)
 Suggested State Legislation (published annually since 1941)

Government Research Service (Topeka, Kansas)
State Legislative Sourcebook (published annually)

Legislative Studies Center, Sangamon State University (Illinois)
Comparative State Politics (published bimonthly since 1979)

National Center for State Courts
State Court Journal (published quarterly since 1977)

National Conference of State Legislatures
Capital to Capital (published biweekly from Washington)
The Fiscal Letter (published bimonthly)
Mason's Manual of Legislative Procedure (1989)
State Legislatures (published monthly since 1975)

National Governors' Association
The Budgetary Process in the States (1985)
Fiscal Survey of the States (published biannually)
Governors' Weekly Bulletin (published weekly)
State of the States Report (published annually)

National Civic League
Campaign Finances: A Model Law (1979)
A Model Election System (1973)
A Model State Constitution (1968)
National Civic Review (published bimonthly)

State Policy Reports
State Policy Reports (published bimonthly since 1983)
The State Policy Reports Data Book (published annually since 1984)

SOURCES FOR INDIVIDUAL STATES

State Blue Books (usually published by the secretaries of state)

State Journals
California Journal (published monthly since 1970)
Empire State Report (published monthly since 1975)
Illinois Issues (published monthly since 1975)
The Kentucky Journal (published 10 times a year since 1989)
New Jersey Reporter (published since 1971)
North Carolina Insight (published quarterly since 1978)

GENERAL SOURCES

Barone, Michael, et al., eds. *Almanac of American Politics*. Washington, D.C.: National Journal.
Published biennially since 1972; by National Journal since 1983.

Beyle, Thad L., and Lynn Muchmore. *Being Governor: The View from the Office.* Durham, N.C.: Duke University Press, 1983.

Duncan, Phil, ed. *Politics in America.* Washington, D.C.: Congressional Quarterly. Published biennially since 1981.

Elazar, Daniel J. *American Federalism: A View from the States.* 3d ed. New York: Harper & Row, 1984.

Gray, Virginia, Herbert Jacob, and Robert B. Albritton, eds. *Politics in the American States: A Comparative Analysis.* 5th ed. Glenview, Ill.: Scott Foresman, 1990.

Key, V. O., Jr. *Southern Politics in State and Nation.* New York: Alfred A. Knopf, 1949.

Legislative Drafting Research Fund, Columbia University. *Constitutions of the United States: National and State.* Oceana, N.Y.: Oceana Press, 1985.

Morehouse, Sarah McCally. *State Politics, Parties, and Policy.* New York: Holt, Rinehart & Winston, 1981.

Peirce, Neal R., and Jerry Hagstrom. *The Book of America: Inside Fifty States Today.* New York: W. W. Norton, 1983.

Price, David E. *Bringing Back the Parties.* Washington, D.C.: CQ Press, 1984.

Rosenthal, Alan. *Governors and Legislatures: Contending Powers.* Washington, D.C.: CQ Press, 1990.

Rosenthal, Alan. *Legislative Life: People, Process, and Performance in the States.* New York: Harper & Row, 1981.

Sabato, Larry. *Goodbye to Good-time Charlie: The American Governorship Transformed.* 2d ed. Washington, D.C.: CQ Press, 1983.

Van Horn, Carl E., ed. *The State of the States.* Washington, D.C.: CQ Press, 1989.

Wright, Deil S. *Understanding Intergovernmental Relations.* 3d ed. Pacific Grove, Calif.: Brooks-Cole, 1988.

SELECTED TEXTBOOKS

Bingham, Richard D. *State and Local Government in an Urban Society.* New York: Random House, 1989.

Bowman, Ann O'M., and Richard Kearney. *The Resurgence of the States.* Englewood Cliffs, N.J.: Prentice-Hall, 1990.

Burns, James M., Jack Peltason, and Thomas E. Cronin. *Government by the People: State and Local Politics.* 6th ed. Englewood Cliffs, N.J.: Prentice-Hall, 1987.

Dresang, Dennis L., and James J. Gosling. *Politics, Policy, and Management in the American States.* New York: Longman, 1989.

Dye, Thomas R. *Politics in States and Communities.* 6th ed. Englewood Cliffs, N.J.: Prentice-Hall, 1988.

Engel, Michael. *State and Local Politics: Fundamentals and Perspectives.* New York: St. Martin's Press, 1985.

Harrigan, John J. *Politics and Policy in States and Communities.* 3d ed. Boston: Scott Foresman, 1988.

Henry, Nicholas. *Governing at the Grassroots: State and Local Politics.* 3d ed. Englewood Cliffs, N.J.: Prentice-Hall, 1987.

Houseman, Gerald. *State and Local Government: The New Battleground.* Englewood Cliffs, N.J.: Prentice-Hall, 1986.

Jewell, Malcolm E., and Samuel C. Patterson. *The Legislative Process in the United States.* 4th ed. New York: Random House, 1986.

Leach, Richard H., and Timothy G. O'Rourke. *State and Local Government: The Third Century of Federalism.* Englewood Cliffs, N.J.: Prentice-Hall, 1988.

Lorch, Robert S. *State and Local Politics: The Great Entanglement.* 2d ed. Englewood Cliffs, N.J.: Prentice-Hall, 1986.

Ross, Michael J. *State and Local Politics and Policy: Change and Reform.* Englewood Cliffs, N.J.: Prentice-Hall, 1987.

Saffell, David C. *State and Local Government: Politics and Public Policies.* 4th ed. New York: Random House, 1990.

Schultze, William. *State and Local Politics: A Political Economy Approach.* St. Paul, Minn.: West Publishing Co., 1988.

Index